Leading the Way

Leading the Way

Young Women's Activism
for Social Change

EDITED BY MARY K. TRIGG

FOREWORD BY MARY S. HARTMAN

RUTGERS UNIVERSITY PRESS

NEW BRUNSWICK, NEW JERSEY, AND LONDON

LIBRARY OF CONGRESS CATALOGING-IN-PUBLICATION DATA

Leading the way : young women's activism for social change / edited by
  Mary K. Trigg; foreword by Mary S. Hartman.
      p. cm.
  Includes bibliographical references and index.
  ISBN 978-0-8135-4684-1 (hardcover : alk. paper)—ISBN 978-0-8135-4685-8
  (pbk. : alk. paper)
  1. Women. 2. Feminism. 3. Leadership. 4. Social change. I. Trigg,
Mary K., 1955–
  HQ1155.L43   2009
  305.42092'2—dc22

                                                              2009008095

A British Cataloging-in-Publication record for this book is available
from the British Library.

Visit our Web site: http://rutgerspress.rutgers.edu

Manufactured in the United States of America

Women will run the 21st century. . . . This is going to be the women's century, and young people are going to be its leaders.
—Bella Abzug

CONTENTS

Foreword   xi
   MARY S. HARTMAN

Acknowledgments   xix

Introduction   1
   MARY K. TRIGG

PART ONE
Learning Leadership: From Life to Activism

1 Going Back Home: Teaching Literature and Poetry to
    Latino and African American High School Students   21
    KRISTY CLEMENTINA PEREZ

2 Soldier in a Long White Dress: Notes from the Battle
    for Same-Sex Marriage   30
    ANDREA E. VACCARO

3 Living While Muslim: Human Rights Advocacy
    in the Post-9/11 Era   39
    ARWA IBRAHIM

4 "What Are You?": Projecting the Perspective of the
    In-Between   49
    INGRID HU DAHL

5 Leading by Example: My Mother's Resilience and
    Power in the Fight against Poverty   58
    ROSANNA EANG

6 Acting on a Grander Scale: Ending Health Care
    Disparities in the Latino Community   67
    CAROL MENDEZ

7   Learning the Meaning of One: Reflections on
     Social Justice Education   76
     JESSICA H. GREENSTONE

                         PART TWO
           Reimagining Leadership: New Models

8   Storybooks and Fairytales from Rural Teso: Leadership
     as Local Problem Solving   87
     SIVAN YOSEF

9   Navigating Identity Politics in Activism: Leading Outside
     of One's Community   96
     ALLISON M. ATTENELLO

10   Finding the Face in Public Health Policy: Leadership
     Learning through Outreach   107
     COURTNEY S. TURNER

11   Eating with a Spoon: Learning from Women at the
     Grass Roots of Society   117
     DAHLIA GOLDENBERG

12   Giving Voice to the Unheard: Writing with
     Women in Trenton   129
     KRISTEN LYONS MARAVI

13   Moving through Message: Feminist Counternarratives
     for Social Change   139
     LIZA BRICE

14   The Transformation of a Chrysalis: Becoming a
     Global Citizen   146
     SASHA TANER

                        PART THREE
          Leadership in Practice: Creating Change

15   Changing the Face of Leadership: Legislators
     at Large for American Women   155
     EDNA ISHAYIK

16   Choosing Nursing: A Feminist Odyssey   167
     JAN OOSTING KAMINSKY

17 Safe Keepers and Wage Earners: South Asian
       Working Women in the United States   174
       ANURADHA SHYAM

18 Blurring the Lines That Divide: Social Change through
       Activism, Politics, and the Space Between   184
       SHIRA LYNN PRUCE

19 Practicing Leadership: The Unexpected Plunge
       into Politics   195
       ALANNA CHAN

20 Stories from the Sidelines: Career versus Family   205
       MEGAN PINAND

21 Creating Knowledge: Feminist Music Scholarship
       as Activism   212
       MARY SIMONSON

       Contributors   223
       Index   229

FOREWORD

The twenty-one young women who tell their stories in this book do not mince words when they catalog the changes they hope to see in the world during their lifetimes. Nor are they reluctant to name themselves as players who need to take the lead if the changes they envision are actually to take place. In fact, even though they are all still in their twenties, the lively and diverse contributors to this volume have already compiled impressive records as young leaders in realms local, national, and global.

The leadership expertise on display in these pages ranges from the public arenas of popular culture—such as filmmaking, sports, the media, music, storytelling, and poetry—to politics, community activism, the corporate workplace, education, human rights, and health care. It also includes the less visible private arenas where leadership is enacted daily, such as households and extended families, friendship networks, and intimate personal relationships, both straight and gay.

These essays offer an extraordinary collection of youthful leadership journeys. Their authors show that they are occupied with much more than gaining entry into a broad range of leadership circles. They reveal the many ways that they are bringing their own distinctive experiences and critiques as educated young women to bear on the multiple worlds of public decision making. Since most are fresh to their varied workplaces, they are only now experiencing firsthand something they read about as students—namely, the scarcity of women in positions of real authority in most workplaces, despite women's greatly increased presence since the late 1960s in male-dominated fields such as business, medicine, politics, and the law. These young professionals make it clear, too, that their top priority now is not simply to fit in, or even to make their way up career ladders just as men have done. They are clearly ambitious, and they do have their eyes on ways to address what they recognize as uneven leadership playing fields for women. At the same time, they are asking tough questions about the rules, spoken and unspoken, of the leadership game itself.

Several of these young women describe how they came to challenge both their own and others' assumptions about these multiple worlds of power and

how they operate. They give colorful narratives of their efforts, whether successful or doomed, to alter these worlds. They are concerned not only to make
workplaces better serve women's needs as well as men's but also to enable
their places of employment to better fulfill their own stated missions to serve
a wider society, whether as government entities or private organizations.
These young women are developing initiatives that are helping transform not
just the "faces" of our leaders but the theory and practice of leadership itself.

As undergraduates, each of these essayists learned to concentrate on such
matters earlier than most of their peers because each earned a certificate in
the now ten-year-old Leadership Scholars program sponsored by the eight
member units of Rutgers University's Institute for Women's Leadership consortium. The program is certified through the distinguished Women's and
Gender Studies department in the School of Arts and Sciences at Rutgers, and
is guided by the wise and committed women and men on its board of advisers,
who are Rutgers' faculty, administrators, and alumni leaders. Given these
young women's accounts of their postgraduate adventures, which are echoed
in the testimony of nearly a hundred additional Leadership Scholars over the
past decade, it now seems clear that this rigorous program offers a highly
effective way to prepare women for leadership in many fields and to accelerate their movement into positions of power and influence everywhere.

The program's components are outlined in more detail in the introduction by the gifted founder and director of the program, Dr. Mary K. Trigg. She
also presents an overview of the varied backgrounds of the contributors and
highlights several intriguing themes in their accounts of how they charted
their multiple leadership odysseys. The Leadership Scholars program com-
bines small seminars, academic course work in each student's major field of
interest, and related research and policy internships. It culminates in an independent social action project that is designed, led, and documented by each
student. Our library at the Institute for Women's Leadership, which doubles as
the Leadership Scholars' seminar room, prominently displays row upon row of
three-ring binders, each full of data on a social action project conducted by
one of our graduates. Together, this repository offers both ideas and inspiration to each new generation of scholars seated around the seminar table.

These young women are part of a new cohort of college undergraduates
who are being prepared and empowered to assume equal leadership roles
with men in all public arenas, and to accept equal responsibility for making
positive social change in the twenty-first century. The accounts here put on
display the new consciousness around issues of leadership that these students
have acquired from their campus experiences. They also show how once they
entered the "real" world of work—in most cases after pursuing postgraduate
studies—they were ready to translate their leadership knowledge and skills
into action, and in fact were excited about taking on the challenge.

Many of the contributors here readily acknowledge that they never intended to study leadership or to become leaders. Edna Ishayik, a political campaign operative and now a veteran of eight state and congressional races, admits that growing up she "was more interested in music, movies, and malls than I was in politics." However, she says she became aware as a college student that women throughout the world were not doing as well as they should. So she took classes in women's studies and on women in politics to learn more. As her senior year approached, she asked herself how she could "begin to untangle the messy knot of women's place in the world." At that point, she decided to pursue what became a life-changing internship in a woman's congressional campaign. As a result of that experience, she explains, "all my thoughts about women, leadership, and politics jelled."

Overwhelmed with new information about the inequities that women still confront, even in more developed societies such as our own, this young woman swiftly came to the conclusion that the surest way to get attention and action on issues that she and other women care about is to get more women elected to public office. "So after graduation I continued working on campaigns for other female candidates. Political campaigns became my career and working to elect female legislators became my raison d'être, my way of changing the world for the better."

The passions of other young women in this collection propelled them in different directions, some working inside existing fields or organizations and others choosing to join or organize activist pressure groups, working from outside traditional structures to promote changes that mattered deeply to them. Whatever arenas they entered, they showed a willingness to take some personal risks to make change happen. Their behavior again and again bears out convictions that inspired our institute members to create the Leadership Scholars program in the first place: that leadership is not a quality that you either have or you don't, that leadership is not a capacity confined to members of the male sex, and that leadership can be learned.

While it is true that some people display greater aptitude for leadership than others, it is also true that both sexes and a broad range of personality types can and do become effective leaders. After all, even those for whom influencing and inspiring others comes easily need appropriate encouragement, support, knowledge, and exposure to opportunity to turn themselves into truly valuable leaders. And in today's fast-changing world, the leaders we need now—whatever their particular fields of expertise—also require at least a working knowledge and awareness of the shifting global power scene. In short, what we need more of these days are precisely those leaders who are made, not born. The demands of a challenging and dangerous twenty-first century world ought to be driving educators more than ever to recognize their responsibility for preparing students who are ready to lead, as the saying now goes, "from day one." This means, among other things, paying special attention to developing and promoting what remains the world's largest single untapped leadership pool: its women.

Initiatives such as the one highlighted here are still young, but as this book shows, they are already making a difference. As they complete the Leadership Scholars program, our students report overwhelmingly in exit interviews that they have acquired greater awareness and information about leadership in addition to expanded self-confidence, improved critical thinking and speaking skills, and deeper expertise in one or more policy areas. Becoming conscious of all the ways that girls, in particular, are still socialized to be passive rather than assertive, and to hide rather than to display their intelligence and abilities, helped many of these students recognize that for them, learning to lead meant unlearning things they had been taught about who women are and how they should act.

At the same time, what is so refreshing in these accounts is these young women's unconditional affirmation of the long and vital female tradition of nurturing and valuing the most dependent members of society—children, the elderly, and the poor. These writers know well that such priorities are too rarely on display in public realms, but they have witnessed such leadership firsthand and recognized it in their families, schools, and neighborhoods. Most often the role models they cite are their fiercely determined mothers, aunts, or grandmothers. Rosanna Eang describes how her family fled Cambodia to escape the genocide of the Khmer Rouge regime, and recounts that her indomitable mother, who is four feet nine inches tall, literally kept her family alive in the jungles of Cambodia, using a machete to hunt for food while the men hid out from Pol Pot's soldiers. When they arrived in Philadelphia, her mother's daily life was more prosaic, though still daunting. She cooked and cleaned for seventeen people in a cramped duplex so that father, aunts, uncles, and children could attend school, find jobs, and learn English. Later, when they moved to Camden, New Jersey, the entire family worked on blueberry farms, and her mother later took double shifts in factories to help send three daughters to college. She once declared that if she could have had an education, she would have become a doctor. Today, one of her daughters—our author—has earned a bachelor's degree in public health and is currently pursuing a degree in medicine. She plans to become a physician in her hometown of Camden, the second-poorest city in the United States.

> Although times have changed, many of my relatives still believe that Cambodian women should be obedient, subservient and dependent on men. For some reason, my mother never fully accepted this ideology, and she taught us something more. She does not want her daughters to

live the life that she has lived. . . . My mother is a great woman, and she is the force that has kept the family alive. Still, she straddles the old world and the new. She defends the tradition of arranged marriage at the same time that she believes women should have choices and be given the same opportunities as men. When Hillary Clinton ran for President of the United States in the 2008 election, my mom said to her sister, "See, in the U.S, who says a woman can't do the same things as a man?"

While reading the feisty, upbeat, moving, funny, and even brash accounts of the twenty-one young women in this book, who graduated from college in the dawning decade of the twenty-first century, I could not help asking myself what the next ten years have in store for them. How different will their lives be then from the lives of their mothers and grandmothers? Will they realize the dreams they confide in these pages, or at least some of them? Will they still be working hard to change the world in 2020 and beyond? I hope so. It will not be easy, but they all know that already. One of them, the political operative, acknowledges that since the first campaign she worked on in 2000, the numbers of women officeholders have "inched forward at a snail's pace." But for now, at least, that tough fact merely serves to spur her on.

Some clues to what might happen to the twenty-one young women here from this so-called millennial generation can be assembled by comparing and contrasting their experiences with the generation of women who came of age in the late 1960s, which contained many who became the so-called second-wave feminists who were among the first women admitted to a range of professional schools and careers. Each of the subjects here, together with her peers, has learned about what happened to the women of the more "establishment" wing of this college generation because all, as participants in my introductory seminar on "Women and Leadership," have viewed and discussed the 1994 PBS documentary *Hillary's Class*. This film uses the occasion of the twenty-fifth reunion of the Wellesley College class of 1969 to explore the experiences of members of that privileged and pioneering group. Hillary Clinton herself is highlighted only briefly in a now-famous commencement appearance where, as the speaker chosen by the students, she electrified her classmates—and scandalized most of their parents—with an audacious, spur-of-the moment rebuttal of guest speaker Sen. Edward Brooke, who had just criticized student radicals for protesting the Vietnam War. The bulk of the film, however, focuses on the other graduates and what happened to them in the years from the 1970s to the mid-1990s.

One woman recalls that at their tenth reunion in 1979, her classmates seemed to her disturbingly smug, exchanging business cards and busily networking in their dress-for-success suits. By their fifteenth reunion in 1984, she reports, the same classmates were confused and less confident, but much more interesting. By then, they were facing the consequences of choices made or not made, marital problems, and more.[1] By twenty-five years out, most of their stories, regardless of outcome, were tales of considerable struggle. One woman who had been a class leader as a freshman, for example, says she might have challenged Hillary as senior class president but by then had already married (in a huge campus wedding attended by her entire class) and had given up plans to attend law school at Yale as Hillary did. By 1994, having acknowledged that she had "never felt like a wife," she had left her husband, at last admitted to herself that she was a lesbian, entered a happy new partnership, and even returned for a law degree. Another woman became a successful banker and was promoted to vice president, taking on the lonely, built-in assignment of role model for all the other female employees. She relates her pain at not being able to handle it all when a baby came along, finally deciding to leave her job while shouldering the added guilt of letting down her colleagues at work. She reports her shock and disappointment at watching how for years thereafter, the bank let the waters close over having ever promoted a woman to a vice presidency in the first place.

The two women profiled from the handful of African Americans in the class, one a successful consultant and the other a prominent professor, reported in 1994 that, unlike the white students, they always knew they would be pursuing careers and never saw dropping out as an option. The professor recalled that as African American students admitted to a predominantly white elite school, they were kept in ignorance when they arrived on campus that their assigned white roommates had been asked in advance if they would agree to room with an African American student. In 1994, describing the tremendous discipline she had needed to combine raising her son with pursuing a high-powered career with a lot of travel, the consultant said that for years she kept to a strict regimen of calling home every single weekday at four p.m. to speak with her son and help him with his homework.

Other women made accommodations of different sorts. One gave up a television career to become a full-time homemaker when her husband was relocated—a bittersweet decision she clearly regrets, despite being devoted to her husband and their three talented children. Another, well-known CBS reporter Martha Teichner, kept the career but explains that just after accepting a promotion at a time when she was in London, she suddenly confronted the likelihood that now she would never marry and have children. She recalls that she wandered out to a nearby park and sobbed uncontrollably for an hour.

The typical response of our millennial to the women they saw in this film was more depression than shock. The women from Wellesley's class were somewhat older than most of their mothers, but not by much. The younger women found it difficult to believe, to be sure, that in the Harvard Law School in 1964, there were just 15 women out of 513 graduates, and that each had been asked individually in her first year by the dean to justify taking the place of a man. (Harvard's Dean Erwin Griswold had used the same question four years earlier on Ruth Bader Ginsburg, the future justice of the Supreme Court. She later recalled: "It was one of life's most embarrassing moments." As Garry Wills observed, it was "meant to be."[2]) The younger women also found the lesbian's story painfully dated; they themselves knew, or were, gay students who had long been out and had even been lesbian-gay-bisexual-transgendered (LGBT) activists in high school. The account of the African American and white roommates also struck my students as both sad and ludicrous. Their school, Rutgers, has among the most diverse student bodies in the nation among research universities, and the Leadership Scholars program featured here itself has 40 percent students of color. Still, they would hardly maintain that their school (or their country) has solved the many remaining challenges around race. And they are fully aware of the dismal statistics on women of color in public leadership.

These twenty-somethings could relate more fully to much else in these accounts of the women of the class of 1969, especially the struggles of combining career and family. Megan Pinand, a finance major now working for a large insurance company, is frightened by what she sees as the sidelining of female colleagues with small children, as well as by pressures they feel after having a baby to return sooner than they would wish in order to keep others from stealing their clients or moving into their offices. "I have come to realize," she says, "that faulty messages of how to treat co-workers with families are being taught in corporate society." But here, as elsewhere, there is a difference in how this generation views its course of action. This young woman has no plans to drop out. She announces that she very much wants to start a family one day, but declares that before she gets pregnant, she will help to organize like-minded fellow workers in a collective effort to confront management and change their views.

Will they, and the others here, succeed? Unlike the privileged Wellesley women ten years out in 1979, these young women are hardly smug at this stage of their lives. They know too much. Nor do they have such a narrow vision of professional success as that implied by the image of eager and clueless networkers exchanging business cards. They have already taken the measure of stunted notions of equality that turn out to have been all along built on male models. For them equality means not just opening the doors to women but redesigning the buildings. Will they be able to handle the skeptics who keep telling them that now is as good as it gets? Most believe that in daring to take the lead they are not alone. Many younger men, they say, are now ready to join them. They are counting, too, upon allies in their parents' generation—cross-sex, cross-race, and cross-class. The stakes in their leadership venture are huge, of course. The next stage of this work could be the one that brings us all, for the first time in history, to something like genuine equality between the sexes. It could—as these young women now fully intend—happen in their lifetimes. I don't know about you, but I am betting on them.

Mary S. Hartman
Director of the Institute for Women's Leadership
Douglass Residential College, Rutgers University

NOTES

1. Some of this description is drawn from Garry Wills, "Lightning Rod," *The New York Review of Books* 50, no. 13 (August 14, 2003), a review of Hillary Rodham Clinton's *Living History* (New York: Simon and Schuster, 2003).

2. Ibid.

ACKNOWLEDGMENTS

Like many books, this has been a labor of love, a product of years, and a collaborative effort. An anthology is not possible without contributors, and I must begin by thanking the twenty-one women who took the time and care to write these essays, and who were willing to share with openness and honesty their own experiences, insights, and life stories. Each one of you continues to encourage and enlighten me.

I want to first thank Mary S. Hartman, the founding director of the Institute for Women's Leadership, for hiring me to direct the Leadership Scholars Certificate Program at its inception in 1998, and for teaching me so generously since then about feminist institution building, women's education, and leadership. I must also express my gratitude to her for bringing this manuscript to the attention of Rutgers University Press. My thanks go to Rutgers University, especially the women's community represented by the eight directors and staff members of the centers and units that make up the Institute for Women's Leadership. I thank you for being such fine and brilliant colleagues, for believing in and supporting the Leadership Scholars program, and for your dedication to the education and advancement of young women. I wish to acknowledge in particular the department of Women's and Gender Studies for accrediting the program, and its current director, Mary Hawkesworth, for her discipline, deep commitment, and tireless work on behalf of feminist scholarship and the department. My appreciation also goes to Rutgers University and the School of Arts and Sciences for the research leave that allowed me to finish this book. To my colleague and friend Lisa Hetfield I extend my gratitude for her unremitting labor in raising funds for the program, and for the invaluable role she has played in shaping it with her vision and wisdom. I thank Wayne Meisel and the Bonner Foundation for their funding and faith in this book project.

My sincere gratitude goes to our generous major donors whose initial and continuing support over the years has helped to make the program possible. These include Anne Evans Estabrook, Gretchen W. and James L. Johnson, Dr. Maurice D. Lee Jr., Adelaide M. Zagoren, Edward L. and Ruth S. Hennessy, Floyd and Helen Bragg, The Bunbury Company Inc., Dr. Jean L. Burton, the

Cape Branch Foundation, the Exxon/Mobil Foundation, the Liz Claiborne Foundation, Rev. Bruce G. and Marjorie Kler Freeman, Mary S. and Edwin M. Hartman, Ruth M. Kurtz and the late Albert Kurtz, the J. Seward Johnson Sr. 1963 Charitable Trust, the Office of the Executive Vice President for Academic Affairs at Rutgers University, the Office of the Vice President for Undergraduate Education at Rutgers University, The Patrina Foundation, Gina A. Valeri and Dario Villani, Dr. Bernice Proctor Venable, and the Wachovia Foundation.

I wish also to extend my appreciation to the many nonprofit organizations that are named in this book, and to all organizations that generously open their doors to accept undergraduate students as interns. The value of these opportunities is clear in these pages.

Both the manuscript and I have benefited enormously from the careful attention and close reading of Marlie Wasserman, director of Rutgers University Press, throughout the writing and editing process. I thank her for her perceptive suggestions and insightful comments on each essay; I have grown as a writer through this process. I am indebted to Cynthia Gorman for her thoughtful counsel and astute suggestions on the book's structure as well as her fine writer's eye. The book is much stronger for both of their contributions. I would also like to thank Christina Brianik at the press for her helpful guidance every step of the way. Finally, I wish to thank the two young women in my family—my daughters, Laurel and Sarah—who inspire me every day with their own commitment to social change work and to pursuing a more just world. And to my husband, Ron Rapp, an unending source of support, friendship, and optimism, I extend my perpetual appreciation.

Leading the Way

Introduction

MARY K. TRIGG

This anthology is a collection of essays written by twenty-one young American women who describe their work, activism, and leadership on social issues, women's policy issues, and women's lives. It responds to critical portrayals of this generation of twenty-somethings as being disengaged and apathetic about politics, social problems, and civic causes.[1] *Leading the Way* is about actual young people leading, living life, and reenvisioning contemporary feminism. It provides a contrasting narrative to assumptions about the current death of feminism, the rise of selfishness and individualism within youthful feminism, and the disaffected millennial generation. Instead it demonstrates the ways that diverse young women in the United States are contributing to the advancement of women and others in multiple spheres and through different avenues at the same time as they themselves are finding their own paths, ways of being, and places in the world. The young women whose voices resonate in these pages are campaign managers, teachers, students, health care professionals, musicians, filmmakers, activists, and employees of nonprofit organizations, corporations, and government. Some of them are new wives in dual-earner households. Others are immigrants or children of immigrants. They are wondering how to prioritize work, family, happiness, social contribution, cultural loyalty, feminism, religious commitment, and activism. They are navigating their own dreams at the same time they are embodying and formulating new models of leadership for the twenty-first century.

In their 2003 collection *Catching a Wave*, Rory Dicker and Alison Piepmeier claim that this generation needs "a politicized, activist feminism that is grounded in the material realities and the cultural productions of life in the twenty-first century."[2] Dicker and Piepmeier's prose captures the profoundly changed culture that young American women today inhabit: they "have developed [their] sense of identity in a world shaped by technology, global capitalism, multiple models of sexuality, changing national demographics, and declining economic vitality. Third wavers often come to feminist consciousness through the academy, an academy shaped by feminism, poststructuralism, and postmodernism."[3] In addition, all of us now live in a post–9/11 world, a world impacted by the American-led war in Iraq, the rise of transnational terror movements, racial profiling, and increasing xenophobia against immigrants. The lives and consciousnesses of the young women writing here have been stained and shaped by these historic events that occurred in the opening decade of the new millennium. At the same time, with the election of Barack Obama to the presidency, an important racial barrier has been smashed, one that young people played a pivotal role in shattering. There is a fresh breath of hope that the United States may be entering a new and optimistic era of change.

To older readers who may feel discouraged at what may be perceived as the passivity and self-centeredness of this generation of American youth, sometimes called the coddled children of baby boomers, this book will serve as a bracing antidote. As Rebecca Walker writes in her foreword to *The Fire This Time*, another collection of essays by young activist women, the media would have us believe that "feminism is dead, the civil rights movement is not happening, communism is taking its last gasp, and educated twenty-somethings, traditionally the most radical of all demographics, are apparently content to sit back and reap the benefits of our parents' world-changing labor."[4] These young women deliver a very different message: they are self-sufficient and hard working; they have rolled up their sleeves and taken action. They believe that creating social change is their individual and collective responsibility, and they are out in communities working, volunteering, and organizing with passion, energy, and astute political awareness. "I must act as through the future of social justice depends on me," Jessica Greenstone concludes in her essay in this volume. "Get Off Yer Ass," the name of a campus-based service-learning organization that one author in this collection created and describes in her narrative, is a fitting emblem of their collective philosophy. There is power in knowing each of us can influence the lives of others. As Anuradha Shyam writes of her work with South Asian survivors of domestic violence, "with some awe, I realized that I had made a difference in at least one woman's life."

This anthology follows in the tradition of the genre of third-wave collections that were published in the mid-1990s, including *Listen Up: Voices from the Next Feminist Generation* (1995), *To Be Real: Telling the Truth and Changing the Face of Feminism* (1995), and *Third Wave Agenda: Being Feminist, Doing Feminism* (1997).[5] Now in a new decade and a new century, the voices in this collection share some of the interests in the cultural issues that fed the third wave a decade ago—the music of the Riot Grrrls and Ani DiFranco; *Sassy*, *Bitch*, and *BUST* magazines; on-line communities; zines; on-campus productions of *The Vagina Monologues*—but in their focus on leadership and public policy, and their concern with increasing the ranks of women in decision-making positions, their emphasis here goes beyond the first-person narrative and is both public and political as well as private and personal. This book demonstrates that memoirs, biographies, and individual narratives are powerful tools for women of all ages to use as they sculpt their own paths in life.

As I gathered the essays that make up *Leading the Way*, the main themes of the volume emerged. The book explores how these young women learned to be leaders, how they reimagine leadership, and how they are practicing leadership in new ways, both in their activism and personal and professional lives. The anthology is organized into three sections. Part 1, "Learning Leadership: From Life to Activism," addresses how we move from the personal to the political (and from being bystanders to actors) by gaining knowledge about leadership throughout our lives, as opposed to a single "ah-ha!" moment. This education and politicization can spring from hardships and struggles, such as painful experiences of exclusion on the basis of religion, race, ethnicity, immigration status, class, or sexual orientation. This section of the book also demonstrates the ways that leadership can be taught: in the classroom, through single-sex programs and institutions, and through internships and other opportunities to interact with mentors and role models who teach by example. It illustrates the ways that feminism, leadership, and activism are dynamic and changing and can evolve with you as you grow.

Part 2, "Reimagining Leadership: New Models," proclaims the importance of leadership and policymaking that is rooted in the lives of those who are affected by the changes being sought. These essays advocate for the need for "local problem solving" and respecting localized knowledge, whether in Teso, Kenya; rural Ecuador; New Brunswick, New Jersey; or Baltimore, Maryland. They argue for remembering the vital connection between theory and practice, research and action, and the need for new models of leadership that bridge differences of age, race, class, health, education, power, politics, and community.

In Part 3, "Leadership in Practice: Creating Change," the authors reflect upon their lives after college as they discuss choosing and embarking upon careers and consider contemporary feminism's relevance to a diversity of professional paths. One way of practicing leadership in the workplace is to advocate for the importance of women in visible leadership roles, whether in the U.S. Senate or on Wall Street. Another approach is to argue for the valuing of work that has traditionally been gendered female, including nursing and motherhood. This section affirms the importance of broadening our understanding of leadership and expanding the "face" of leadership.

Transitions

Although being young is often romanticized, our twenties can be a difficult decade for women as we struggle to determine who we are, what we love, where our passions lie, what our ambition should be, and how to, in the eloquent words of Mary Catherine Bateson, compose a life.[6] The transition out of college can be challenging because of both the exciting opportunities and the stressful decisions that come with building a new life outside the comforting, familiar structure of sixteen years of formal education.

College-educated women, who make up approximately one-third of young women in the United States ages twenty-five to thirty-four, still face difficult choices about career path, whether to marry and have children—or to have children without marriage, and the level of their ambition.[7] Young women are increasingly moving into professional positions; according to the Bureau of Labor Statistics, the number of women between the ages of twenty-five and thirty-four in managerial and professional jobs has increased 14.6 percent to 5 million in the last five years.[8] Yet, their career expectations do not always match with the reality of workplaces that are still gendered in their assumptions and structures.[9] At the same time, younger Americans of both genders are more likely to be pessimistic about their future prosperity compared to their parents' generation, and more negative about their children's material prospects.[10] Some scholars and journalists suggest that young, highly educated women are choosing not to move in traditional leadership directions because the pressured, often brutal environments of political life or corporate leadership are simply not appealing to them.[11] Although the media and popular literature continue to describe an "opt-out revolution"—a return to the home by young, elite, professional mothers—the reality of young, college-educated women's attitudes, experiences, and choices toward work and in the workplace are most likely much more complex than this and deserve further exploration.[12] This book addresses these national conversations through the voices and ideas of the young women authors.

One commonality that unites the authors in this anthology is that they are all graduates of Rutgers University, the State University of New Jersey. Each completed a two-year certificate program in women's leadership that draws on the rich scholarship in women's studies to train young women to reimagine leadership, to accelerate their own leadership, and to prepare them to make a difference in the world.[13] Some of the essays are about undergraduate education, and the growth in learning, maturity, and leadership that can come from internships, independent projects, research opportunities, and student activism. These experiences can be life changing and can serve as a bridge that helps facilitate the passage from college to "the real world." Other essays examine life after the bachelor's degree as the authors begin careers, build families, and enter medical school, doctoral programs, or the workplace.

I solicited the essays by inviting alumnae who I believed would be thoughtful about their work and evolving leadership, and who were willing to write personally and honestly about their lives. I sought diverse voices, not only those that were racially and ethnically diverse but also those that represented perspectives that would be varied due to differing professions, majors, and life pursuits. In the call for papers that I distributed, I described the anthology as a collection of essays written by women in their twenties about their work, activism, leadership, and learning on social issues, women's policy issues, and women's lives.[14] I was interested to learn and share with a broader audience how these exceptional, inspiring young women moved from finding their way to leading the way, as I believe they have done. To my delight, nearly everyone I invited to write for the collection responded with enthusiasm, which they maintained through rounds of revisions. The book took seven years to complete; the authors graduated from Rutgers between 2000 and 2008 and wrote their essays in different years, resulting in some variation in chronology between the chapters.

This anthology is not only a collection of personal narratives, it is also—unintentionally—a series of stories and snapshots of New Jersey: the industrialized, struggling cities of Perth Amboy, Newark, Trenton, New Brunswick, Camden; and the affluent towns and suburbs of Montclair, Morristown, and East Brunswick. New Jersey diners and malls even make appearances in these pages. Reflecting the diversity of the state university and the highly urbanized, most densely populated state in the nation, these authors speak as Latinas, Jewish Americans, Chinese Americans, African Americans, South Asians, Euro Americans, and as young women who understand themselves to be leaders and social actors. They address contemporary feminism's insistence on a racially inclusive movement that defies media stereotypes. The experiences they describe also transport us beyond New Jersey, the New York City metropolitan area, and the United States to the global: they include working as a Fulbright Fellow in Ecuador, teaching English to fourteen-year-olds in rural Kenya, interning at the Knesset in Israel, and conducting interviews with young Iraqi war refugees in Jordan. Ten of the authors in this anthology are either immigrants or second generation Americans: they or their parents come from Cambodia, Hong Kong, Poland, Colombia, the Dominican Republic, Israel, Iraq, China, Taiwan, and India. The essayists write about building intellectual, intercultural, and interracial understanding, and reflect the third wave's roots in U.S. third-world feminism as well as scholarship by academics that identifies gender, race, ethnicity, class, and sexuality as interlocking modes of oppression. They demonstrate that there is no one shared identity

called "woman," just as there is no common identity called "American."
Immigrant Arwa Ibrahim writes in these pages, "I came to realize that our
shared experiences are inevitable; they result from the increasing fluidity of
barriers and borders that deny anyone an 'authentic' eternal homeland to
cling to as their sole identifier and barrier against 'the Other.' In a sense, we
are all travelers who face dispossession and dispersion, so let us work together
toward the realization of justice and equality as a shared humanity."

New Models of Leadership

Leading the Way considers the ways we think about and define leadership,
women's leadership, and leadership for social change.[15] The anthology highlights the Leadership Scholars Certificate Program and the Institute for
Women's Leadership (IWL) at Rutgers University as a model and laboratory for
women's education and for the advancement of young women as leaders and
agents of change. The institute is a unique collaboration of eight academic
centers and units that came together in 1991 around the shared mission of
examining and advancing women's leadership in education, research, politics, the workplace, the arts, and the world. Institute members include
Douglass Residential College; the department of Women's and Gender Studies;
the Center for American Women and Politics; the Institute for Research on
Women; the Center for Women's Global Leadership; the Center for Women
and Work; the Institute for Women and Art; and the Office for the
Advancement of Women in Science, Engineering and Mathematics.[16]
According to director Mary S. Hartman, the institute strives to actualize a
vision of leadership that has been articulated in feminist thought but rarely
realized. "Women's leadership does not begin with the world 'out there' and
with attempts to educate women to become equal players in existing political,
social, and economic structures. Instead, through approaches rooted in
women's and gender studies, it encourages women and men alike to perceive
the world differently, to become capable of making different judgments
because their view of the world includes a more complete picture of women."[17]

The voices of the young women in this collection articulate new ways we
can envision and define twenty-first century women's leadership. One way to
do this is by expanding our notion of what we consider leadership to be, as
Edna Ishayik suggests in her essay.

> Leadership must include social roles that do not involve titles, money,
> or power. When thinking about women's leadership in particular, the
> definition must make room for the ways that mothers, sisters, grand-
> mothers, and first ladies have been organizing their families, and com-
> munities throughout history. We should be able to apply the term to

teaching fifth grade classes, balancing the family checkbook, demanding a cross walk at a dangerous school crossing, or increasing profit margins of a corporation.

These authors describe women's leadership in multiple and inclusive ways: as collaborative, community-based, intergenerational, and fueled by passion and humility. It is important to think about leadership not as an individual endeavor but as a collective process. Collaboration is exemplified in the work of the Institute for Women's Leadership—which is a consortium of multiple organizations—and our approach is reflected in students' learning and in their own practice of leadership after graduation. Alumna and current Institute for Women's Leadership staff member Sasha Taner optimistically remarks, "Young feminists can fill our current leadership void and pave new pathways to lead our societies into better models, based not on competition but on collaboration." In her essay in this volume describing her outreach work with needle exchange programs for intravenous drug users, Courtney Turner writes, "In this environment, leadership is defined as a collaborative effort because of the strong dependence on resource sharing. . . . I learned the value of collaborative leadership and its strength to facilitate positive change." Liza Brice characterizes her contributions publicizing and distributing feminist films at Women Make Movies by declaring, "I am part of a team of leadership."

A collaborative model of leadership involves working as a team, affiliating and cooperating with others, and learning from those whom programs and initiatives intend to serve. The contributors to this volume believe that leadership should be linked to action and social change, and connected to the real lives and circumstances of people. Reflecting on her college service-learning experience establishing a library in Teso, Kenya, Sivan Yosef reflects: "The women of Teso have an incredible wealth of knowledge about their resources, capacities, strengths, and weaknesses, and I do not. . . . Only the Atesos have the localized knowledge of their own community." She asserts that acquired knowledge (through education and books) and localized knowledge (through living) together equal the ability to solve both theoretical and everyday problems. "In this way," she concludes, "leadership is local problem solving." In her essay discussing her work with grassroots women's organizations in Ecuador, Dahlia Goldenberg concurs. "It is important for feminists, academics, and practitioners working on international issues or doing development work to have a clear understanding of the lives and circumstances of the people they intend to help."

The contributors recognize that leadership requires specific skills—a few they name include public speaking, listening, self-reflecting, modeling, mentoring, collaborating with local knowledge, fundraising, and organizing a group—and that a multitude of activities can be considered leadership, from conducting interviews, researching and writing, to building consensus and contributing to social movements and organizations. Arwa Ibrahim concludes from her research on dislocated Iraqi youth: "I learned that leadership often means knowing when to take an active role in informing others and when to actively learn from others." Urban high school teacher Kristy Perez agrees that leadership often requires more humility than hubris. "Being a leader does not mean knowing everything all at once," she writes. "It does not even mean you will always have the answers. Much of the time you may never have the 'right' answers; however, leadership means being willing to take risks by putting yourself out there, even if it means not getting it right the first few times you try."

The new models of leadership these Rutgers graduates propose involve bridging differences of all kinds that separate us. Allison Attenello writes of her activism striving to connect the university and the local New Brunswick community: "My hope was to facilitate resource sharing between college women and Latina immigrants." Kristen Maravi describes her own growth as a result of the writing workshops she facilitated with poor women in Trenton: "I had an invisible barrier of difference in my own mind, which kept me from feeling that I could interact meaningfully with low-income people." Although not without encountering obstacles along the way, these young activists are striving to move beyond identity politics and envision leadership as inclusive, grounded, honest, self-reflexive, mutual, and egalitarian. "In addition to being able to empathize," Liza Brice writes, "wanting to be a social change agent also includes a shift from living solely for self-preservation to working for the preservation of the community, as we grow to see these as inextricable from each other." This is a hopeful image of future leadership that challenges traditional, masculine notions of leadership that often center on the acquisition and leverage of power, authority, resources, and that celebrate the cult of the individual. These authors suggest that leadership looks different when women practice it and that gender can be a powerful lens for viewing and changing the world.

The contributors to this volume are asking new and different kinds of questions about leadership. If activists do not belong to a particular community, should they join and play leadership roles in an organization that represents that community? Must a leader hold a formal position or title within an organization? Must leaders have a staff or a following? Must they produce something quantifiable like money or laws? Must they be well known? What is the best way to enact leadership for social change? Is it by reshaping existing social institutions by entering and eventually transforming them, or is it by working for change from outside of the mainstream? Is it possible to pursue both approaches at once?

They understand that, as young women leaders, they face the challenge of being taken seriously by a society—and sometimes a feminist movement—that is quick to dismiss them. In her essay "Soldier in a Long White Dress: Notes from the Battle for Same-Sex Marriage," Andrea Vaccaro comments, "Young women leaders must constantly prove themselves, and they do not have the successes behind them that older people often do; younger women leaders also meet a great deal of resistance to their more innovative, heterodox approaches to leadership." Now mostly in the work world, the authors of these essays notice and criticize the paucity of women in leadership positions in corporations, politics, the arts, health care, education, academia, and human rights work, as well as the unfair burdens women are often asked to carry in the home. They also acknowledge the particular obstacles they have encountered as young women in the workplace. The young women of color writing here recognize the double discrimination they face; while women in decision-making positions in the United States are in the minority, the numbers become more rarified for women of color. I echo here the call for the importance of a twenty-first century feminism that addresses the lack of women in leadership positions. Dicker and Piepmeir write in *Catching a Wave*, "The scarcity of highly placed women in university administrations, corporate America, and government—to name only the most obvious institutions—demonstrates our very real need for continued feminist activism."[18] Dicker and Piepmeier argue for a feminism that "aligns itself with second-wave strategies for recognizing and addressing structural inequities" and that is not afraid to utilize the earlier activist tradition of consciousness-raising, which offered a place for women to come together to share their life experiences and feelings, and to recognize the political in the personal.

Intergenerational Leadership and Feminist Waves

We are now at a new moment in the history of women in the United States. The young women carrying the feminist movement forward live in a profoundly changed world from the one their mothers and grandmothers inhabited at their ages. In her history of American feminism from the 1960s to the end of the twentieth century, Sara M. Evans placed third-wave feminists in a broader historical context.

> Born between 1965 and 1974, the very years when Second Wave feminism was hurtling across the landscape, they grew up believing they could do anything. Legal barriers to education, work, and athletics, which enraged their mothers, were long gone. They . . . came of age when feminism was visible primarily as a stereotype. . . . Multiplicity and contradiction, "lived messiness," these are recurrent terms in the

stories of those who name themselves Third Wave. "Third Wavers waver," as one writer put it. "As Gen-Xers we have no utopias," writes another. Like the founders of women's liberation, Third Wavers need to tell their stories (even against an academic culture that now disparages personal storytelling), to articulate the distinguishing aspects of their life stories, the ways in which their generational experience demanded a different feminism.[19]

The women writing in this collection were born between 1977 and 1987, a little more than ten years after the third wavers Evans described above. Dubbed by some journalists and scholars as belonging to the millennial generation, the college years of these authors coincided with women's increasing visibility in positions of public leadership, from holding national elective office, to heading institutions of higher education and corporations.[20] At the same time, shrinking numbers of Americans are living in "traditional" households that consist of a man, a woman, and children, and our population is becoming increasingly racially and culturally diverse. At nearly 15 percent of the U.S. population in 2006, millennials are the most diverse generation in history: approximately 33 percent of children under eighteen are racial or ethnic minorities and about 20 percent of high school age students are immigrants or children of immigrants.[21]

Although the wave metaphor that charts the history of U.S. feminism has been criticized and may be reconceptualized by scholars, a number of the contributors here do place themselves within this continuum and consider the ways that third-wave (or contemporary) feminism differs from second-wave feminism.[22] In considering her decision to apply her undergraduate women's studies major to a career in nursing, Jan Oosting Kaminsky states, "Third wave feminism has not taken a stand on nursing specifically, but this generation of feminists in general is more inclusive of women making radical or traditional decisions for themselves, including the decision to choose a field of work that is still dominated by women." Another perceptive author writing here notes the more inclusive nature of youthful feminism: "We remain trapped in feminist agendas and acts of the past, unable (and perhaps unwilling) to step outside the tactics and styles of our predecessors and develop our own. . . . As a new generation, we must cease to be controlled by the media, the generation gap, and society as a whole. We must define our own feminisms, our own ways of acting as feminists as more inclusive, individual, and personal."

What "counts" as activism? The ways in which women in their twenties are expanding the issues, bringing a global and multicultural perspective to them, and enlarging what we consider to be feminist work is central to this anthology. Those writing here describe political campaign work, health education and the crafting of health policy, antipoverty work, nursing, human rights activism, music scholarship, filmmaking, independent media, urban education, gay marriage advocacy, and the development of work–life policies in corporations as sites for feminist activism. Mary Simonson asserts, "As I read more and more accounts by third-wave feminists, I am drawn to a common message: we need to stop questioning what is and is not true feminist activism, what counts and what doesn't count, which acts are the most important and which don't matter at all. We need to ignore charges that young women (and our generation as a whole) are inward-looking slackers, and follow our own passions, whether they fit into the socially constructed boxes of 'feminist action' and 'social change' or not."

The women writing in *Leading the Way* reject the media-fueled conflicts between younger and older women. Instead they are interested in and appreciative of mentors: they point to the importance of role models of earlier generations in helping them learn who they are and who they can become. These include their mothers, grandmothers, internship supervisors, professional colleagues, professors, writers, scholars, and public and historical figures. They are watching the women around them closely to see what is possible, how far they can strive, how they should define success. Their essays demonstrate the ways in which contemporary young women are reaching not just across differences of race, class, and communities but are also working with and learning from women of other generations. Although not without their challenges, these cross-generational relationships can be pivotal. A progressive high school teacher, a caring guidance counselor, a committed internship supervisor—mentors in general—can make the critical difference for young women: they may introduce us to potential career paths, stages of ambition, and push the envelope of what we believe to be possible, whether it is the level of education we can attain, the kinds of personal lives we can create, or the amount of social change that can be achieved.

The mother–daughter metaphor has been invoked to depict generational tension between feminists.[23] In her critique of the wave categorization of the U.S. women's movement, for example, Nancy Naples states, "this metaphor often takes the form of, on the one hand, complaints about a petulant daughter who does not appreciate what her foremother has sacrificed for her freedom versus a controlling mother who judges her daughter's approach to feminism as ineffectual and self-absorbed."[24] Founding editor and publisher of *Bitch* magazine, Lisa Jervis, suggests we say goodbye to feminism's generational divide.

> Much has been said and written about the disagreements, conflicts, differences, and antagonisms between feminists of the Second and Third waves, while hardly anything is ever said about our similarities and continuities. Older women drained their movement of sexuality;

younger women are uncritically sexualized. Older women won't recognize the importance of pop culture; younger women are obsessed with
media representation. Older women have too narrow a definition of
what makes a feminist issue; younger women are scattered and don't
know what's important. Stodgy vs. frivolous. Won't share power vs.
spoiled and ignorant.[25]

Although exaggerated, these kinds of judgments and tensions do not just exist
between generations of women who are feminists; they are simmering in the
workplace as well, between women in their fifties and sixties who believe their
personal sacrifices and workaholic habits paved the way for women in their
twenties and thirties who can afford the luxury of a more relaxed work ethic.
Rather than dwelling on the potential difficulties of cross-generational relationships however, the authors in *Leading the Way* suggest instead the importance of establishing and maintaining them. They pay homage to their older
mentors and understand clearly the importance of fostering ties and networks
with women of all ages at the same time that they reenvision a contemporary
feminism that is relevant to their own lives and desires. We have much to
learn from one another. As Shira Pruce notes of her education at the Institute
for Women's Leadership, "I was supported all the time by staff that was simultaneously learning from the young women scholars while we learned from
them."

The Power of Women's Studies

In addition to an exploration of women's leadership, this is a book about
women's studies, the potential and power that the women's studies classroom
has to open eyes, change consciousnesses, and transform lives. In educating
high school and college students about the history of feminism, the efforts
that have gone into securing hard-fought gains often assumed as givens, and
the inequities that women continue to face nationally and globally, women's
studies has reshaped the ways that young women (and men) live their lives,
make choices, and perceive themselves as actors in the world. A former
finance major writing here describes taking a women's studies class as a sophomore because it would fill an elective requirement and she thought it would
be an easy "A." Instead she found it to be a pivotal experience in her undergraduate education: "It taught me a great deal about women's rights and gender differences that I never heard in history classes or on the news," Megan
Pinand writes. "I left the semester with many questions concerning the status
of women in this county, how they are treated in the workplace, and how they
are treated in their home lives." Another contributor recalls first understanding feminism, and understanding herself, after participating in a women's
studies class offered by her progressive suburban high school. In "Practicing

Leadership: The Unexpected Plunge into Politics," Alanna Chan writes of her awakening and the memorable high school teacher who inspired it. "She was the one who taught me the fundamental meaning of feminism—the belief that men and women should be considered equal: financially, professionally, politically and socially. . . . While learning about women's suffrage and about the first- and second-wave feminist movements and how they applied to current events, I found my niche. I realized that I did not have an attitude problem; I just had a different attitude." Medical student and immigrant rights activist Carol Mendez, who was born in Colombia and immigrated to the United States at age two, describes feminism as providing her with an expression and a unifying concept for the ideals that had guided her throughout her life.

> I did not know what the term "feminism" meant until I went to college and sat in weekly discussions with other IWL scholars. I always believed in equality, fair treatment for all, and social justice. However, in those weekly discussions I was able to place a name and a scholarly theory behind the values that had been driving my life for as long as I could remember. It was feminism that empowered me and allowed me to analyze my life, the lives of my family members, and the women I wanted to serve and strengthen in my community.

Like Jean O'Barr and Mary Wyer in their anthology *Engaging Feminism: Students Speak Up & Speak Out*, I am interested in understanding the women's studies enterprise from the students' point of view. My conclusions concur with several of theirs: that there are multiple ways that students engage ideas in the women's studies classroom, that a sense of self-worth emerges in a feminist learning environment, and that students are "in the class of knowers" from whom we can all learn.[26] The personal narratives gathered here attest to the continuing relevance of feminism, of women's studies, and of single-sex institutions and women's centered spaces in higher education and in society at large.

Reenvisioning Contemporary Feminism

The young women writing here do not represent a trend trumpeted in the media that argues that antifeminism and resistance to labels are abroad in the ranks of disengaged American youth. For example, in *The F Word: Feminism in Jeopardy*, Kristen Rowe-Finkbeiner writes, "Few young women want to be called 'feminist' these days. It's so taboo that even some women's magazines jokingly use 'the f-word' when referring to feminism, and the word is often hurled in insults on talk radio—think 'feminazi.'"[27] In *Sisterhood Interrupted*, Deborah Siegel claims that many of the conflicts that characterize public debates about the meaning and relevance of feminism are generational.

"Feminism is not yet dead, but our memory of its past is dying," she writes. "Younger women run from the word 'feminist' without quite knowing why, or what the word has stood for. The movement's architects are aging, some are dying, and the names of others are hardly known."[28] Most, if not all, of the authors in this anthology comfortably describe themselves as feminists and agree that the need for an organized women's movement that will challenge structural inequalities in economic status, the family, control of our bodies, and access to power and decision-making positions is still very real. Dawn Lundy Martin, one of the founders of the Third Wave Foundation, and Vivien Labaton, its first executive director, wrote of the need to expand and remake feminism for a younger generation of women.[29] "Feminism needed an elective surgery—a face-lift, a remodeling—but it also needed an ideological expansion so that it could be more pertinent to contemporary realities and attractive to younger activists. Yes, we were interested in helping to obliterate media-constructed perceptions of feminism (a militant, irrelevant sect of man-hating dykes), but most of all, we wanted a movement that addressed our races, sexualities, genders, and classes."[30]

These essayists demonstrate their rejection of the individualistic feminism that has been deridingly dismissed as "me-too feminism." In her provocative 1998 *Time* magazine article "Is Feminism Dead?" journalist Ginia Bellafante described the feminism of the late 1990s as "wed to the culture of celebrity and self-obsession."[31] She portrayed contemporary feminism—the feminism of young women in their twenties and thirties—as flighty, silly, and self-absorbed. The young women's voices in this collection could not be further from this critical and pessimistic assessment.

Personal Narratives and Feminist Politics

Personal narratives are central to feminist politics. Autobiographies, accounts of real lives, have motivated women in particular to break out of the social conventions that have long constrained them. Autobiographical narratives, in Jill Ker Conway's words, "make us both more reflective and more decisive about working on the inner script with which we construct the meaning of our own lives."[32] When I was in my twenties, I read a book that had a profound impact on me, a collection of essays edited by Sara Ruddick and Pamela Daniels titled *Working It Out: 23 Women Writers, Artists, Scientists, and Scholars Talk about Their Lives and Work.*[33] Originally published in 1977 and now out of print, the book is a collection of autobiographical essays by women in early mid-life, many of them eminent in their fields, who wrote personally and powerfully about their struggles and discoveries as they strove for self-understanding through their work and carved out what their own contributions to the world would be. Their insightful accounts considered the place of

chosen work in women's lives, and reflected on their efforts to define and pursue work of their own, and to overcome the obstacles—both internal and
external—to the legitimacy of such work. The authors included second-wave
feminist luminaries such as Adrienne Rich, Catherine R. Stimpson, Evelyn Fox
Keller, Alice Walker, and Tillie Olsen, and the anthology captured a moment
in the history of the women's movement in the United States. This book was
published the same year that I, at twenty-one, graduated from the University
of Michigan (where I had majored in natural resources and taken my first
women's studies course), married my high school sweetheart, and followed
him across the country to his first job in Los Angeles. I resonated strongly to
this book because it spoke to what my mind and spirit were caught up in. Who
was I? Who should I be? How could I best contribute to the world? What was
the overlap between work and love? What was the work I could love and was
meant to do? How could I be courageous enough to claim it? What did it mean
to be a young woman in 1977—a feminist, a new wife, a white, middle-class,
college educated American who wanted to have chosen work, a meaningful
career, and had hopes of changing the world? What could I learn from women
trailblazers who came before me? There was an urgency to these questions for
me then that I will never forget. *Leading the Way* was inspired by that earlier,
personally influential book.

Thirty years ago, the issues of women and work were in much public
discussion—as they continue to be today. Women's unpaid labor in the home,
the importance of work to self-realization and adulthood, the artificial separation of private and public spheres, and the need to balance work and family
have been addressed by feminist writers for at least a century.[34] Questions
asked by earlier generations of women still resonate in the minds of young
women in the early twenty-first century. "How can I 'have it all'?—close family,
a successful career, fulfilling work that fosters women's leadership, a happy
married life, and children (someday)?" one young feminist writing here asks.
In comparison to their mothers at the same ages, young women in their twenties today are better educated, more likely to combine work and family, and
are choosing a greater variety of household and living arrangements.[35] They
still, however, face a gender gap in wages, the stress of role juggling, and a
desire to move ahead in organizations whose leadership is dominated by men.
Public opinion still holds that for women (and not men), ambition and chosen
work are selfish needs, rather than human needs.[36] The young women authors
in this collection speak to these complexities.

In *Working It Out*, Ruddick and Daniels argue that chosen work is essential
to being human, which was perhaps their most powerful message to me as a
young woman. They wrote in their introduction, "These essays do not pertain
to women alone. They are resonant with a human need to make a difference,
to make one's mark in the world by producing with dignity something of use

to others."[37] Like their feminist mentors, the young authors in this anthology are intent on making their marks in the world through their work to produce with dignity something of use to others. As music scholar Mary Simonson writes in this collection, "Social change comes by breaking through the constraints, exploring the answers to our own questions, understanding why we are passionate about our work, and sharing these passions, these beliefs, these ideas with everyone around us. . . . As we each act in our own ways, staking claims, naming fields and works as places for feminist change, we define what it means to be feminists in our time." It is my hope that the passion, intelligence, courage, and conviction of these young American women leaders will find its way into the hands and minds of other young adults as they think about how they too can lead the way in the twenty-first century.

NOTES

1. See for example Robert D. Putnam, *Bowling Alone: The Collapse and Revival of American Community* (New York: Simon & Schuster, 2000).

2. Rory Dicker and Alison Piepmeier, eds., *Catching a Wave: Reclaiming Feminism for the 21st Century* (Boston: Northeastern University Press, 2003), 5.

3. Ibid., 14.

4. Vivien Labaton and Dawn Lundy Martin, eds., *The Fire This Time: Young Activists and the New Feminism* (New York: Anchor Books, 2004), xiii.

5. Barbara Findlen, ed., *Listen Up: The Next Feminist Generation* (Seattle: Seal Press, 1995); Rebecca Walker, ed., *To Be Real: Telling the Truth and Changing the Face of Feminism* (New York: Anchor Books, 1995); and Leslie Heywood and Jennifer Drake, eds., *Third Wave Agenda: Being Feminist, Doing Feminism* (Minneapolis: University of Minnesota Press, 1997). See also Daisy Hernandez and Bushra Rehman, eds., *Colonize This! Young Women of Color on Today's Feminism* (Emeryville, CA: Seal Press, 2002).

6. Mary Catherine Bateson, *Composing a Life* (New York: Grove Press, 1989). See also Lia Macko and Kerry Rubin, *Midlife Crisis at 30: How the Stakes Have Changed for a Generation—And What to Do about It* (New York: Rodale, 2004).

7. Martha Farnsworth Riche, "Young Women: Where They Stand," in *The American Woman 2003–2004: Daughters of a Revolution—Young Women Today*, eds. Cynthia B. Costello, Vanessa R. Wright, Anne J. Stone (New York: Palgrave MacMillan, 2003), 43–67; at 60.

8. Ellen Joan Pollock, "In Today's Workplace, Women Feel Freer to be Women," The Black Collegian Online, http://www.black-collegian.com/career/wsj/workplace1100.shtml, May 2, 2003.

9. Anne Machung, "Talking Career, Thinking Job: Gender Differences in Career and Family Expectations of Berkeley Seniors," *Feminist Studies* 15, no. 1 (Spring 1989): 35–58; see also Virginia Valian, *Why So Slow? The Advancement of Women* (Cambridge, MA: The MIT Press, 1998); and Joan Williams, *Unbending Gender: Why Family and Work Conflict and What to Do about It* (New York: Oxford University Press, 2000).

10. Tamara Draut, *Strapped: Why America's 20- and 30-Somethings Can't Get Ahead* (New York: Anchor Books, 2005).

11. Ruth B. Mandel, "A Question about Women and the Leadership Option," in *The Difference "Difference" Makes: Women and Leadership*, ed. Deborah L. Rhode (Stanford, CA: Stanford U. Press, 2003), 66–75.

12. Lisa Belkin, "The Opt-Out Revolution," *New York Times Magazine*, October 26, 2003, 42–47; Pamela Stone, *Opting Out? Why Women Really Quit Careers and Head Home* (Berkeley: University of California Press, 2007).

13. See Mary K. Trigg, "Educating Women Leaders for the Twenty-first Century," *Liberal Education* 92, no. 1 (Winter 2006): 22–27.

14. Questions I asked the authors to reflect upon included

> What is/was your work, activism, and/or leadership?
>
> What is the meaning of your work, both to you and to others?
>
> What is it like to be a young woman doing this work?
>
> What did/do you do, and how did/do you learn from it?
>
> How did you personally grow, both as a leader and a young woman, from it?
>
> What do you get from this work, and what do you give back?
>
> How does this come out of your life? Your generation? Your racial or ethnic background? Your education?
>
> How do you understand and define women's leadership? Leadership for social change? Feminism?

15. Sources on women's leadership include Deborah L. Rhode, ed., *The Difference "Difference" Makes: Women and Leadership* (Stanford, CA: Stanford Law and Politics, 2003); Sue J. M. Freeman, Susan C. Bourque, and Christine M. Shelton, eds., *Women on Power: Leadership Redefined* (Boston: Northeastern University Press, 2001); Constance H. Buchanan, *Choosing to Lead: Women and the Crisis of American Values* (Boston: Beacon Press, 1996); and Marie C. Wilson, *Closing the Leadership Gap: Why Women Can and Must Help Run the World* (New York: Penguin Books, 2004).

16. See the institute's signature book, Mary S. Hartman, ed., *Talking Leadership: Conversations with Powerful Women* (New Brunswick, NJ: Rutgers University Press, 1999). For more information on the IWL, see our Web site: http://iwl.rutgers.edu.

17. Mary S. Hartman, "A Vision of Women's Leadership," http://iwl.rutgers.edu/vision.html.

18. Dicker and Piepmeier, *Catching a Wave*, 3.

19. Sara M. Evans, *Tidal Wave: How Women Changed America at Century's End* (New York: Free Press, 2003), 230–231.

20. The millennial generation is comprised of young people born between 1977 and 1997. Of the 75 million twelve to twenty-nine year-old citizens in the United States in 2006, there were 41.9 million eighteen to twenty-nine year olds. "Young Voters by the Numbers: A Large, Growing, Diverse, and Increasingly Active Electorate," Fact Sheet produced by Young Voter Strategies, February 2007. Young Voter Strategies is a nonpartisan project in partnership with the graduate school of Political Management at George Washington University. Data cited is from the U.S. Census Bureau's March 2006 current population survey (CPS). Fact Sheet is available at http://www.rockthevote.com/assets/publications/research/rtv_young_voters_by_the_numbers-2007.pdf.

21. Ibid.

22. See Kimberly Springer, "Strongblackwomen and Black Feminism: A Next Generation?"; Nancy A. Naples, "Confronting the Future, Learning from the Past: Feminist Praxis in the Twenty-First Century"; and Ednie Kaeh Garrison, "Are We on a Wavelength Yet? On Feminist Oceanography, Radios, and Third Wave Feminism," all in *Different Wavelengths: Studies of the Contemporary Women's Movement*, ed. Jo Reger (New York & London: Routledge, 2005). See also Melody Berger, ed., *We Don't Need Another Wave: Dispatches from the Next Generation of Feminists* (Emeryville, CA: Seal Press, 2006).

23. See, for example, Cathryn Bailey, "Unpacking the Mother/Daughter Baggage: Reassessing Second- and Third-Wave Tensions," *Women's Studies Quarterly* 30, no. 3/4, (2002): 138–154.

24. Naples, "Confronting the Future," 220–221.

25. Lisa Jervis, "Goodbye to Feminism's Generational Divide," in *We Don't Need Another Wave*, ed. Melody Berger (Emeryville, CA: Seal Press, 2006), 14–15.

26. Jean O'Barr and Mary Wyer, eds., *Engaging Feminism: Students Speak Up & Speak Out* (Charlottesville: University of Virginia Press, 1992).

27. Kristen Rowe-Finkbeiner, *The F-Word: Feminism in Jeopardy* (Emeryville, CA: Seal Press, 2004), 5. Rowe-Finkbeiner argues that the term itself might have become the obstacle in the post-Friedan, post-seventies era that lacks a mass women's movement.

28. Deborah Siegel, *Sisterhood Interrupted: From Radical Women to Grrls Gone Wild* (New York: Palgrave Macmillan, 2007), 2–3.

29. The Third Wave Foundation is a multiracial, multi-issue, and multicultural activist organization devoted to feminists between the ages of fifteen and thirty. See their Web site for further information: http://www.thirdwavefoundation.org.

30. Labaton and Martin, *The Fire This Time*, xxiv.

31. Ginia Bellafante, "It's All About Me!" *Time*, June 29, 1998.

32. Jill Ker Conway, ed., *Written by Herself: Autobiographies of American Women: An Anthology* (New York: Vintage Books, 1992), xiii.

33. Sara Ruddick and Pamela Daniels, eds., *Working It Out: 23 Women Writers, Artists, Scientists, and Scholars Talk About Their Lives and Work* (New York: Pantheon Books, 1977).

34. See, for example, Charlotte Perkins Gilman, *Women and Economics* (Boston: Small, Maynard & Co., 1898); Lorine Pruette, *Women and Leisure: A Study of Social Waste* (New York: E. P. Dutton & Co., 1924); Betty Friedan, *The Feminine Mystique* (1963; repr., New York: Bantam Doubleday Dell, 1983).

35. Riche, "Young Women," 43–67; Institute for Women's Leadership, "Challenge and Change: Younger and Older Women in New Jersey," *NJ WomenCount*, August 2007 (New Brunswick, NJ: Institute for Women's Leadership, Rutgers University).

36. See, for example, Anna Fels, *Necessary Dreams: Ambition in Women's Changing Lives* (New York: Anchor Books, 2004).

37. Ruddick and Daniels, *Working It Out*, xxvi.

PART ONE

Learning Leadership

From Life to Activism

1

Going Back Home

Teaching Literature and Poetry to Latino and African American High School Students

KRISTY CLEMENTINA PEREZ

(Journal entry: August 16, 1997)

> I am all that I am not meant to be. . . . Here I am at the waterfront, the place I grew up and was pulled away from. . . . I am here hoping I can bring back a piece of myself that I have lost. My Latina. . . . Never did I think I was going to be a college student and become somebody. It is very difficult and at times, I wish I could sit down with someone and talk to him or her and see if they understand. Someone who has been there and knows what I am feeling.

I was nineteen years old, fresh from my first year of college, and wrestling with how to bridge my traditional Dominican upbringing with my American values and ideals. I remember going to the Perth Amboy waterfront, sitting alone on a bench, and wondering, "Did I make the right choice?" I knew college was going to be academically challenging, but I never expected to feel so disconnected from my culture, my womanhood, my family, and my community. Yet it was the same disconnection and struggle to define my identity as a Dominican American woman that led me back to Perth Amboy High School to teach American literature and poetry to students who also struggle finding their place in this world.

Growing up in Perth Amboy was mostly a positive experience for me. I lived right next to the waterfront, known as "la playita." My summers were filled with jumping rope and playing tag, "Mother May I," "Red Light/Green Light." Like most Latino families, my cousins were my first friends. We lived in a three-family home. My grandparents lived on the third floor; my aunt and uncle lived on the first floor; and my parents, siblings, and I lived on the second floor. A typical day found my grandparents, aunts, and cousins sitting on the front porch, reminiscing about Dominican Republic, gossiping about the old lady next door or who's not talking to so-and-so in the family. I loved those days. They were before I was old enough to realize that life was imperfect, before I knew that some people's lives were more difficult than others' lives. It was before I added the words "difference" and "inequality" to my vocabulary.

And yet, there were differences and inequalities within my own family and community. My father worked outside the home as a security guard and my mother stayed home taking care of my siblings and me. I grew up believing it was normal for the man to work and the woman to stay home with the kids. My father always went around the house saying, "I am the king of the castle." As a little girl, I never saw anything wrong with that. I believed he was the king of the castle.

My father made all the decisions in our home. He determined everything, from what we wore to how we should speak and behave. As a good Dominican daughter, I was supposed to be polite, friendly, and respectful and not embarrass the family name.

My father also instilled in me a strong appetite for learning and knowledge. He is the person responsible for introducing me to books and ensuring that I read. He enrolled me in book subscriptions, and each month I received a box full of books, including *Danny the Dinosaur*, *Sammy the Seal*, and *The Adventures of Little Bear*. I loved reading. It also allowed me to relate to my father in a way that the other females in my family did not. My father was, and still is, an avid reader of American history, politics, and the social sciences. I grew up watching him spend most of his free time reading in his bedroom or on the living room couch. Although he never went to college, he valued education and saw himself as a thinker. He taught me to question the world.

Watching television programs with my father was never an easy task. He constantly pointed out that there were not enough Latinos or African Americans on the TV shows. He would ask, "Kristy, do you notice anything wrong with this show?" and I would respond, "No, dad, I don't." Then he would begin a long lecture on how the Latino and African American community are greatly underrepresented in this country and how we needed to come together and change this.

Although I found these mini-lessons annoying during my favorite episode of *Full House*, my father's words and lectures seeped into my consciousness and altered my point of view. I began to see the imperfections existing within my own country, culture, community, and family. With my new set of eyes, I saw the women in my family struggling financially, emotionally, and mentally. Most of my aunts were single mothers in unhealthy relationships. My own mother did not have a voice in our household and depended on my father for money. I was expected to get an education but also work toward being a good wife and mother myself one day. Although I did want to fulfill those roles and obligations, I did not want to be like my aunts and my mother. Deep down inside, I knew that the women within my family were viewed as "less than," and this made me feel powerless.

A pivotal incident for me was discovering that my grandmother could not read or write in English or Spanish. I was only six years old and already had access to a world larger than my grandmother could ever imagine. That day was like any other when she came into our house: she gave her ritual blessing, kisses, and hugs and then walked over to my father. She asked him to read an important document for her and after he finished, he told her to write the letter X on the dotted line. I asked, "Mama, why don't you sign your name?" Her name, Clementina, was also my middle name. She smiled and replied in Spanish, "*Por que yo no se escribir or leer*" (Because I don't know how to read or write).

How could someone go his or her entire life without knowing how to read or write? My six-year-old brain could not understand. After prodding my father for answers, I learned that she never went to school because she had to work on the family farm in Dominican Republic. I also became aware that two of my aunts from my father's side only finished the third and fourth grades, and his youngest sister completed the eighth grade. My father was the only one of the five children in his family to have finished high school.

As for my mother, she received her general equivalency diploma (GED) when she first came to the United States, but when she was growing up, education and future careers were not priorities for girls like her. Instead she was taught how to cook, clean, and take care of others. My mother once told me that she had wanted to be a nurse, but her dream was not encouraged. To prevent me from following in her footsteps, she told me every day to do well in school and said I would have a good life if I did.

These are the reasons why I am so committed to women's issues and education. I witnessed early in my life women's disempowerment and their lack of resources as a result of not being formally educated. I also learned that because I was born in the United States, I was privileged and offered many opportunities unavailable to the women who surrounded me; this made my experience different, which gave me hope.

Yet I continued to struggle with the mixed messages I received on a daily basis. On the one hand, I was told to do well in school and challenge the stereotypes placed on people of color in the United States. I was also expected to uphold the Dominican traditions of finding a good husband and raising a good family. I was never informed that I could do both.

It was not until my mid-teens that I began seeing my mother as a woman independent from her husband and children. As a result, I discovered she had a story of her own—one she never had an opportunity to voice. It was when my mother began sharing with me her hardships and struggles that I started to visualize and construct the woman I wanted to be. I wanted to be an educated Latina who inspired and promoted the learning and advancement of other women of color. I did not want women to believe that they did not have choices in creating the lives they wanted to live.

However, the path toward realizing this vision was not an easy one. I was a mediocre student until the ninth grade. I did just enough to get by. I found school boring and a waste of time. My father constantly yelled at me for bringing home Cs, Ds, and Fs on my report cards, but I did not see the point of doing well. If I did try to excel, it was only to please my parents; after a while, I just hated doing all the work. I was in remedial classes for a few years, which made me feel stupid. For a long time, I believed that I was. As a result, I withdrew into myself and started keeping a journal at age thirteen.

Writing not only transformed my life, it saved it. Many young people who are lost or have low self-esteem become caught up in self-destructive behaviors. They may choose drugs, violence, sex, or unhealthy relationships to escape from their pain and self-doubt. I chose words. When I began writing in my journal, I did not envision the role that language would play in my life. Initially, I wrote to release my inner thoughts and feelings. I did not feel as if I could talk to anyone. As time went on, I developed as a writer and discovered a new and powerful self: one who had a lot to say and who possessed goals and dreams. I liked this self, but at the same time I was afraid of sharing this secret passion of mine, fearing it would be mocked and challenged, so I chose to keep it hidden.

I was drawn to literature and poetry during my first year in high school and read everything assigned by my English teacher. I fell in love with *The Count of Monte Cristo* and "The Cask of Amontillado." While reading I was no longer just a girl from Perth Amboy, I was a part of something bigger. I was someone invited to participate in the lives and experiences of others and was offered the gift of seeing the world through their eyes. As a reader, labels and expectations did not limit me. I could do and be anything, which led me to believe that I could also do and be anything in my own life.

Literature and writing led me to think creatively and to imagine a life where I could be more than a wife and mother. Although I still valued those roles, I no longer felt confined by them; I could create an identity of my own. I began to think about college during my freshman year of high school, after receiving straight As for the first time. By the end of my sophomore year, I applied to the Advanced Placement English and history programs at my high school. After being accepted, I found that the voices of women writers and the Latino and African American experience were missing from the conversation. All my English teachers were white, and men wrote most of the literature we read. I wondered, was it possible for a Dominican girl from Perth

Amboy, New Jersey, to go to college and become a writer? Who would want to know about her story or experiences? I had no idea that Latino or Latina writers were out there.

When I was a senior in high school, I was told by a guidance counselor to attend a community college because my parents could not afford to send me to a four-year school. It did not matter that I was an AP student or in the National Honor Society. One can only imagine what was being told to students who did not excel academically. Fortunately, I did not listen, and I found amazing mentors at college who provided me with financial aid and other resources. Many other students, however, choose not to pursue their dreams because they listen to those who tell them that they cannot achieve their goals. Many urban Latino and African American teens are denied the opportunity to fulfill their personal greatness.

It was not until I was in college, majoring in English, that I heard of the writers Sandra Cisneros, Julia Alvarez, Miguel Algarin, Miguel Pinero, Judith Ortiz Cofer, Sandra Maria Estevez, Junot Diaz, and others. Discovering these writers validated my own claim to write. However, I resented the fact that I did not learn about these writers until I was in college.

My feelings of isolation inspired me to reach out to teenagers. My first opportunity to work with urban Latino and African American high school students was during my third year at college. I was an intern at ASPIRA (which means "to aspire" in Spanish) in Trenton, New Jersey. ASPIRA is a national nonprofit organization that empowers and educates urban Latino and African American students through leadership development training, cultural awareness, and college readiness programs. I was interning there as a requirement for the Institute for Women's Leadership Scholars Program. I specifically selected ASPIRA as my fieldwork site because of its holistic approach to working with young Latinos and African Americans.

Many of the students I worked with felt helpless, frustrated, and isolated because of the realities of living in a poor inner city. Some did not believe they had anything to offer to their community or families. They expressed deep feelings of hopelessness and self-hate, which led many to believe that going to school was pointless. In speaking with my Aspirantes, I heard complaints about teachers who did not care, and about how hard it was to grow up in unsupportive homes and communities. The students wanted to succeed and create better lives for themselves and their families, but they could not envision it happening.

Much of our work during the weekly club meetings, leadership retreats, and training sessions aimed to counteract those feelings of powerlessness by instilling a strong sense of community and family within the members. The Aspirantes were expected to take on leadership roles and required to do service learning projects. They were personally invested in each other's lives and built a strong support network among themselves. They also knew that the staff was committed to their success.

While at ASPIRA I recognized the importance of publicizing the stories and experiences of urban Latino and African American teens. Writing is a powerful tool in creating social change, and I wanted to offer that instrument to young people as a means of reclaiming their self-worth and place in the world. This theme has followed me throughout my own personal and professional life.

After my internship, I began to construct a vision in which young urban Latino and African Americans would have access to quality education and opportunities. I imagined a world in which their voices would be heard and acknowledged. I wanted to be someone who motivated, inspired, and stood for the empowerment of urban youth in America. Looking back, I see how this experience and so many others led me back to my hometown of Perth Amboy, which is something I never expected. Like most teenagers graduating from high school, I told myself I would never go back.

Teaching for Change

Over the years, I have learned that it is my story and personal struggles with education, identity, and self-worth that have led me to be an advocate for young people of color. My experiences are the source of my commitment to empower and educate Latino and African American students. I intentionally chose to return to Perth Amboy and teach at my old high school because I recognized the need for students of color to see that it is possible to be both educated and successful. I knew that many of them did not see themselves possessing leadership skills, academic abilities, or influential roles within or outside of their communities. As a teacher and writer, I set out to inspire them to go on to college and to continue creating positive social change.

Young people of color need a space in which they can fully express their thoughts and opinions. They need to know and believe that their words and voices can make a contribution, and can play an important role in transforming not only their own lives but also the lives of others. The experiences of urban youth of color must be acknowledged and validated; their stories play a crucial role in shaping the choices made about their futures. It is not only a disservice to them but to this country if we do not offer them the opportunity to showcase their gifts, concerns, and deepest dreams.

When I started teaching American literature, I was determined to expose my students to the voices and experiences of women and writers of color. It is important that young people—especially those who are marginalized—see their stories and lives reflected in literature. It gives them the opportunity to identify with the characters and it validates their existence. I wanted to give my pupils the opportunity to create identities of their own outside of their circumstance or past constraints. One of my biggest challenges as an English teacher is convincing my students that literature and writing can be an avenue to escape from the negative stereotypes surrounding Latino and African American teens. Before entering my class, most of my students viewed literature and writing as boring and irrelevant because the works they studied did not apply to their own experiences or perceptions of the world. I have made it my mission not only to teach classical American literature but also to find sources that reflect and address the issues my pupils must confront on a daily basis.

During my second year of teaching, I taught an after-school course to students who failed freshman English more than once and needed this class to graduate. Unmotivated and low-level readers, they were taking this as their last opportunity. I had to be creative and experiment with various teaching methods to capture their interests. All of my students were Latino, so I decided to teach novels, short stories, and poems written by Latino and Latina writers.

The first novel I chose to teach was *Bodega Dreams* by Ernesto Quinonez. This was the book my students loved the most. They identified with the characters and the issues that they faced: the class discussed violence within schools and communities, racism, sexism, and poverty. It was rewarding to see teens who once said they hated reading evolve into individuals who could not wait to get into the next chapter, and kids who never spoke in class share their thoughts and opinions. I was reminded that any student can be engaged in literature and writing as long as he or she can see its relevance.

One of the disheartening realities I face as an educator is hearing students say that being American means being white. This year when I introduced a research paper assignment to my juniors, I told them they could read any works written by American authors and I gave them a list of multicultural writers from whom to choose. Many of them were amazed when they saw Latino and other ethnic writers on that list. I have to constantly remind them that being a citizen of the United States makes them American. If they choose to be writers and poets, they will be considered American writers.

Leading the Way in Education: Cultivating Global Thinkers and Leaders

As someone who is committed to education, I recognize that I play an important role in shaping the minds of young people, as well as influencing my colleagues. When I first started teaching, I was the youngest and only person of color within my department. Although some of my associates were my former teachers, I still felt isolated and alone. Many of them were strongly attached to traditional teaching methods and assigned literature that I did not believe was conducive to students' reading or interest level. I found myself struggling with the same issues I had confronted in high school, only this time I was the educator. I did not have Latino or African American English teachers until I was in college, and even those individuals were rare. I was not completely comfortable in my role as an educator and teacher of American literature. It was hard for me to take ownership of the role because deep down inside, I still believed I was less than and not good enough.

However, my commitment to the empowerment and advancement of Latino and African American students has always been stronger than my own insecurities and fears. This is one of the most important lessons I have learned about leadership and creating social change. Being a leader does not mean knowing everything all at once. It does not even mean you will always have the answers. Much of the time you may never have the right answers; however, leadership means being willing to take risks by putting yourself out there, even if it means not getting it right the first few times you try.

Standing in front of a group of teenagers on a daily basis can be frightening and overwhelming. Sometimes, I have neither the energy nor the stamina to keep up with them, however there is nothing like having a student come back and thank you for being their teacher. A few of my students have told me that they want to be English teachers too one day, which is powerful to hear. We need more people of color and female educators at the secondary and university levels, and those of us who are already there must encourage our young people to pursue higher education and leadership roles. They need our support because so many of them are falling through the cracks.

Although I teach American literature and poetry, my role is much bigger than that. In my classroom my students begin to discover and accept who they are and where they come from. They are given the freedom to express and voice their thoughts and ideas. I am in the business of training and developing global thinkers and leaders through literature and writing. Over the last three years as an educator I've learned that change takes time and patience. The fight for racial, social, gender, and educational equity cannot be won overnight. I have discovered that to be an effective leader, I must be authentic and vulnerable, willing to take risks and fail. I have had to give myself to this cause and be open to whatever challenges come my way. No matter how hard or how much I love a student, the choice to excel and overcome life's obstacles must be her or his own. Young people will select their own paths; even when we have the advantage of seeing the bigger picture, they sometimes cannot understand that. I believe that a true leader gives the power of choice to his or her followers.

It is important that I teach my students to stand up for themselves. Sometimes I want to carry them on my back and lead them to the "other side," especially those I think may not make the journey. In the beginning of my teaching career I believed—because I wanted to create an environment where all students could succeed—that I was solely responsible for realizing that ideal. I became overworked and burned out as a result, and my vision became blurred and distorted, causing my students and myself to become unmotivated and stagnant. A leader must enroll others in his or her vision and pass it on so they can continue fulfilling the cause and step into that role.

Being a teacher has taught me how to be a better human being. It has pushed me to look beyond individual personalities and learn acceptance and compassion. For me, teaching has always been more than just an academic exercise; it is a conversation and an opportunity to cocreate with my students. And in that process we are both empowered. Even when I tried to resist my role as an educator, I was still being transformed and learning new things about my students and myself. There is much that I still want to accomplish in education, writing, and social justice; toward that goal, I am currently pursuing a master's degree in community organization, planning, and development.

I look at education and low-income communities at a macro level, especially focusing on young women of color. I want to try to understand how we ensure that girls in particular are supported and given the opportunity to complete their educations. The same issues I faced as a teenager are still present today. Young girls of color are still invisible. I believe that education is the way to address the wage gap and tackle social issues such as welfare reform and poverty. My intention now is to create programs and curricula for Latina and African American girls that will consider race and class, and that will bring forth the power already present within them. Although I never considered myself interested in politics, I now feel that the only way to truly serve as an advocate for young people of color is to bring the policy issues that affect them to the table as well as to *be* at the table. I have come a long way from that nineteen-year-old girl sitting alone on that bench by the Perth Amboy waterfront. She was someone who had no idea which direction her life would go and never imagined she would make a contribution to others. She serves as a model to me—and hopefully to others—that anything in life is possible.

2

Soldier in a Long White Dress

Notes from the Battle for Same-Sex Marriage

ANDREA E. VACCARO

One sunny afternoon, I convinced my father to go with me to David's Bridal on a quest to buy a ninety-nine dollar wedding dress. We made a beeline for the sales rack, picked out several ornate gowns and one simple one more to my liking, and proceeded to the fitting room. The sales consultant, beaming with excitement, smiled and asked, "When is the Big Day?"

As I held the dresses, I felt the power of heterosexism. She assumed I was buying a dress for my wedding and was engaged to a man, in love, and searching for the perfect ivory or white centerpiece to celebrate my rite of passage into adulthood. In actuality, I was a twenty-year-old lesbian college student who had cofounded Marriage Equality New Jersey (MENJ), a nonprofit grass-roots organization. I was buying the wedding dress to wear to protests and rallies with the hope of gaining same-sex couples the right to marry.

While girls are socialized to imagine someday being brides in white dresses amid hundreds of flowers and smiling relatives, I am excluded from this culture. I am an outsider looking in because I am gay. I am encouraged to have a "wedding" but not allowed to have a marriage. A marriage certificate costs only twenty-eight dollars, yet it provides 1,138 federal benefits and responsibilities, such as hospital visitation rights, access to spouses' health insurance and pensions, automatic inheritance, tax benefits, and legal guardianship of spouses' children.[1] Civil unions, which gay and lesbian Americans are allowed to have in New Jersey as well as in a handful of other states, cost the same amount but only grant the couple access to state bene-fits. The woman asked again, "When's the Big Day?"

"Hopefully soon," I answered, knowing that gay Americans currently live in a context in which same-sex "marriage," although "legal" in several states, does not grant federal rights and protections to these "marriages" at all, including basic household privileges such as filing joint federal income tax returns.[2] The Defense of Marriage Act (DOMA), passed in 1996 under the Clinton administration, is the primary reason the federal government does not recognize same-sex marriage; this U.S. law limits marriage to a union between a man and a woman and gives states the right to refuse recognition of a same-sex marriage approved by another state. In addition to being unabashedly discriminatory, the title "Defense of Marriage" strongly implies and positions gays as a "threat" to heterosexual marriage, which serves to polarize not only straight people but also the gay and lesbian community, some of whom feel the fight for same-sex marriage is too heteronormative for our community. DOMA also creates confusion surrounding what same-sex or "gay" marriage actually is as well as the specific liberties to which it entitles people. For same-sex marriage to truly be legal and fully equal to heterosexual marriage, DOMA would have to be proven discriminatory and overturned in the court system. Until then, despite the legality of gay "marriage" in a few states, it is nothing more than a rhetorical category intentionally covering a long trail of inequalities toward gay and lesbian Americans.

"Hopefully soon," I repeated, half to myself, knowing that Lambda Legal Defense and Education Fund, a nongovernmental organization dedicated to defining and pursuing civil rights equality for gay, lesbian, bisexual, and transgender (GLBT) individuals, had just filed a case in June 2002 suing New Jersey for marriage rights, a case that resulted in New Jersey's civil union decision of 2006.[3]

The woman looked confused. "You mean you don't have a date yet?" she asked, attempting to justify my presence in the store, trying to give me false social validity for buying the dress, even though there was no ring on my finger, no happy gleam in my eyes, only a look of steel and a will that refused to be shattered.

"This dress is symbolic and political," I said. "There will be no wedding for this dress." My father piped in, "Can you yell in it, sweetheart?" I breathed in and out deeply, moving my diaphragm, and knew I could yell loudly in the dress. The gown was white, simple, long, and delicate, yet I would have to be strong when I wore it. I would not only be Andrea, I would be representing the gay community, a marriage activist, and a radical in a country that suffers from an overwhelming fear of change or progress.

I bought a wedding dress to help my cause be noticed. The dress is a symbol of our culture and its values, and the contradictions that forced me—a young woman leader from Montclair, New Jersey—onto the front lines of political activism in the late 1990s and early 2000s. I bought the dress because I believe deeply in the equality and pursuit of happiness this country promises me. In that beautiful, white gown, which is sure to become stained and torn, I will be a soldier. My imaginary army will be clad in rainbows with people of all colors: some female, some cross-dressed gender-benders, some straight, some HIV positive, some old, some disabled, and all wanting the freedom of equality. My cause and the people I love who share that with me will be in vivid color in contrast to my stark white dress, and it will be beautiful.

The Front Lines

Women's leadership is fought for, not earned. Women must work harder than men to get three quarters of what men have; to be leaders takes incredible strength in addition to these daily struggles. Being taken seriously, commanding an audience, organizing a group, fundraising, meeting with important people, and creating change are considered masculine privileges. Men are assumed to know how to do all of these things; women are socialized to follow. Young women leaders have the additional challenge that young people, in general, are not taken seriously. Young women leaders must constantly prove themselves, and they do not have the successes behind them that older people often do; younger women leaders also meet a great deal of resistance to their more innovative, heterodox approaches to leadership.

At sixteen, while I was just starting to understand my own sexual identity, I had my first experience with leadership when I was elected president of Montclair High School's Gay and Straight Alliance (G/SA). Leading a queer youth organization amidst the perfunctory heterosexuality of high school made visibility crucial. Because I think in metaphors, the idea to organize a Day of Silence at my high school came easily. To participate, a student simply had to sign up, wear a sticker, and hand out small cards, which explained that she or he pledged silence all day to represent the silencing of GLBT individuals. To my surprise, more than six hundred people—one-third of my school—participated. The eerie silence that day was forceful; it taught me the power of vision.

The G/SA met every Tuesday to discuss programs, fundraising ideas, and experiences, but the organization was never just a weekly thing for me. In addition to running meetings, I came to school an hour early every morning to tape up signs with slogans such as "Gay is OK" or "Straight not Narrow," which were inevitably torn down by the end of the day. I came back to school three nights a week to run bake sales at the adult school from six to nine in the evening, and I set up a pseudo crisis hotline from my home phone. Every once in a while I saw how my visibility helped others; people I never met before would approach me and say things like, "I'm gay, but no one knows; where can I meet people?" or "Thank you so much. I could never come to a meeting, but I'm gay too, and I just wanted to let you know that those signs help me every day." My father asked me why I spent so many hours working for the G/SA, and the answer is still the same: I did it for those who couldn't.

Because I firmly believe in allies, I also helped Columbia High School in South Orange, New Jersey, establish and maintain their G/SA by meeting with the electoral board on a monthly basis. The legacy I left Montclair, however, was its now-annual tradition of marching in the New York City Gay and Lesbian Pride Parade. I organized a group to design our first banner and ended up sewing it by hand with only two others. I wanted our group, along with GLBT youth in general, to have visibility in our community. About twenty people marched both years I was president, and the tradition continues each June.

When I graduated from Montclair High School, I thought of activism as something very important to me; it enabled me to speak in front of fifteen hundred people with ease, make appointments with administrators, challenge policies I thought were unfair, and get in touch with my community. Activism became my primary identity; it gave me something to stand for that was bigger than myself as well as a strong sense of purpose. Activism taught me never to lose my ideals. I learned that a little action every day makes a big difference. Despite the daily struggle, I never stopped putting up "Gay is OK" posters in the high school hallways; after two years of doing so, I saw some very positive results from my efforts. By the time I brought a female date to the prom, my peers truly accepted me. When I went back to visit several years later, I saw signs still up in the late afternoon: change is slow but possible. I loved the G/SA for the two years I was running it and felt that I would never be able to do something of that magnitude again.

On my second day at college, however, I was offered an interview for an internship at the Gay and Lesbian Political Action and Support Group (GayPASG), a small nonprofit organization in Edison, New Jersey, dedicated to working toward marriage rights and civil equality for GLBT individuals. I received the internship and worked there six to ten hours a week my first semester at school. My internship at GayPASG opened my eyes to the more global community struggles outside my college bubble. I remember thinking that it was very strange that so few people at that time (2000) were fighting for marriage rights. I am still perplexed by how many people in my community are unconcerned about this important civil rights struggle.

By mid-October, I decided to go to the second meeting of the Bisexual, Gay, and Lesbian Alliance of Rutgers University (BiGLARU), where the female co-president quit on the spot, leaving the group in a predicament. When the male co-president asked if anyone would be interested in running, I stood up and gave an impromptu speech about my previous experiences and internship. I never mentioned that I was only a first-year student, and no one asked. I was elected within five minutes. Before even knowing how I would do academically, I had taken on two challenges most seniors never have the occasion or opportunity to shoulder.

I had to learn a great deal quickly. The next day I started handling a large budget and gave myself a crash course on programming and politics at a university I barely knew my way around. Within my first week in the position, I spent a total of twenty-five hours cleaning the office, meeting with key people, and organizing an event that was to take place in a little more than a month. I was back to leading meetings every week, which was something I was very accustomed to doing, but the members were apathetic. Because of our limited membership, the other GLBT groups on campus viewed BiGLARU as a washed-up organization with little power. I had the added pressure of having two thousand dollars allocated that had to be spent by the end of the semester. The group decided that we should flex our muscles, and I came up with an idea to do a queer-focused World AIDS Day event in December.

Everyone shot down the idea at first but then decided it was worth a try. More than eighty people attended BiGLARU's four-hour event; there were five speakers, a segment of the AIDS quilt, and a project that the group made, our own AIDS memory quilt. World AIDS day ended up being the most successful queer event of the semester and became my legacy at Rutgers; it is still celebrated by the gay community in an event every December 1.

After less than a month of running the BiGLARU, I noticed that the gay community, particularly at the youth level, was desperate for leadership. The amount of inertia was overwhelming. In the two years I headed the organization, I had four different male co-presidents. I think many people underestimate the amount of time and energy good leadership requires. It was not uncommon for me to sleep only four to six hours a night and spend fifteen to thirty hours a week devoted to the group.

By the end of my first year at college, I had a 3.85 GPA. I had also successfully run three major events at my university, including organizing BiGLARU to march in the New York City Pride Parade. I was accepted to the Institute for Women's Leadership (IWL) and was selected to be both a live-in academic mentor and a college writing tutor, two positions I held until graduation.

My acceptance to IWL made me absolutely confident that I wanted to major in women's studies; I loved the intellectual and theoretical lens my courses at Douglass College gave me, which opened my mind in a new way. I came to understand hierarchies in their multiple forms as the dominant force in many of my social worlds, which started me on a now lifelong quest to challenge and expose often-invisible systems of power and privilege. Douglass College taught me to question the status quo as well as my own relationships and convictions. As a result, I became inspired to envision and pursue a more just world.

I began IWL with an internship at the Gay and Lesbian Alliance Against Defamation (GLAAD) in New York City, an organization that promotes accurate and inclusive media representation for gays and lesbians. My direct supervisor, Connie, was one of the founders of Marriage Equality USA. She was impressed by my activist record and concern for GLBT marriage rights, and we often engaged in conversations about marriage politics during our lunch breaks. By the end of the internship, I decided to take on her challenge, which was to form a satellite group for Marriage Equality USA in New Jersey. Both Connie and I knew that if any change were to happen on the East Coast, it would happen in New Jersey. One of my friends from college, Ariel, who was very influential with BiGLARU, was a willing accomplice. She was just as eager for social change as I was and was a brilliant businessperson.

We filled out the paperwork and became a chapter according to Marriage Equality USA in April of 2002. Ariel and I sewed a huge banner with our logo, mass produced educational brochures and literature, and started planning events. I decided with this new challenge not to run for a third term as president of BiGALRU, which by that point was a well-established organization again. Ariel and I spent the entire summer getting contacts for our mailing list, trying to recruit members, and putting our name in or around every gay function in New Jersey. I remember going to New York City Pride with brochures, only to go to New Jersey Pride a few weeks later, and Trenton Pride a month after that. Tabling was one of our key methods of giving out information. We also made key contacts with more established organizations such as Lambda Legal Defense and Education Fund, the Pride Center of New Jersey, and the Human Rights Campaign.

Our first big break happened that June when Lambda Legal decided to sue New Jersey for marriage rights in 2002. They also began to hold town hall meetings, informational get-togethers about marriage rights and the legal cases throughout the state. Marriage Equality New Jersey hopped right on the bandwagon as one of the hundred-plus cosponsors, and a representative spoke at two of the gatherings. People seemed excited; most of the town hall meetings could not accommodate the number of attendees. People would stand for the full hour and a half just to see what was going on and how they could help make social change. It was amazing, but it was not enough.

While I knew that most GLBT people wanted marriage or at least equal legal rights for their relationships, most straight people were unaware that we could not marry or have the same rights. I wanted more visibility in the New Jersey community, not just the New Jersey GLBT community. I brought this up at the November Marriage Equality New Jersey meeting, and my idea was met with overwhelming support. The group brainstormed, and we decided to have a series of events at New Jersey malls. Malls and diners in New Jersey are the two main social outlets for people under forty, so we knew there would be plenty of spectators. We would be in full wedding apparel and would hand out literature and talk to people. We spent hours working out the logistics but were denied permits by all six of the malls we contacted. However, we did have a small educational event in December.

By February, I felt discouraged and started to have second thoughts about running a statewide group at the age of twenty. To make matters worse, no one had attended our January or February meetings. I remember sitting with Ariel for nearly the entire hour and saying, "maybe people are just late." Those two occasions felt like the longest fifty minutes of my life. By the last ten minutes, we were debating how much of a donation to leave for the Pride Center. Then it was back to either Ariel's apartment or my dorm room, both of which served as our headquarters.

By March 2003, I knew Marriage Equality New Jersey needed to flex its muscles, so Ariel and I planned a tax day protest in downtown Trenton in front of the main post office. April 15 is one of the few days of the year that the post office is open until at least midnight, so I knew we would get a sizable audience. I got a permit from the city to peacefully gather and recruited seven people to be there. Ariel and I both wore wedding dresses; my partner, Lauren, and another woman, wore suits; and three other protestors dressed casually. Nevertheless, I insisted that everyone wear a veil.

We got to Trenton, only to find the post office closed and the streets abandoned. We stayed twenty minutes, just long enough for a person driving by to yell profanities about my girlfriend and I being fags. Since the people who gave us the permit left out the important detail of the post office being closed that day, Ariel and I decided to go up to the main post office in Middlesex County and protest without a permit. We all got back into the cars for another hour's drive; upon arrival, we were told we were not allowed within 100 feet of the premises. We set up 101 feet away, on the side of a busy road right across the street from the post office, and held up signs saying "Civil Marriage Now." Ariel and I stood on either side of the banner in our wedding dresses and veils. People did jeer and called us dykes, fags, or queers. Some supported us; some even got out of their cars and joined us. Others yelled that we were going to hell, that God would punish us, but we stood proud, strong, and together. We were visible; thousands of people saw us there.

At around eleven o'clock at night, we were causing too much traffic and a group of police officers approached. Seeing riot sticks at their sides, I started to run because I knew from history that peaceful protesting is not generally broken up calmly. I ran, my long white stained but still beautiful dress trailing behind me, my train dancing in the wind. I yelled to my group, "Follow me." We all ran with our banner flying behind us. The moon was bright that night and the moonlight streamed onto my dress—my battle suit—and reminded me that, even with a slight retreat, I was still very strong. I got everyone into both cars before I piled my dress and myself inside. We drove without headlights through factory roads until we lost the police; then, around midnight, we did what any New Jersey group of young adults would have done after such a memorable night: we went to a diner and ordered a feast befitting a victorious army.

By the next year, Marriage Equality New Jersey was just a memory. Ariel and I could no longer do it alone and we were not getting enough help. I was not particularly proud of letting my organization go, but I knew that it had to be done. Maybe I was too young; I had not even finished college at that point. Maybe I had too much on my plate: I was working two jobs, going to school full time, writing a senior thesis, and composing two columns in a biweekly progressive magazine. Maybe I just could not deal with the apathy; we rarely had more than seven people attend our meetings, and few did anything besides talk about how much they wanted marriage. Maybe I did not have the money to spend on lavish events or a name that would make people want to even attend. I do not really know why exactly an organization dies or why Marriage Equality New Jersey did: I know the dream did not.

In August 2008, I put my dress on again, this time for my wedding. Despite some criticism, I stood up, and vowed to cherish and get "civil unioned" to Lauren, the love of my life. I did so with the grace of a bride and the will of a soldier. The only battle gear I needed was that same simple, long white dress. My rainbow army was there, at least in my mind's eye, and the day was filled with vivid colors that contrasted my pale dress. I crossed over that day from activist to participant in the struggle for same-sex marriage equality. When I threw my bouquet, I passed the torch and helped a close friend of mine come out publicly for the first time at age sixty-three. The ceremony gave me more vision and a deep personal connection to the cause.

Although this was the most beautiful day of my life so far, it was also the most bittersweet because I entered a committed and loving relationship knowing it will be treated as a second-class union, knowing that people—even those closest to me—do not have the language to call us "spouses" or "wives" but rather "partners," as if we are at a square dance. Only other people who have walked this path can truly understand how condescending and linguistically awkward society can be about my "special relationship" with Lauren. We are not treated as a married couple because we are not a married couple. We are "civil unioned," a complete abstraction from the binaries "single" and "married" on which our society is based. Civil union certainly is not the answer; it is simply a way of reinforcing second-class citizenship.

The ring on my left hand, also a symbol of heterosexual marriage, forces me to either be automatically assumed straight or to explain civil unions to each new person I meet. People generally assume I am a nice mid-twenties heterosexual woman with a husband at home unless I choose to mark myself as different, which is not a choice I always have the luxury of making. When this happens, it chips away a little piece of my heart every time. It forces me into an invisible space that is both isolating and painful; it prohibits me from experiencing true social participation. Just by being me, I live this struggle every day; I fight this fight every moment. Leadership has enabled me to survive and be who I am. Leadership helps me navigate the front lines. Leadership has made me a soldier.

I still have my long white dress—complete with stains—because I believe stains are history and should not be erased so quickly. It stays in my closet, but I know that one day soon this dress will come out again. I will put on my long white dress and my pride rings, and I will proudly display my second-class citizenship. I will again be a soldier, and the dress will be transformed from a lifeless, long white cloth into my battle gear. My rainbow army will reemerge behind me. And maybe one day my long, stained white dress will be the centerpiece of my legal and equal marriage not for its cultural significance but because it is part of my history; it is the uniform in which my battle will be won.

NOTES

1. See the Web site of Marriage Equality USA at http://www.Marriageequality.org (accessed October 31, 2008).
2. "What Gay Unions Don't Guarantee," *New York Times*, October 31, 2008; see also "Civil Unions Are Discriminatory," Lambda Legal, http://www.lambdalegal.org/our-work/publications/facts-backgrounds/civil-unions-discriminatory.html.
3. http://www.Lambdalegal.org (accessed October 31, 2008).

3

Living While Muslim

Human Rights Advocacy in the Post–9/11 Era

ARWA IBRAHIM

As an Iraqi-born American citizen who grew up in Baghdad during the first Gulf War, I will never forget the hardships I faced as a child: the lack of electricity, the limited food available to my family, and the U.S. military warplanes flying overhead as they dropped bombs in my neighborhood. One specific incident still haunts me. On the eve of the U.S. bombing campaign in 1991, my family went to a local bomb shelter in hopes of staying the night. After realizing that adult men were not allowed to stay, my parents decided that they would rather be together as a family. They returned home. Later that night, U.S. Air Force planes dropped two "smart bombs" on a nearby shelter in the Amiriyah neighborhood. All 408 people inside, mostly women and children, were burned alive.[1] At only four years of age, I learned my first lesson in American foreign policy.

The economic and security situation in Iraq was so dire, and the promise of the "American dream" so alluring, that my family applied for and obtained refugee status and hastily began a new life in the United States. Ten years later, I was faced with the U.S.-led occupation of Iraq, another inescapable hardship involving both of my homes. As I coped with the increasing violence affecting my family in Iraq, I felt myself on the defensive in response to the growing hatred against Arab, South Asian, and Muslim Americans post-9/11. A high school student during those definitive years, I made an important decision early on to channel my individual experiences into broader collective objectives. I began contributing to consciousness-raising campaigns that sought to contextualize and humanize violence and discrimination, both in Iraq and in the United States. Yet it was my time as a college student that propelled me to become a spokesperson and human rights advocate. This is the story of my personal journey toward finding my place in the global movement for justice and equality.

During my first year in the Institute for Women's Leadership (IWL) scholars program, I decided to focus my social action project on Iraqis' living conditions in order to contribute to consciousness-raising efforts that seek to humanize the U.S.-led occupation of Iraq. I spoke with Iraqi youth and wrote an article that shared their stories with American young people. The article was published on two online news forums, *WireTap* and *The Nation*, and reached at least sixty thousand readers nationwide.[2] In a strange twist of events, the discrimination I faced upon my return to the United States after speaking with Iraqi youth in Jordan initiated the second topic I currently address in my human rights activism: the increasing hatred toward Arab, South Asian, and Muslim Americans.

Humanizing Iraqi Experiences

I find myself in a difficult situation as an Iraqi American: I struggle with the fact that the United States, the place I now call home, is the instigator and primary actor of the devastation of my country of origin, Iraq. It was not long after the start of the U.S.-led occupation of Iraq in 2003 that my family began to receive reports of kidnappings, injuries, and deaths of our family members who still resided in Baghdad. It all began when my grandmother called to tell us the tragic news: unknown persons kidnapped my mother's cousin, and the family still had not heard of his whereabouts.

"Do you think the kidnappers will return your cousin to his family?" I asked my mom. She shook her head. "He has a heart condition. He needs to take his medicine daily, or else he can't live. It's already been a week. It's too late," my mother replied. She was right. Now five years later, we still have not heard from him.

The disheartening news did not stop there. A year later, my father received a call from his sister. She told him of their nephew's recent troubles. My cousin Iyad, struggling to study and work in Baghdad under the difficult circumstances, found his troubles spiraling out of control one fateful day.[3] While driving near his neighborhood, he was caught in crossfire between the Iraqi government and local militias. Shrapnel bore through the car's exterior and punctured his back, all in front of his devastated mother, who had feared the loss of her only child after already losing her husband during the Iran-Iraq War. A passerby who seemed to take sympathy in Iyad's condition offered him a ride to the hospital. Iyad, moved by the man's generosity, volunteered to repair the stranger's car without charge, "if I manage to survive," he thought. Instead of alleviating my cousin's hardships, this stranger only complicated Iyad's predicament. Two weeks after my cousin left the hospital and a week after he received the stranger's car for repair, the man wrongfully accused Iyad of stealing half a million dinar, which he claimed he had left in the trunk of his car. He threatened Iyad with death, so my cousin, in fear and desperation, collected the money from family members and quickly handed it over.

The constant flow of bad news led me to ask myself: How can I quietly accept prospering in a country that began this whole mess anyway and that was indirectly responsible for taking the lives of members of my own family?

As I pondered this thought, I observed the discrepancy between the news I obtained from my family and the methods used by the American mass media to cover the U.S.-led occupation of Iraq. I noticed that the corporate-run news sources were actually engaged in the act of covering up the human impacts of a brutal war and occupation. Even when human lives were considered, the dialogue was framed around the question, are American lives at stake? I wondered, how can we as Americans, many of us more secure than the majority of people in the world, ignore the people who are disproportionately impacted by this war, Iraqis, especially women and youth? The sadness and frustration inspired me to take advantage of my position as an Iraqi American and to use the resources available to me to humanize the victims of war. Suddenly I found my topic for the IWL scholars program's social action project. I would attempt to raise awareness about the experiences of Iraqis living under the U.S.-led occupation.

I decided to interview five Iraqi youth and use their personal stories as the basis for an article I hoped to write. Due to the extremely dire and insecure circumstances in Iraq, I spoke instead to recent refugees in Jordan during the summer of 2006. At the time of the interviews, more than seven hundred thousand Iraqis had been displaced to Jordan since the start of the U.S.-led occupation, with forty thousand to fifty thousand people fleeing their homes every month.[4] With such a high number of refugees, I felt confident that I would be able to hear from at least five young Iraqi refugees. I soon realized I was mistaken.

One of the major challenges of my project became finding youth to participate, largely due to my place as an outsider in terms of what it meant to be an "authentic" Iraqi. Some of the people I solicited wondered, what is her motivation? while others thought, is our safety on the line? These concerns are part of the larger ongoing dialogue in the social sciences. Feminists in particular have focused on the issue of power, namely power inequalities stemming from the different positions of the researcher and researched, and the power exerted by the researcher during the research and post-fieldwork period.[5] I became aware of existing literature that attempted to forge a feminist methodology based on ethical and socially responsible practices within research. The widespread reluctance by the Iraqi refugees I encountered forced me to reassess my role as "researcher" as I attempted to shift the disparate power dynamics between the people I interviewed and myself.

Another obstacle to my research was my inability to find young women who would agree to participate. Due to the extreme rise in violence against women and other forms of gender inequities since 2003, many young women began to seek refuge in their homes.[6] I had to rethink my project due to this major setback, but I was able to interview two very passionate young men from Baghdad.

What were the living conditions during these three years of occupation that turned even the most ardent supporters of the United States against the Americans? The young men, Ahmad and Qasim, described the deterioration of infrastructure and basic services in Baghdad, including electricity, potable water, sewage systems, health care, and education.[7] Sixteen-year-old Ahmad moved to Amman, Jordan, in early July 2006 with his family for temporary relief from the occupation. His father, a lawyer, remains in Baghdad until he can find work in Amman. Eighteen-year-old Qasim also moved to Amman in July 2006 with his brother to attend medical school. His father currently works in Bahrain as a veterinarian while his mother and sisters remain in Iraq, but they all hope to eventually converge in Amman.

Baghdad residents complain that one of the major problems they struggle with on a daily basis since the start of the occupation is access to electricity.[8] I learned that since the start of the U.S.-led occupation, access to electricity diminished significantly. In 2004 (just one year into the occupation), 92 percent of households in Baghdad reported unstable electricity supply.[9] Ahmad said that when he left the country in June of 2006, his family was receiving only thirty minutes of service per day.[10]

These two teenagers also spoke to me about overcrowding at public hospitals due to the mounting injuries caused by U.S.-led coalition troops, Iraqi government death squads, and local militias.[11] Ahmad told me that when a member of a local militia shot his older brother while he was driving home, his family had to frantically search for a private clinic and pay the extra costs because they knew they could not rely on the public hospitals to help. If his family had not had the extra money, it is likely his brother would have died.

Another major concern is the crumbling education system in high-violence areas such as the neighborhoods in which Ahmad and Qasim resided. Although the public schools and universities have not closed down in these areas, the quality of education has suffered greatly. The physical act of going to and returning from school is dangerous due to violence at military check-points and the threat of kidnap. The boys explained that being inside the classroom is also dangerous because there are frequent militia attacks against Americans in nearby areas, and American troops and Iraqi police forces often retaliate by directly targeting the schools. Because of this constant threat of violence, students and teachers often cannot attend school. As a result, education is increasingly devalued. This has led to an increase in illiteracy rates, school dropouts, and the overall quality of public education.[12]

Both Ahmad and Qasim gave accounts of school-targeted violence. Ahmad described one such instance to me, stating: "The Americans got targeted [one day] so they retaliated by hitting [my] school. They shot through the window and a boy inside was hit; I think the bullet pierced him from behind. The little kids in the school were scared, yelling and crying from the fear and the Americans. The teachers took [the injured child]. He was fifteen. There was blood everywhere. We returned home and went to school the next day." Qasim's account was strikingly similar, but it was an Iraqi police officer that fired at his school and injured a student.

The testimonies above allude to a problem greater than lack of adequate education: the general lack of security. I was surprised and frightened to hear the many stories that a sixteen- and an eighteen-year-old could tell of their friends and family getting shot, kidnapped, and tortured. I was particularly struck by a story Qasim told me about his father's near-death experience. Only one week after the war officially ended in 2003, Qasim's father and his driver were returning to Baghdad by car. His father's driver mistakenly drove through an American checkpoint without stopping due to heavy fog that obstructed his view of the soldiers. Qasim's father was shot by U.S. troops. His driver unfortunately died. The troops took his father to a prison to interrogate him and treat his wounds. He was not released for almost two weeks. Qasim said: "Our family was expecting him, but he didn't come. I was praying [one day] and I heard the doorbell ring so I answered it and I saw my father with his legs covered with bandages. I thank God for this. For a week and a half, I thought he was dead."

At one point in my interview with Ahmad, he asked me why I kept inquiring about personal stories of kidnappings, death, and torture. For Ahmad and Qasim, I realized, these stories are common and often unsurprising. Instead of allowing my growing sadness and hopelessness to overtake me, I came to another realization: I must share these powerful stories with a wider American audience.

The process of speaking with Ahmad and Qasim and presenting their thoughts on paper was as much of a crash course on leadership as it was a method of gaining and relaying information. Initially I realized that I could successfully blend my skills and interests in academia and activism by writing an article that could reach and affect a wide audience. The article was published in *WireTap* online, a national news and culture magazine by and for socially conscious youth. *The Nation* online also carried it. Another lesson in leadership was realizing that a personal project could be a powerful one. I embraced my personal connection to Iraq as a catalyst to create awareness. Most importantly, I learned that leadership often means knowing when to take an active role in informing others and when to actively learn from others. I reassessed the power dynamics between myself as researcher and the "researched," and I refused to view Ahmad and Qasim merely as victims. Their stories told of strength and hope in spite of such odds, and it was precisely their hopes that motivated me to be more ambitious and persistent in completing the project. "What can we as Americans do to help Iraqis?" I had asked Ahmad when we first spoke. "Let the Americans know what is really happening to us! Make our voices loud," he replied. With sixty thousand estimated readers of the story, I took a strong first step toward fulfilling their hopes.

Advocacy against the Discrimination of Arabs, South Asians, and Muslims in the United States

Upon my return to the United States from Jordan in August of 2006, I was detained and interrogated at John F. Kennedy Airport in New York by customs and border protection agents. It was five days after the August 10 London Airline bombing plot scare, in which a supposed plan to blow up ten U.S.-bound planes was exposed.[13] My process through customs began with a seemingly standard security procedure. My family and I handed our passports to the customs agent. Instead of directing us to proceed to the baggage claim, the agent asked my family to proceed to an enclosure and await further instructions. I looked around me and began shaking my head. We were in a de facto holding cell. Surrounding us were approximately three hundred Arab and South Asian Americans, many obviously Muslim by their dress. I glanced around and spotted some of the Anglo-American passengers from our flight—they were on the other side of the barrier, grabbing their suitcases off the luggage belt and heading for the exit. As I saw them freely leaving the airport one by one, I felt like a prisoner, held indefinitely with little knowledge of my rights and clueless of what to expect.

We were told by the Homeland Security officers to hand in our passports and wait for our names to be called. We waited five hours. We were only allowed to leave the overcrowded holding area to use the restroom facilities. We were prevented from using any electronic devices, including phones to call our friends and family members to alert them of our delayed arrival. Purchasing food and drinks was also prohibited. Our questions to the customs and border protection agents went unanswered, and we were threatened that we would be held longer if we did not keep quiet.

Eventually, our family was called for questioning. Our responses were transcribed on the computer, possibly as a part of the controversial post-9/11 government record collection programs. We were asked intrusive questions about the details of our lives, some of which were politically charged. My sister was asked about her political views on the Iraq war. Did she support or oppose it? After being detained and interrogated, our baggage was thoroughly searched. Eventually, after six hours, we were finally free to exit the airport.

I was in shock and felt both sad and powerless. I had just been racially profiled by my own government. I held an American passport and considered New Jersey home, yet a clear message had just been sent: no matter how many papers you have telling you otherwise, you will never be an American.

The thought of trying to continue "life as usual" without addressing the injustice I had just faced seemed unacceptable. My family contacted the Council on American Islamic Relations (CAIR), a grassroots civil rights and advocacy group that works to promote a positive image of Muslims and Islam in the United States while protecting Muslims' rights.[14] A staff member of the organization asked if we would be willing to participate in a press conference about the heightening discrimination against Muslims.

At the press conference, I learned that the discrimination conducted against my family felt wrong to me because the detainment, interrogation, and searches were all illegal. I also learned that our family's experience fit into a larger trend of growing discrimination against Arabs, South Asians, and Muslims since the events of 9/11 as well as an even larger pattern of alienation of oppressed groups of people due to their ethnicity.[15]

The press conference led to a wave of television, print, and Internet coverage of my family's story. We had traveled at a time in which the use of controversial security practices was on the rise, and a rush of media interest surrounded their efficacy, legality, and morality. Shortly after we reported our experience, news of other incidents began to emerge. Just a few days later, two groups of Muslim men were arrested for attempting to buy cell phones, and later released. In November, six imams were taken off a national flight and detained for hours because of complaints of "suspicious behavior," which the imams claimed was an illegitimate classification of the prayer they conducted before boarding the plane.[16] Whether anti-Muslim discrimination reached new levels in the last months of 2006 or more incidents were being made public is unclear, but it is apparent that Americans were beginning to become aware of the unjust difficulties Muslim Americans were facing.

I took the lead in my family and participated in most of the interviews, appearing on the FOX 5 Evening News, the syndicated daily news show *Democracy Now!*, and the *Montel Williams Show*. While I had little time to prepare for interviews—sometimes as little as thirty minutes after accepting the invitation—I felt confident and motivated to share my story because of my previous training in public speaking. I cannot deny that the process was nerve-racking, with bright lights shining on me, a microphone clipped to my shirt, and a reporter who preferred to ask about how I felt rather than what I thought. However, I used the opportunity to move beyond telling my story;

I attempted to raise consciousness about the illegality and dangerous impact of rising discrimination against Arab, South-Asian, and Muslim Americans.

After the flood of media interest died down, I was left with a few hundred results when searching my name on Google and a couple of interested peers. Had I really accomplished my goal of preventing Muslims from facing the same unconstitutional, illegal discrimination at the hands of the government that my family and I had faced? Absolutely not. Instead, I view my actions as small but important first steps that propelled me to become an active participant in the movement to defend the human rights of all Americans, regardless of their race, ethnicity, gender, or religion. I now approach my activism with a different perspective, aware that local successes make up the core of global struggles and solidarity movements. There are multiple setbacks, and defending human rights is never anything short of challenging; yet persistence guarantees that however slowly, gains will be made.

Conclusion

When I talked with Ahmad and Qasim in July of 2006, they had only been refugees for two weeks, which was apparent by their expectations for the future. They both believed they would be able to return to Iraq within a year, not yet realizing the extent to which the unfolding circumstances in both Iraq and Jordan would worsen. Without realizing it, Ahmad expressed the common struggles that displaced people face when he said to me, "I can't think about or decide on my future now. I don't know yet. Will I continue school here; will I continue in another country, return to Iraq, will Iraq return to normal? One cannot decide now. I want Iraq to return to normal and for the Americans to leave." Ahmad recognized that his desires and the reality of the situation were at odds, leaving him in a precarious situation. The instability of "home" will likely contribute to his feelings of homelessness and alienation as a refugee.

In Ahmad and Qasim's concerns I remembered my own. I too wondered the same things years ago, as I awoke early in the morning to a bedroom I shared with my entire family, anxiously awaiting the sound of the alarm clock, which I knew would usher in a daunting eight hours at an unfamiliar school with strangers I could not understand. My life as a refugee began with uncertainty and fear like theirs, yet I had found my way by embracing what Gloria Anzaldúa coins the "mestiza consciousness," Homi Bhabha calls the "hybridity of being," and Vijay Agnew terms the "double consciousness."[17]

These alternative identity configurations are potential solutions to the struggles of displacement. Edward Said and Jean Mohr offered a similar solution when they argued, "since the main features of our present existence are dispossession, dispersion, and yet also a kind of power incommensurate with our stateless exile, I believe that essentially unconventional, hybrid, and

fragmentary forms of expression should be used to represent us."[18] Through
Qasim and Ahmad's testimonies and through the discrimination I faced by my
own government, I realized that I had already embraced Said and Mohr's sug-
gestion. My refusal to adopt a singular national identity is a personal and
political act of resistance. It makes it possible for me to defy normalizing and
oppressive agents. More importantly, it allows me to reclaim identity as a tool
of social change across borders. However, these alternative identity configurations are not only applicable to immigrants. I came to realize that our shared
experiences are inevitable; they result from the increasing fluidity of barriers
and borders that deny anyone an "authentic" eternal homeland to cling to as
their sole identifier and barrier against "the other."[19] In a sense, we are all
travelers who face dispossession and dispersion, so let us work together
toward the realization of justice and equality as a shared humanity. This has
been the most important realization in my journey toward becoming a
spokesperson and defender of human rights.

NOTES

1. The exact number of deaths remains contested. While it is now believed that the
   number is closer to 408, estimates by American and European news agencies and
   organizations at the time of the incident were lower. Human Rights Watch put the
   death toll at 200 to 300 civilians in their 1991 report, "Needless Deaths in the Gulf
   War: Civilian Casualties during the Air Campaign and Violations of the Laws of
   War." http://www.hrw.org/en/reports/1991/06/01/needless-deaths-gulf-war.

2. Arwa Ibrahim, "Iraq: Innocent Targets," *WireTap Magazine*, March 13, 2007. http://
   www.wiretapmag.org/stories/43039/.

3. Name has been changed.

4. UN High Commissioner for Refugees, "Supplementary Appeal, Iraq Situation
   Response: Protection and Assistance to Iraqi Refugees in Neighboring States and to
   IDPs and Non-Iraqi Refugees in Iraq," January 2007, 5.

5. Diane Wolf, "Situating Feminist Dilemmas in Fieldwork," *Feminist Dilemmas in
   Fieldwork*, ed. Diane Wolf, 1–55 (Boulder, CO: Westview Press, 1996), 2.

6. In the 2005–2006 school year, 75 percent of Iraq's children attended school.
   However, there was a dramatic decrease in the 2006–2007 school year with only 30
   percent of Iraq's 3.5 million students attending classes. According to the 2006 Iraq
   Ministry of Education report, a majority of the 70 percent of Iraq's children who do
   not attend school are girls and young women. While there are many elements that
   may explain the difficulty of finding young women to interview, it is important to
   avoid adopting what Ålund describes as the "otherizing" notion of "third world" and
   "immigrant women" as "largely subordinated, passive and driven solely by tradition." Aleksandra Ålund, "Feminism, Multiculturalism, Essentialism," in *Women,
   Citizenship, and Difference*, eds. Nira Yuval-Davis and Pnina Werbner, 147–162 (New
   York: Zed Books, 1999), 150.

7. Names have been changed.

8. Prior to the occupation, although they were getting up to twelve hours of electricity a day, electrical service was on a predictable schedule that families could incorporate into their daily routines.

9. UN Development Program, *Iraqi Living Conditions Survey 2004*, Baghdad, 2005, 18.

10. Both Ahmad and Qasim lived in neighborhoods like Al-Amiriyah, Al-Doora, and Hay Al-Jihad, in which there is a high rate of militia activity against U.S.-led coalition troops.

11. Dr. Bassim al-Sheibani, Najah R. Hadi, and Tariq Hasoon, "Iraq Lacks Facilities and Expertise in Emergency Medicine," *British Medical Journal*, October 21, 2006. http://www.bmj.com/cgi/content/full/333/7573/847.

12. UN Development Program, *Iraqi Living Conditions Survey 2004* (Baghdad, 2005).

13. John Anderson and Karen DeYoung, "Plot to Bomb U.S.-Bound Jets Is Foiled," *Washington Post Foreign Service*, August 11, 2006.

14. See CAIR's Web site for more information: http://www.cair-net.org.

15. Michael Welch, *Scapegoats of September 11th: Hate Crimes & State Crimes in the War on Terror* (New Brunswick, NJ: Rutgers University Press, 2006), 5.

16. Leslie Miller, "At National Airport, Prayers Against Profiling," *Associated Press*, November 28, 2006, A10.

17. See Gloria Anzaldúa, *Borderlands/La Frontera: The New Mestiza* (San Francisco: Aunt Lute Books, 1987); Homi K. Bhabha, *The Location of Culture* (New York: Routledge, 1994); and Vijay Agnew, "Introduction," in *Diaspora, Memory, and Identity: A Search for Home*, ed. Vijay Agnew (Toronto: University of Toronto Press, 2005) 3–17.

18. Edward Said and Jean Mohr, *After the Last Sky* (New York: Columbia University Press, 1999), 6.

19. Idea presented in poem by Vivian Slioa, "Clay Tablets," from the author's collection, *Ahzan al-Fusul*, Sweden, 1997.

4

"What Are You?"

Projecting the Perspective of the In-Between

INGRID HU DAHL

Sometimes I'm back there, to moments in time sitting in the family room with my parents and brother, a kid watching classic American films on the television. Fred Astair dancing, Audrey Hepburn transforming in front of Henry Higgins, Auntie Mame displaying her vibrant personality, Gene Kelly living as an American in Paris, Marilyn Monroe embracing a man in drag, and Charlie Chaplin attempting to fit into the world—these films brought my family together. I remember looking at each member of my family, whose contented gaze flickered in the shadows of images. We watched the same movies over and over. Although the images, roles, messages, and stories entertained us while influencing our ways of seeing, the characters never reflected who we were. Our lifestyles and culture had no representation—the nod to racial diversity was fabricated in stereotypes. There were no racially mixed actors in any of the classic films I saw growing up. So here we were—an interracial family watching films that just did not fit. Not fitting in was far from our minds as we viewed these famous performances, yet right outside of the picture, it was a reality and a struggle.

It all began at a bus stop. I was six or seven when an older, popular neighborhood boy called me out on my racial background. It floored me. I remember feeling very accused and put on the spot, as if I had done something wrong. I continued my day quietly, distant from those around me as though I had been painted over with transparent pigment. As I grew up, I fell in and out of silence as I tried to balance a friendly, outgoing personality with my hesitation to appear out of the ordinary. As the years went by, the looks on people's faces continued to show a sense of confusion. The persistent question I was asked in my youth was: "What are you?" This always caught me a bit off guard. If I explained, "I'm half Chinese and half Norwegian," I would have to endure the awkwardness of the inquirer looking at me, making a comment, or even taking a step back as though I were a painting to examine.

I started to develop a critical eye on all that I observed. Coincidences felt strangely planned or clichéd; everything began to seem rehearsed, as if the world were one big compilation of actors performing the same series of films over and over again. It was redundant and boring—but the experience of a total stranger trying to make sense of my genetic make-up was just so strange and easy to both challenge and fall victim to. My life was different. It was not just because I was the only mixed race kid as far as I could see in affluent, suburban Hillsborough, New Jersey. It was also that my parents had unusual roles compared to those typical of my peers' mothers and fathers.

When my mom was home, I would admire her perceptive ways of seeing. She was strong, determined, and accomplished; the breadwinner in the family, her job required that she travel extensively. She is Chinese and grew up in Taipei, Taiwan. My mother braved sexism and racism in the workplace—I witnessed the painful toll they took on her, being marginalized because of her accent and missing out on directorships because the traditional hierarchy of leadership and power couldn't accept a woman as the director. She constantly witnessed outside hires—always male—being selected and promoted instead of her. This reinforced the glass ceiling she faced. Because of what she—as a woman and a woman of color—had to prove through long work hours, I rarely was able to see my mother in my youth. My father, a Euro-American mix but primarily Norwegian, is a kind and humble man who studied theater and dance but, once married, switched to geology and started his own business at home. My dad was there when I came home from school crying for being called names, for being different—not knowing slang or excerpts from mainstream TV—for being hard to categorize, and for forming *chinglish* sentences. He had to face the assumption that he had married my mother while in the service (he was never in the military) because people accepted that as justification for interracial marriage. My dad had a difficult time acknowledging that he was not the primary wage earner when public norms so strongly expected him to fill that role. I have witnessed the cruel effect of social expectations—they can twist people who do not fit in the most awful ways.

When I entered my high school years, I did not yet know how to react to the racism and sexism that affected me. During those early teenage years, I received much unwanted attention for "being pretty," "exotic," and again, "different." I was desperate to hide from the spotlight at school, to find a piece of myself to claim as my own. It felt as if I was being picked over at an all-you-can-eat buffet. I was mad and wanted to have a chance for people to get to know me, but I did not quite understand how to work around the barriers that set us apart and targeted me as "other." I slowly released my anger and confusion through drawing, painting, and fashion. When I flip through artwork I did in high school, my self-portraits are really interesting. Some studies consisted of my entire face, others, just of my nose or mouth. I am surprised at how convincing they look—as if I had drawn myself from careful study after careful study, over and over. They were a testament to wanting to see me for who I was, rather than through the reactions and assumptions of others. The need to classify is frustrating but on some level very human and understandable. I think we all have unconscious means to fit what we see into categories—it is a way for our brains to make sense of the world. But this must be challenged, especially when race and identity politics influence our need to label based on assumptions. In drawing and "viewing" myself, I attempted to challenge the underlying "slippage" (which refers to the in-between, or a contradiction) of that question—"What are you?"[1] A social change activist can use the power of that slippage—in this case, an unconscious xenophobic moment that can be challenged or used to educate—to transform our understanding of difference.

When I look back, I realize that in fact my difference was a gift—it enabled me to perceive things in a fresh way. I saw solutions, hopes, battles, quests, and movements within people. After observing so many faces trying to read the surface of my own, I tried to see beyond exterior stereotypes. What are the hidden thoughts and emotions on the faces of strangers? I imagined cause and effect and the variety of "otherness" that we all feel. And I realized that I needed to spread the refreshing perspective that otherness provides.

My difference also became a mentor. The "what are you" question forced me to think about my response, to analyze the deep down, nitty-gritty of the self and realize that I am strong, dynamic, special, important, insightful, intelligent, determined, charismatic, and forgiving. Rather than feeling like an outsider—a member of society who "passes" and yet does not belong—instead I felt engaged to become more aware, thoughtful, and accepting of difference.

Learning to Name "Difference"

After high school and a brief stint at U Mass–Amherst, I attended Douglass College of Rutgers University and was required to take a women's studies class. I signed up in the fall to get it out of the way; for the first few weeks, I hated that course, partly because of the unspoken pressure from my peers to dislike a class on gender but even more because it is so difficult to hear the truth. That class held nothing back when it came to critiquing sexism and power, and it had the theory and analysis to back it up as well as the voices and words of feminist leaders across the spectrum. When you do not know about women's history and feminism—when you yourself have felt isolated and hopeless—you get angry that somehow you missed the boat. How did such a movement happen? Was I left out of it? In our current social climate, women are left behind, without a sense of community or true allies among one another. The media pays handsomely to highlight young women's doubts and anxieties, yet we all desire friendships as much as we want to be heard, recognized, and respected.

In this class, new ideas and terms—such as sexism, otherness, and standards of female beauty—resonated with me as I began to understand how they had affected my own life. It was more work than you could imagine, but by mid-semester, my hate was replaced with hunger. I wanted to learn more about the theory, experiences, and voices of feminists, women of color, and warriors who had the courage to speak and, as a result, changed history. I found the course strengthening, confidence boosting, and eye opening; it expanded my mind and reshaped all that I had known. I now had language and theories to name "difference" as it had been applied to gender, race, and class. I ended up majoring in women's and gender studies, embracing myself as a feminist, and working against the grain. But it was not clear to me yet that I could be a leader like the women I read about—that I could be, like them, an agent for social change.

The instructor of that gender studies class encouraged me to apply for a two-year leadership program at the Institute for Women's Leadership, and I remember feeling the impact of being recognized. It was awesome. I was soon accepted and introduced to an all-female space that I found both intimidating and exhilarating; it was full of diverse, deep thinkers who were part of a collective. Having an intelligent, compassionate group of women as my colleagues, friends, and mentors helped me trust and value friendship with women. We offered one another support, insight, time, and sincerity. We took risks and ricocheted between insecurity and determination. The director of the program, noticing my initial reluctance to accept such a community (uprooting the affects of sexism takes time), offered me the position of social activities chair, which strengthened my ability to embrace my membership in the group and actively bring people together. Through this role I realized that I could mobilize others and influence them in positive ways.

Throughout my college coursework, I learned about sexism and racism in art and society, about feminism and backlash, struggle and continuity. I studied leadership and how women have been involved in almost every movement in history, how they have been great scientists, artists and politicians, and they continue to work toward social change despite the challenges they face. I understood the agency of third world women and how that relates to the state, and I discovered ways of taking action myself, and expressing my own voice.[2]

Women in the Arts

Participating in the Leadership Scholars Program influenced my understanding of how I fit into the world as a female leader. The skills development component of the program (which provided mandatory public speaking and negotiation workshops) further developed my self-confidence and leadership abilities. In the Institute for Women's Leadership, we each studied and addressed different policy areas that affected women's lives. My area was women in the arts, and I took courses on film, feminism, and art history that encouraged me to make transformations—academically, personally, and artistically.[3] While taking these courses, I learned about cinema and how film can be a tool for social change. For example, under the guise of being pro-Communist, Chen Kaige's 1984 film *Yellow Earth* was able to convey anti-Communist messages to the public. Chen designed an innovative way to appear conformist while actually sending a radical message. This made a lasting impression on me; I will never forget the closing scene where a young boy runs against the tide of soldiers marching en masse just to reach the one soldier who had touched his life.

After watching this film, I wanted to know more about the other movies we would be viewing in the course and was surprised to learn that there were none on the list by women. My female professor was dismayed when I asked if she could include Chinese women filmmakers on the syllabus. Her response was worrisome: she did not know of any. Partly out of disappointment and partly out of humor, I told her that if there were no great female Chinese filmmakers, I would become one. And so I registered for a course on women and film and discovered the world of women screenwriters, producers, and directors and the ways in which they created works that expressed, influenced, taught, and artfully showed their audiences new modes of seeing. Films such as *Les Rendez-vous d'Anna* (1978) by Chantal Ackerman opened a door for me to the ways we perceive and reiterate stories on screen from a feminist perspective. This affirmed for me that film and art are powerful tools for social change.

For my senior honors thesis, I wrote about the African American conceptual artist Adrian Piper, a woman who plays with performance, race, identity, and xenophobia through a variety of strategies in art.[4] In her works, she explores her mixed race identity. Her performances, installations, drawings, photos, and videos offer insights into the stages of coming to understand her racial ambiguity, and she asserts that in fact, we are all essentially "mixed." Her art made me realize that there can be inventiveness in sharing the concept of "being mixed"; I learned how to use a "double vision" both personally and politically to eradicate the fear of difference that entraps so many people.

I had to unlearn oppression and practice empowerment—developing a new lens and new themes. I had to practice how I was going to be a leader in my own life. If my life were a film, who would be my target audience and what would be my message? Who would be my allies, actors, and fellow agents of change? All that I had experienced, studied, and performed prepared me to be a leader—but it was time to craft something, to create a tangible piece of leadership and give it back to the world.

Seeing with Our Own Eyes

When it came time in the women's leadership program to think of a social action project—the culmination of our scholarly work—I decided to give myself a challenge. I determined to write, shoot, and direct a short film that would illuminate my life experiences and observations. I would focus on young people between the ages of sixteen and twenty-one and show them internally questioning social norms and working to debunk stereotypes. *A Third Eye Opening* would be the title, a reference to both wisdom and a new perspective or way of seeing. After drafting a proposal, I was awarded funding by the Institute for Women's Leadership and the office of the New Jersey governor, through the Governor's Award for Young Women's Leadership, which I received in 2001. These two grants, along with the support of friends and a film student at the Mason Gross School of the Arts, made this twenty-minute short possible.

A Third Eye Opening is my own interpretation of the lives of four young people in their teens or early twenties whom I had observed in real life. I filmed segments of their everyday experiences, setting up the mise-en-scène and building themes that questioned notions of identity, gender, race, media, and culture. Included in all four segments are readable texts similar to those used in Charlie Chaplin silent films. Rather than representing what the characters were actually saying (or even thinking), I wanted to symbolize the beginning of taking control, the act of questioning what we come to accept as the "norm." In making this film, I played with the viewer's perceptions and stereotypes of "others." I explored how no one enjoys fitting into the boxes of femininity, masculinity, race, or class—unless of course, they benefit from them.

A Third Eye Opening is a silent, visual narrative, mostly black and white, where I use text to represent a few of the thoughts and questions raised in my generation. Some of these have the capacity to create political change and encourage new ways of being in the world. The unspoken queries include the following: Are these roles we perform everyday our own or are they constructed for us? If so, who created them and why? How can we impact the world as unique individuals and change society? How can we see with our own eyes? Young people can make a powerful wave of change but we need encouragement, support, and recognition. I hoped I would represent this in *A Third Eye Opening*. I used a variety of different types of film—33 millimeter/Bloex camera, HD film, and digital. The film is converted to VHS (keeping it old school, like the days of my eighties youth) and is kept in parts in film and HD. Therefore, even the texture of the image changes along with the characters. Clips of the filmmaker editing 33 millimeter, examining frames and putting them together, divide each narrative.

The viewer watches the main character in each section of the film based on particular themes: the politics of housework; the punk rock, mixed race other; the blonde bombshell trapped in daily gendered routines; and an Indian American woman defying stereotypes of ethnicity, nationality, and culture. I captured rhythms of their everyday lives. I inserted words that spoke for their thoughts—aiming to instill in the viewer the idea that there is more than what we see, more that lies within the minds and experiences of each individual. We cannot base our understanding on assumptions. I hoped that with the images, themes, silence, and projected words, like artists and filmmakers before me, I would send out a message.

The first actor in the film is a young man—a nontraditional male feeling confident in who he is despite the fact that he is both sexualized and shown as a homemaker. He is displayed bare chested, washing dishes, and then ironing a shirt and touching the fabric delicately, almost petting it in a deep trance, as though this act brings him a moment of clarity, reflection, and memory.[5] The second character is a stereotypical beautiful blond female whom we watch getting dressed, putting on makeup, and sitting at a café while other young women study her, either directly or through the reflection of mirrors. In the text interspersed with her scenes, she informs the viewer that she is tired of this routine—she is uncomfortable with our gaze and is waiting for us to stop staring at her, to see her beyond her looks.[6] In the third segment of the film, the viewer watches a mixed race, punk-styled teenager (my brother) sitting between a Chinese mother and Caucasian father, not speaking. He does not feel that he belongs, yet through writing and interacting with technology he discovers his own identity and unique perspective.[7] In the fourth and final section, a strong, bicultural South Asian woman is shown in her living room, shaking her head at magazines that commodify non-Western cultures. The closing shot shines a spotlight on Indian Barbie while the text informs the viewer that the actor is discovering she will only be represented correctly if she represents herself. She is playing with toys and consuming the images radiating from the media, but she is thinking about them critically.[8]

My hope is that by seeing the filmmaker construct and create these stories, other young people will believe they too can make a film and share their observations and messages through art. Film is unique because it documents a moment of your life and what you believed in at that time. One of the best tools a person can bring to film or art is individual experience—to embrace the "outsider within" perspective, which can create personal and social change.[9] As Patricia Hill Collins has demonstrated, people of color often have "insider" relationships with predominantly white institutions and groups, but at the same time, their "outsider" status gives them a unique perspective on self and society. *A Third Eye Opening* is used now in women's and gender studies courses at Rutgers and shares the story I wanted to tell to affect my community and to contribute to social change. As a filmmaker, I am a spokesperson to those I represent through the messages I craft. The meaning of this film derives from my belief that young people are the foundation for social change, but they must carve out their own journeys and design projects to share their findings with the world.

As in all art, you give a piece of yourself along with your vision, perspective, and empathy when you make a film. I do this with a sense of responsibility and leadership because I am a sounding board for what I have experienced, witnessed, and learned. I am the representative of the multiple perspectives I have gained as a unique, different, observant individual. It has taken leadership to use my own experiences as a way to express my opinions, vision, and lessons learned. No two paths are the same, and there is much to learn from each person's perspective, no matter what we, as viewers, see on the outside. Leadership takes courage, friends, and collaboration, and is worthwhile even when the challenge feels intimidating, overwhelming, or impossible. It is about taking a risk and not letting resistance prevent you from trying out a new way of seeing or acting. It involves a willingness to change, confront, accept, readjust, determine, inform, and question. Leadership is stepping out of what you know or what is comfortable because something inside matters enough to motivate and inspire you to make a difference.

Through my development as a feminist, a filmmaker, and a leader, I have realized what (and who) I am. If we take all our experiences and everything we have learned from childhood memories, hardships, identity formation, and education, we can affect social change. It is not easy to swim against the tide, to unlearn so much that is part of who we are, what we've recited, memorized, and claimed. A leader grows tired of performing the same old routines—the same lines of the same films—and picks up the tools necessary to create new ones that may alter the experiences, self-understanding, and vision of those who follow closely in her footsteps.

NOTES

1. On the concept of "slippage" see B. Spivak and Gayatri Chakravorty, "Can the Subaltern Speak?" in Cary Nelson and Lawrence Grossberg, eds., *Marxism and the Interpretation of Culture*, 271–313 (Urbana: University of Illinois Press, 1988).

2. One way I expressed my own voice was by creating the indie rock band World Without Maps with three guy friends I had met at Rutgers, which was a different kind of leadership experience. Eventually, these two threads—music and women's empowerment—would lead me to become a founding member of the Willie Mae Rock Camp for Girls in New York City. Through that affiliation, I work with girls aged eight to eighteen to help them find their voices, question identity and image, read

the media, create their own messages, and discuss sexism. For more information, see their Web site: http://www.williemaerockcamp.org. See also Ingrid Dahl, "'I Want to Rock Out!' On Acting Rather than Appearing: The Rock n' Roll Camp for Girls," M.A. practicum paper, Department of Women's and Gender Studies, Rutgers University, May 2005.

3. These courses included Theories of Women in Film, The Chinese Cinema, Women and Leadership, Comparative Feminism, Women and Art, and The Dynamics of Race, Class and Sex.

4. See Adrian Piper, *Out of Order, Out of Sight* (Cambridge, MA: The MIT Press, 1999); Adrian Piper, Maurice Berger, and Jean Fisher, *Adrian Piper: A Retrospective* (University of Maryland, Baltimore County, Fine Arts Gallery, 1999); Ingrid Dahl, "The Outsider Within: The Space of the Mixed-Race Artist," undergraduate honors thesis, Department of Women's and Gender Studies, Rutgers University, April 2002.

5. This character continues to enjoy household chores and lives in his own apartment in Jersey City, New Jersey.

6. Years later, the woman who played this character informed me of a similar experience as she ended a relationship that objectified and degraded her.

7. My brother is currently a film major at Hunter College in New York City; we often discuss our different experiences and responses to our mixed race and our respective genders.

8. This character is currently pursuing a Ph.D. and writing about queer stories of displacement post-Katrina. She has worked with a number of South Asian organizations.

9. See Patricia Hill Collins, "Learning from the Outsider Within: The Sociological Significance of Black Feminist Thought," in Sandra G. Harding, ed., *The Feminist Standpoint Theory Reader: Intellectual and Political Controversies*, 103–126 (New York: Routledge, 2004).

5

Leading by Example

My Mother's Resilience and Power
in the Fight against Poverty

ROSANNA EANG

Poverty has a staggering effect on the lives of women and children, stripping away human dignity. My own experiences of poverty as well as my mother's example of strength and resilience in the face of great odds have shaped my outlook on leadership and activism as well as my career goals. This is a story about my mother, my life, and my passionate pursuit of helping women and children living in poverty.

In November of 1981 my parents, two brothers, sister, grandpa, aunts, uncles, and cousins first arrived in America, in the City of Brotherly Love, after they had fled three years of civil war and starvation in their home country of Cambodia. The brutal genocide of the Pol Pot Khmer Rouge regime had taken more than one million lives, including those of many of my aunts and uncles as well as my grandparents. My father became a monk at nineteen and lived in the temple for five years before he left. He and my mother had an arranged marriage, which is customary in Cambodian traditions. My mother and father are actually first cousins, which is also quite common. My father was twenty-five and my mother twenty-three when they were married in their rural town of Poom Peanne, Cambodia.[1] Although my mother was pregnant eleven times, she has only five surviving children. She gave birth to her eldest son when she was twenty-four. My second brother was born seven years later, a few years before the war began, and my older sister was born during the war. My family is only here today because of my mother's determination. During the war in Cambodia, she kept my two older brothers and sister alive while my father went into hiding because the Khmer Rouge was executing all the men who were educated or were formerly monks. My mother and siblings slept in jungles along the mountainsides, and my mother used her machete to hunt for food to keep her children alive.

Despite my mother's courage and strength, she, like other Cambodian women, was expected to abide by the traditional gender roles that are central to the culture. Women are supposed to marry early and remain in subservient, care-giving roles. In Cambodia, girls are usually married between the ages of sixteen and twenty-five, but sometimes even younger. It is also typical for the groom to be older than the bride by twelve years or more. The Wats, or temples, serve as the religious, cultural, educational, and social centers of the country. Men usually become monks first and then marry after they leave the monastery. The elders make marital decisions and often the groom has some say, but the bride can never go against decisions made for her. My mother always said she never had a choice in her marriage.

Childhood Lessons

My younger sister and I were considered lucky to be "American," meaning that we were born in the United States. I was born in 1983, and my younger sister was born in 1984 in West Philadelphia. My parents had moved many times all over Philadelphia, but my most vivid memories are of when we lived in a three-floor duplex. The second and third floors were occupied by my three orphaned cousins, two brothers, and my aunt's and uncles' families. My mom and dad, two sisters, and I slept in the first-floor dining room, and my grandpa slept in our tiny den. The house was old, and its walls were covered with lead paint; I remember the chipped green paint and the dark, dirty, dingy basement. No matter how ancient, ugly, and crowded the house was, my parents appreciated the American freedom and tried their best to raise their five children.

My dad, aunts, and uncles attended adult school in Philadelphia and learned English, but my mother did not receive formal education. She stayed home and did housework, including all the cooking and cleaning for seventeen people. While my brothers attended junior high school and my older sister was in kindergarten, my dad worked on many farms throughout New Jersey and my mother took care of my younger sister and me, and my ailing grandpa. My mother's limited English skills and the lack of an interpreter led, she later believed, to the death of both my grandfather and my eight-month-old sister, who died of sudden infant death syndrome. When my mother took her to the Philadelphia hospital, she signed papers she was unable to read, and consented to medical procedures she could not understand. After her passing, my sister's body was returned to my mother in a small, tightly sealed white box. My mother had unknowingly consented to a medical study of my sister. After the deaths of my grandfather and sister Philly, my mom worked in the blueberry and plant nursery fields with my dad.

My father became a crew leader and drove a big blue bus full of other Cambodians or immigrants to and from the many farms where they worked. On weekends, my entire family boarded the bus and headed out to the farms. I remember not knowing how to pick blueberries; my hands were so tiny that no matter how hard I tried to pick and hold on to them, the berries would fall through my fingers and onto the ground instead of into an aluminum juice container that served as a bucket tied around my small waist. At the blueberry farms, everyone was always tired from picking and from the hot sun, but I was so short compared to the tall bushes that I was in the shade all day. When the inspectors looked for underage children working, my frantic parents told my sisters and me to sit quietly under the shrubbery. We were never afraid. We were too young to know it was against the law for us to work.

During the week, my younger sister Rosalie and I were dropped off every morning at six at my aunt's apartment after a noisy, bumpy bus ride through the streets of Philadelphia. My mom opened the door with her key, and we went in and curled up under a thin blanket on the couch in front of the small television set. We just lay there and whispered to one another about our plans for the day and stared at the ceiling because we weren't sleepy anymore after the bus ride. My aunt lived on the third floor of a five-story apartment complex. It was a creepy place for three- and four-year-olds; drug dealers and junkies lived in the building, hookers stood at the first-floor entrance, and homeless men and women slept on the stairways. Even though we were brought to our aunt's home for care and attention, we were never really super-vised. My sister and I wanted to go outside and play, but day after day were forced to stay indoors. My mom bought us two bikes with training wheels, one red and one blue, after we had whined about how bored we were all day. We rode the bikes inside the apartment and our aunt often yelled at us.

What haunts me the most is what happened one day when I was at my aunt's house. The vivid memories of the events that occurred, that no child should ever experience, return. Flashbacks of sexual abuse and neglect run rampant in my mind and my body chills. There was an old, Cambodian man who often came to visit at our aunt's residence. He was not a relative, he was just a stranger who lived on the streets and suffered from a mental disability. While my aunt was busy with her chores, she left us alone with him. I vividly remember the time he made us touch his private parts. When I recall that incident, I feel anger and I feel hurt. I have to compose myself. This is my childhood experience. I am not proud of it, and I am not yet healed of it. I know, however, that I can overcome this because I have already been through the hardest part—surviving the bad childhood.

We also experienced racism in our West Philadelphia neighborhood. One evening when I was four years old, we were gathered in the living room to watch *Wheel of Fortune*, our favorite game show because everyone was trying to learn English. I was sitting on my cousin's lap, and he had just whispered the answer in my ear and I screamed out, "Dee Pi is in Dee skiiY!" when suddenly a brick came crashing through our window, flew above our heads, and landed in front of the TV. The shattered glass and loud noise filled the room; my mom grabbed my sisters and me and ran into our bedroom. My dad yelled, "Get down! Get down!" My uncles and male cousins grabbed an old lamp, someone else ran to get a baseball bat, and they all rushed outside. I was scared but did not understand why someone had thrown a brick through our window as a sign of hate.

Life in Camden City

When my parents finally saved enough money and were fed up with the old duplex and the racism, violence, and discrimination in West Philadelphia, they moved across the bridge to Camden City, New Jersey. They bought a three-bedroom house for their family of seven, plus my three orphaned cousins, my father's younger brother, and my uncle's family of six. Even with everyone crammed into a small house, it still seemed better than the West Philadelphia duplex. The house was packed; there was literally no empty space. When that summer ended, I was five years old, so my mom bought me a pink Minnie Mouse backpack, and with my uncle translating, she enrolled me in kindergarten at the H. H. Davis Elementary School two blocks from my house.

I was eight years old when I began doing full-time manual labor during the time I was not in school. Beginning from second grade, I spent all my summers working on my brother's ten-acre farm located in the "blueberry capital" of Hammonton, New Jersey. It was a family business but the profit never surpassed the effort that we put in. It was such hard work. My brother still owns the farm today, and I go whenever I can for good, grinding exercise. I hoed the ground ten hours a day, from seven a.m. to five p.m. When the summer ended, my mom worked in factories. I accompanied her and stood in the same production lines every weekend and every day when school was not in session. We earned $4.50 an hour under the table working in both freezing cold and sweltering hot factories. To date, I have worked in more than ten different factories at jobs ranging from packaging foods, assembling products, and breaking boxes, to paper and dry cleaning operations. Some days when school ended at three o'clock, I ran home to get on the van and go to work with my mom; we often labored two or more shifts. This experience not only forced me to be an adult at an early age but it also did much harm to my health and my body.

On the farms, as I hoed the ground with my parents, I knew I did not belong there. I felt so hopeless standing out on the field, in the scorching sunlight. But when you are a child, you do what you are told and feel obligated to help your parents. I often asked them what they would do differently if given the opportunity. My dad said if he could go to college, he would study agriculture because farming was all he had known and he loved it. My mom screamed, "No! If I had a chance to go to school, I would become a doctor. I would not be working in blood and sweat with my daughter here in the burning sun. I will make a better life for my children and myself." Standing at four feet, nine inches tall, and weighing only 105 pounds, my mother may not have heard of the word feminism and may not understand its meaning, but she exemplifies woman power.

My life really began when I attended the public schools of Camden City. Every morning and afternoon, as I walked to and from school, I observed my surroundings and knew it was not a pleasant environment for children. In Camden City, which is now the poorest city in New Jersey and the second-poorest city in the nation, growing up was tough. While my parents struggled to pay the bills and our family drifted apart through domestic violence and disagreements, I paid attention to getting an education. I learned at an early age that for change to happen, you must be active and voice your opinions. In eighth grade I won an essay competition, declaring: "I can be mayor of Camden City right now at the age of fourteen . . . and will be able to rebuild Camden better than any previous mayor has." (This was after the current mayor had been indicted and sentenced to house arrest.) I was quite a radical.

Today, Camden City has roughly eighty thousand residents, and the median family income is well below the state average. Almost six thousand houses are vacant and more than 70 percent of residents do not have high school diplomas. The city has the largest percentage of children in poverty and the highest unemployment rate in the state, and more than a third of the population is on some form of public assistance. In addition, health care needs are not being met, and the school system continues to deteriorate. This was the environment in which I lived between the ages of four and eighteen.

When summer was over and the farming season ended, we went on public assistance while my mom continued to work in the factories for cash. I remember standing in welfare lines with my father and interpreting for him while he was interviewed by the caseworker. The only time my parents, siblings, and I had any medical care was during the months we received welfare benefits and Medicaid. We collected $500 from Temporary Assistance for Needy Families and $250 in food stamp benefits for a family of seven. When President Clinton signed the Personal Responsibility and Work Opportunity Reconciliation Act in 1996, the welfare system and its requirements changed. My parents followed the new guidelines to receive assistance: my father had to do volunteer work and was sent to an employment agency for training; my mother attended adult school. It was very difficult. She went to school in the morning, worked nights, and somehow found time in between to care for her family. This was the only schooling my mother ever received, and she was able to learn some English. After my sisters and I got home from school, she boarded a van to go work in the blistering factories. At times we would not see her for an entire week, because she left before we returned from school. My sisters and I took care of ourselves and focused on our education.

Throughout high school, I was very active in my community and school. I participated in science fairs and competed in oratorical and art contests. I learned that competition does not just involve winning and losing; it builds leadership and the foundations of self-learning. I was engaged in student government, which gave me experience conducting school fundraisers and food, clothing, and toy drives for the local homeless shelter. Mobilizing my classmates to get involved with their community taught me leadership skills at an early age. A student representative to the Camden City Board of Education my senior year, I had the opportunity to interact with board members and the Superintendent of Schools. I was curious about almost every subject at school, but science, especially medicine and healthcare, interested me the most.

Transitioning to College

When I first came to college, I felt nervous, scared, and eager all at once because I had not seen much of the world outside of Camden City, and yes, I was embarking on something that wasn't expected of a Cambodian girl. I had graduated in a class of sixty students from Dr. Charles E. Brimm Medical Arts High School, three days before the summer Educational Opportunity Fund (EOF) Program began. EOF, designed to help socioeconomically disadvantaged students in college, was my family far from home. I remember when my older sister Sean, the first woman in the family to attend and graduate from college with a Doctor of Pharmacy degree, was driving me to campus. She told me to chill and relax because she was sure that everyone else was feeling the same way or maybe even worse. Then we laughed about our relatives being in shock over how there had been one girl in college and now there were two, and in another year there would be three.

I had never heard of the word feminism and never knew there was a major called women's studies until I went to college and took an introductory women's and gender studies course. I used to consider feminism a negative or bad thing because I did not know what it meant, but when I realized it was associated with women's rights, I began to identify as a feminist. There is no set definition of feminism. Naming yourself a feminist and claiming your own understanding of what it means makes you stand out as an individual. When young women discover themselves as feminists and become active leaders, change happens. I believe there is a feminist in every woman across all racial and cultural boundaries, but we do not recognize this because of misconceptions about the term. Although we may have divergent definitions, we are all connected in the pursuit of obtaining gender equality and bettering the lives of women and children. My older sister and I often have long talks about women's issues, and when we get to the word feminism, she always makes this statement: "If you are a woman and you believe in your rights as a woman, then you are a feminist!"

During my fifth semester at college, I took a course on feminism, poverty, and public policy. On the first day of class, the professor asked, "What is poverty and with what do you think it is associated?" That was when I sank a little lower into my chair. She said she wanted everyone in the room to introduce themselves and share their thoughts on poverty. At that point, my heart was racing and my palms were wet. The question about poverty terrified me because I had so many answers from personal experience. This course, as well as others I took in women's studies allowed me to reflect on my life experiences and to analyze them in relation to larger social structures, including race, gender, and class, as well as welfare and immigration policies. Women's studies also encouraged me to see a connection between the classroom and the community.

Taking Action in the Community

One of my greatest experiences at college was being a scholar at the Institute for Women's Leadership, which gave me the opportunity to create such interventions and to exercise my skills as a young woman leader. The program exceeded my expectations: I had the chance to meet and work with remarkable, smart, funny, talented, and committed young women. Their passion and convictions will have a lasting impact on me; when I think of them I smile because I know they are out there causing trouble to make our lives better. I met friends and mentors through the program.

Through an internship and a social action project, I have grown and healed and become a better leader. During my first year in the program, I interned at the Eric B. Chandler Health Center, a federally funded clinic located in New Brunswick, New Jersey, where I worked on projects to support teen mothers, parenting education, domestic violence support groups, prescription assistance, and a self-esteem workshop for patients. As I sat in the office of a social worker at the center, listened to the patients' stories, and participated in the support groups, I felt empowered and moved to help.

During my second year, I established a pediatric literacy program at the health center as well as a student volunteer organization, Reach Out and Read (ROAR), at my university. ROAR enlists college students to read to children while they are waiting to be seen at the clinic. It makes early literacy part of pediatric practice, a necessity in a health center serving an impoverished community. Starting this organization was a way for me to get other students involved in helping low-income, immigrant children achieve educational equity. It gives college students the opportunity to learn something no textbook can teach: the volunteerism, service, and compassion they share with the children and parents at the health center will have a lasting impact.

My childhood years left me scarred in many ways; to help those in the same situations that I had experienced is liberating. Starting a program and an organization has taught me that leadership requires vision, commitment, patience, and perseverance. I have learned that healing does not always require medicine; it calls for programs and initiatives that intervene to prevent the social determinants that deplete the health of individuals living in poor communities.

Learning from the Past, Looking to the Future

If someone were to tell my relatives eleven years ago that one day Rosanna and her sisters would be college graduates and feminists, their jaws would have dropped, thinking it was impossible for these three Cambodian girls to get that far. Although times have changed, many of my relatives still believe that Cambodian women should be obedient, subservient, and dependent on men.[2] For some reason, my mother never fully accepted this ideology, and she taught us something more. She does not want her daughters to live the life that she has lived. She has worked nights, weekends, and double and triple shifts at two to three different jobs at a time to make sure there was food on the table and a shelter over our heads. My mother is a great woman, and she is the force that has kept the family alive. Still, she straddles the old world and the new. She defends the tradition of arranged marriages at the same time that she believes women should have choices and be given the same opportunities as men. When Hillary Clinton ran for president of the United States in the 2008 election, my mom said to her sister, "See, in the U.S., who says a woman can't do the same things as a man?"

It has been hard growing up and it will be challenging to slowly change the cultural beliefs about gender that seemed once to be written in stone. It is difficult to change certain attitudes when so many Cambodians, especially women, accept them. To end this cycle, women must adopt leading, decision-making roles in both the home and the workplace. My mother has taught us that when women are able to define their rights and embrace the feminist within, they will lead by example. This is what my sisters and I are doing. We have all grown up to be like our mother: we refuse to conform and we are throwing gender roles out the window.

As a recent college graduate with a bachelor of science degree in public health, my career objective is still to become a physician in Camden City, New Jersey, and help improve the health and well-being of women and children living there. I am currently a student at the Ohio University College of Osteopathic Medicine, working toward this long-held goal. I find that every day is an opportunity to learn new things, to try to forgive, and to understand that our past does not dictate who we are. Our past does not make us weaker but pushes us to be stronger, and to further define ourselves and realize our rights as women. I am now a quarter century old and I have found my own definitions, voice, and path in life. My experiences of poverty, abuse, and child labor have left me marked in many ways. But my mother's example of courage, strength, and resilience inspires me. After surviving war, genocide, starvation, hunger, abuse, injustice, gender violence, discrimination, hatred, and extreme poverty, she continues to fight for her daughters. My sisters and I have inherited her will and we will continue her legacy.

NOTES

1. This small village, which runs along the Sangkier River, is in the town of Mong Russey in Battdambong Province. This spelling is sounded out from the Khmer language.

2. A traditional Cambodian saying compares girls to washcloths and boys to diamonds, and expectant mothers and fathers often express disappointment if their baby is female.

6

Acting on a Grander Scale

Ending Health Care Disparities in the Latino Community

CAROL MENDEZ

From my early childhood in the poorest neighborhoods of Bogotá, Colombia, to my adolescence as an uninsured, undocumented immigrant in the United States, to my young adulthood as a medical student, I have witnessed the inequities of healthcare disparities and the power of activism to address these. During all the stages of my life up to now, the social inequalities and injustices around me have driven me to become an active participant in the solution to our problems. I have found feminist activism to be a powerful framework to use in efforts to eliminate health care disparities and social injustice, and to work toward a better world for all. I have learned that we can be engaged at different stages of our lives in different communities. We need to look for continuities and connections in the issues. Wherever we may be in our careers or personal development, there is always a need to demonstrate leadership by working along with others toward a shared goal.

My longstanding commitment to the poor, to immigrants, and to equal health care began when I was a young girl growing up in Bogotá, Colombia. My mother was murdered in a carjacking when I was two years old; because of this horrible act of violence, my maternal grandmother raised me. My grandmother is my inspiration and role model; she worked many difficult jobs, including cooking for children at a day care center, cleaning houses, and serving as an elevator attendant at a city hospital. She suffered a great deal because she was poor, and she raised four grandchildren after rearing five children of her own. In addition, she was a victim of domestic violence in a gendered, strictly patriarchal society. She taught me by example. In our house, we had running water and food at all times, but our neighbors did not, so they would line up in front of our home with buckets to get clean water. My grandmother always gave and gave, as much as she could. There was a clear sense of the "haves" and "have-nots" around me in Bogotá; we were on the side of the "have-nots," but even then she managed to share the little we did have. She taught me to be self-sufficient, to work earnestly for advancement, and to serve others.

When I was ten, my grandmother was no longer able to care for me, and although I had neither documentation nor knowledge of English, I came to the United States to live with my aunts. I had talked to my aunts on the phone, but had never lived with them. I came to live my American dream because I believed that anything in the United States was better than growing up in Colombia. I quickly learned English and adapted to an exciting and challenging new culture and family in Morristown, New Jersey. Within two years of this novel life, my two-year-old cousin, whom I lived with, was diagnosed with meningitis due to tuberculosis, a disease of poverty that immigrated with my great-grandmother. At twelve years old, I experienced firsthand the need for bilingual, Hispanic physicians as well as health care professionals who are sensitive to cultural and linguistic barriers. My desire to become a doctor became more concrete as I assumed the role of interpreter between my very frightened family and my cousin's physicians. Sadly, a few months later my cousin suffered a stroke and consequently had to undergo years of physical, speech, and occupational therapy. As a result, my role as an interpreter between my family and health professionals continued. I was both proud and deeply influenced by the experience.

The Possibilities of Activism

My interest in immigrants and health care deepened throughout my high school years. I attended a large urban high school in northern New Jersey with a racially and ethnically mixed student body. When I was a senior, I volunteered with Wind of the Spirit Immigrant Resource Center in Morristown, New Jersey. This organization helps immigrants and nonimmigrants come to know each other, to be enriched by one another, and to advocate for the human rights and dignity of all people regardless of immigration status.[1] In my time there, I heard many horror stories from undocumented men, women, adolescents, and children who were recent immigrants as well as from those who had been here for many years. They did not speak English or have access to services, and they lived their lives in fear. They worked very hard at jobs that most people would not do because employers demanded so much and paid so little. The skills that I possessed at that time allowed me to serve others at the center as an English teacher, a translator for a court case, an organizer, and an example to other young people who felt they had no future ahead of them. I had a lot of time as a high school student to work at the immigrant resource center; this beginning helped me to solidify what I wanted to do with my life and gain skills that would later help and motivate me.

While a volunteer at the center, I lobbied and helped raise awareness about the Development, Relief, and Education for Alien Minors Act (the DREAM Act), S. 2075 in the U.S. Senate and the American Dream Act, H.R. 5131 in the House of Representatives. These similar pieces of federal legislation would allow undocumented high school students the opportunity to obtain permanent residency, attend institutions of higher education at in-state tuition rates, and give them a path toward citizenship.[2] The passage of these laws would be significant because they would benefit society as a whole; if our high school graduates are strong students, they should be given the opportunity to follow their dreams and become full contributors to the country by sharing their talents with us. There were many times during this period when I felt that all my hard work was going unnoticed: I was afraid that after finishing high school I would work cleaning offices or at a fast food restaurant. I even considered dropping out of high school like many of the other intelligent undocumented teens in the United States. Through my volunteer work I met other young undocumented students who were valedictorians or star soccer players, well-rounded individuals who spoke English better than Spanish yet could not attend college. They were ready and willing to work hard and study to become the nurses, primary care physicians, scientists, law enforcement officers, and teachers, which our society needs. Through lobbying for this legislation, I learned a lot about the U.S. legislative system. I organized at a local and national level with others who felt passionately about our youth and the future of our country and sat across the table from senators and representatives sharing my story and asking for their support. Despite much effort by many volunteers and advocates, these bills have not passed to this day. The reader is therefore encouraged to contact local elected officials for their support in passing these legislations.[3]

The people who started the immigrant resource center were my leadership and social justice mentors and they opened up my world to activism. They connected the sense of justice and righteousness that I had learned at church and at home with action, and with making a difference. They gave me the tools I needed to connect with other students who had immigrated to the United States, and to ask them to make statements in support of the legislation. I argued for the importance of publicly disclosing one's deepest secret and identity, the most vulnerable point of our lives, which we had been told to never mention out of fear of being deported. My fight for undocumented students to attend college was personal because I was one of them.

Every stage of my life up to now has been possible because others believed in me and thought it was important that I have a chance to achieve my dreams. In fact, I almost did not attend college: I did not even know what the SAT was, did not qualify (as an undocumented student) for financial aid, and worried that it was unsafe to apply out of fear of deportation. My high school guidance counselor actually drove me to the college campus for a recruitment day specifically for women of color. She assisted me in filling out my application and did everything possible to help me find private scholarships and funding. She believed that changing society begins with young people and worked to ensure we were heard, validated, and given guidance and tools to advance to higher educational levels. Had it not been for her, I would never have applied to college; had it not been for my scholarship foundation and all the people who donate to it, I would not have been able to attend.

New Venues for Activism and Learning

When I went to college, I wanted to continue to work for immigrants' rights and for the elimination of racial and ethnic disparities in health care. One-third of the residents of Middlesex County, New Jersey (where Rutgers University is located), speak a language other than English at home, so I was in an environment that allowed me to continue my activism for the causes I believed in, but in a new way.[4] When it comes to health care and efficient patient care, immigrants face language barriers as well as cultural obstacles that, if not addressed correctly, can lead to fatal outcomes. Young women leaders who want to work toward minimizing racial and ethnic disparities in health care can do so by getting involved with their local communities. I became part of the New Brunswick Community Interpreter Project where I learned the nuances of interpreting as well as practical procedures for facilitating health care between Spanish-speaking patients and their doctors. Professional training is essential because, according to Dr. Glenn Flores, "ad hoc interpreters, including family members, friends, untrained members of the support staff, and strangers found in waiting rooms or on the street, are commonly used in clinical encounters. But such interpreters are considerably more likely than professional interpreters to commit errors that may have adverse clinical consequences."[5] The New Brunswick Interpreter Project trained me in medical interpreting; it only took a few hours in one afternoon. The project works toward eliminating medical errors by connecting trained students with local clinics and hospitals. In addition, it gives undergraduates opportunities for community service and growth.

My undergraduate internship at the Eric B. Chandler Health Center (EBCHC) gave me a new venue for activism and learning, and for continuing to address the needs of medically underserved Hispanic women. The EBCHC is a New Jersey federally qualified community health center that is operated by the Robert Wood Johnson Medical School–UMDNJ and the EBCHC Community Board. This center offers many high-quality, affordable services including primary health care, community outreach programs, and nutrition and health education. In 2005 the EBCHC provided more than fifty thousand

encounters: 71 percent were with Hispanic patients, 52 percent with the uninsured, and 40 percent with Medicaid patients.[6] The racial breakdown is significant because 16 percent of the residents of Middlesex County, New Jersey, are
of Hispanic or Latino origin.[7] A large percentage of the Hispanic residents
attend centers like the EBCHC for their health care and utilize them as community resources for other services as well. I was given the opportunity as a
premed student to work with its staff to administer a patient survey to learn
more about their needs, concerns, and health status. Based on the findings
from the surveys I distributed as part of my internship, I created a series of
classes for Hispanic women about maintaining healthy lives through exercise,
nutrition, reproductive health, preventive health, and the care of their
children.

The opportunity to do this type of education and community outreach as
a college student was unique because it gave me access to a health care system
where I could gain valuable experience and skills. Organizing this series of
classes was a great learning experience for me, but it was also a service to the
center and the women who utilize it because the project's curriculum could
be used repeatedly. I was able to work with the staff and learn from their experiences in community organizing and health education. As a leadership
scholar at the Institute for Women's Leadership, I was given these opportunities (a credit-bearing internship and social action project) and I also gained
knowledge from the faculty and staff of the institute about creating such a
project and writing up a grant proposal for funding.

The institute not only offered me the tools and structured curriculum to
participate in these educational experiences but also gave me a framework for
learning more about feminism, leadership, and activism. Through rigorous
studying of women's leadership and their roles in social change, I started to
relate academic writings and theories to my own life and my perspective of
the world. I did not know what the term "feminism" meant until I went to
college and sat in weekly discussions with other IWL scholars. I always
believed in equality, fair treatment for all, and social justice. However, in
those weekly discussions I was able to place a name and a scholarly theory
behind the values that had been driving my life for as long as I could remember. It was feminism that empowered me and allowed me to analyze my life,
the lives of my family members, and the women I wanted to serve and
strengthen in my community.

Like feminism, the idea of leadership was an exciting one for me in my
college years. Leadership involves recruiting people who are dedicated to your
cause, motivating, helping, and guiding them to create programs that are
sustainable. It is finding the right people and bringing out the best in them,
using their skills toward serving the common cause, focusing their efforts to
maximize their potential. I believe that women leaders have the power in

their hands to make a better world; they have the insider's view on the compassion and pain women have been forced to feel through a gendered society
and through the history of gender inequity. As a young woman who has had
the privilege of studying women's leadership I have been exposed to many
women-led initiatives, created as a response to gender inequalities and social
injustices around the world. The progressive women leaders I have both met
and read about think in a global perspective; they take into account issues
that are integral to life, viewing children as the future of our society, and education and health care as rights and tools of empowerment.

Many women leaders are activists for causes they believe in. I began to
understand that activism is dynamic and changing: it can evolve with you as
you grow. Once I was accepted to college, I did not have the time to continue
volunteering at Wind of the Spirit because I had to maintain my scholarships,
which were awarded to me by private foundations based on my academic performance, involvement in my community, and financial need. I also had to do
well in my rigorous premed studies and be active in my new local community,
which made it difficult to go back to Morristown enough to really be involved
in a project there. However, I was able to participate in college organizations,
share my beliefs with even more students, and focus on other issues affecting
young people. I was able to use my new setting to organize a different kind of
agenda but still focus on the same core goals.

By looking for connections, we can continue to act and organize for the
causes we most believe in but apply them in new ways and in new settings.
Activism can be expressed in multiple ways: by organizing at your place of
worship or at campus dining halls, setting up an information booth, expanding your knowledge, attending rallies, and educating others through confer-
ences, op-eds, or distributing an interesting article. In *Grassroots: A Field Guide
for Feminist Activism*, Jennifer Baumgardner and Amy Richards define activism
as "consistently expressing one's values with the goal of making the world
more just. . . . An activist is anyone who accesses the resources that he or she
has as an individual for the benefit of the common good."[8] With this definition in mind, anyone who is interested in Latina women's health issues can
take action and make a difference. Activism includes educating our communities about their health risk factors, modes of prevention, and the importance of early screening. By working toward the shared goal of healthy and
happy lives for all racial and ethnic groups, everyone in our communities will
benefit.

Becoming Part of the Solution

Now that I am in medical school, I have even less time to volunteer and organize, but I have tried to take advantage of new and exciting opportunities that

have arisen; consequently, I have grown as a person and affected even more people in different ways. The summer after my first year of medical school I went to Philadelphia to start a GED program in Spanish, teach ESL classes, serve as an interpreter, and learn the public systems there to aid others in their immediate needs. Some of the benefits I find in being young come from not having serious attachments like children who are settled in their schools, or a job. I am flexible enough to literally pick up and move to another city for the summer. I have lots of energy and drive to keep going; it motivates me to begin new programs, and it reaffirms what I believe in most deeply.

My focuses now are on cultural competency and how to deliver effective, high-quality health care to my community. This reflects my earliest experiences in Colombia, my youthful role as a medical interpreter for my family, my activism for immigrants' rights as a high school student, and my interaction with patients at the community health center as a college student. Racial minorities have poorer health outcomes than their white counterparts in many preventable diseases. Health is not only impacted by medical ailments but is seriously affected by our societal realities. For example, although Latinos in the United States have lower cancer rates than that of the non-Hispanic white population, their cancers are more likely to be at advanced, less treatable stages when they are diagnosed.[9] Other factors that negatively impact Hispanic health include elevated exposures to environmental risk factors in their homes, neighborhoods, and workplaces; lower education and health literacy; lower income; limited proficiency in English; reduced use of screening services; and lack of insurance. Undocumented immigration status can further compound the factors that make Latinos a vulnerable population because it makes them hesitate to seek health care for fear of deportation.[10]

Academic medicine must make the elimination of health care disparities a critical part of its mission. This can be done by collecting and reporting patient data by race and ethnicity, supporting language interpretation services in the clinical setting, increasing awareness of disparities in health care, augmenting the proportion of underrepresented minorities in the health care workforce, integrating cross-cultural education into the training of all professionals, and incorporating teaching on the impact of race, ethnicity, and culture on clinical decision making.[11] It is my responsibility as a medical student to follow these recommendations, and there are many levels at which I can become part of the solution. For example, the initiative Healthy New Jersey 2010 and its more local initiative Healthy New Brunswick 2010 aim to increase the quality and length of healthy lives, and eliminate disparities in health outcomes based on race or ethnicity. As a student, I can join the community partnerships that are working together toward meeting the initiative's goals.

Healing others and doctoring is not just treating a cold, headache, or other illness; it should mean thinking on a grander scale. Working with

Latinas on health education and awareness must be accompanied by active involvement with the deeper issues that affect the undocumented community. This can include contacting public officials and elected representatives to tell them about these issues and reminding them of the positive contributions immigrants give to the community. It can mean asking for driver's licenses so that patients can get to work every day, and earn enough money to send their children to college, be able to visit their dying parents in their home countries, and reunite their children with their siblings who simply could not make it across the border. As my grandmother's example taught me, we have a responsibility to share what we have with those who have less and to serve others.

Now as a medical student, I reflect on my life and where it all began. I am thankful for all of my experiences so far and still cannot believe sometimes that I reside in this country and that I am living my American dream. I believe that our deepest commitments and life pursuits often come out of our own lives and experiences, as mine have. No matter what city I have lived in, I have seen the same issues facing low-income immigrant Latinas and Latinos: no health insurance, no childcare, few resources, no places to meet or take classes, and people who oppose what you are trying to do. I have tried to address these problems in a variety of ways. I hope that my contributions will positively affect women and families who have the same struggles, dreams, and hopes for a better future that my family does. The communities that motivate me to keep going are the ones that raised me and taught me the values I live by.

The challenges that my family faced twelve years ago still exist; now more than ever we need culturally competent and sensitive medical care. To address the health disparities that exist in the United States and that deeply affect Latinas, we must raise awareness about immigration issues and support legislation that leads to citizenship and equal access to services. We should do a better job training our medical care providers in cultural sensitivity and follow the recommendations given by so many studies on moving toward an equal health care system with no racial or ethnic gaps. My life experiences have shaped and influenced my activism, which continues to change and evolve as I do. I believe those of us who are committed to social change and to empowering our communities can make the difference—no matter what our life stages or physical locations—so that one day we can all live in a world of justice, freedom, and equality.

NOTES

1. See Wind of the Spirit Immigrant Resource Center, http://www.windofthespirit. net/index.html.
2. National Council of La Raza, *DREAM Act Overview*. http://www.nclr.org/content/policy/detail/1331/.

3. A 35-member panel appointed by Gov. Jon Corzine in 2007 to consider ways New Jersey can better integrate immigrants into society has recommended that undocumented students should be allowed to pay in-state college tuition. If this recommendation becomes law, New Jersey would join California, Illinois, New York, and Texas in allowing the children of undocumented immigrants to attend college at in-state tuition rates. Jeff Diamant, "Panel Wants New Rights for Illegals," *The Star-Ledger*, March 31, 2009, 1.

4. U.S. Census Bureau, State & County Quick Facts. http://quickfacts.census.gov/qfd/states/34/34023.html (accessed October 6, 2006).

5. Glenn Flores, "Language Barriers to Health Care in the United States," *New England Journal of Medicine* 355, no. 3 (2006): 229–231.

6. Robert Wood Johnson Medical School–UMDNJ, Eric B. Chandler Health Center (Statistics) http://www2.umdnj.edu/chandweb/statistics.htm (accessed October 4, 2006).

7. See note 4.

8. Jennifer Baumgardner and Amy Richards, *Grassroots: A Field Guide for Feminist Activism* (New York: Farrar, Straus and Giroux, 2005).

9. U.S. Department of Health and Human Services, *National Institutes of Health News*, http://www.nih.gov/news/pr/sep2006/nci-06.htm (accessed October 4, 2006).

10. Ibid.

11. Joseph R. Betancourt, "Eliminating Racial and Ethnic Disparities in Health Care: What Is the Role of Academic Medicine?" *Academic Medicine* 81, no. 9 (2006): 788–792.

7

Learning the Meaning of One

Reflections on Social Justice Education

JESSICA H. GREENSTONE

An incident that occurred when I was in sixth grade marked the beginning of my path as a social justice educator and activist. The setting was the middle school cafeteria. It was the beginning of the year and I was fresh out of elementary school. I had just begun the critical process of starting to forge friendships with a group of girls who I imagined would become my lunch companions and more for the remainder of the year. What at the time seemed like a mundane activity—the exchange of the day's gossip—abruptly changed when Lisa, who was describing an argument she had with another student, attributed the girl's role in the argument to her being Jewish.[1] "All Jews are snippy and obnoxious," she said nonchalantly, as if this was a well-known fact that would clarify to everyone at the table the cause of the argument. Her words pierced me like arrows and my stomach tightened. I grabbed the Star of David necklace that always hung visibly around my neck and reminded her, almost rhetorically, "I'm Jewish, you know!" She responded with sincerity and the same justification that allowed her to believe it was okay to make such a comment in my presence: "Yeah, but you're not like them." Lisa believed that through this explanation I would see that she had assigned me a special status, which I should take as a compliment. Her response made me even more angry and offended.

Although I did not have the language for it at the time, years later as a college student studying the psychology of prejudice, I would come to understand that Lisa was exercising a form of rationalization of stereotypical beliefs that Gordon Allport referred to as "re-fencing."[2] She regarded me as an exception to the category she had constructed for Jews, but she held intact the set of characteristics she assigned to Jews other than me. I was an individual who did not exemplify all of the attributes that Lisa associated with Jews, yet she was unable to challenge her beliefs, instead she held to them unwaveringly. Her use of the word "them" not only placed me outside of her classification but also created an "us" of her and me, thereby placing me in her in-group. The use of that one small word, "them," spoke volumes. It assigned a set of traits to her construct of the category "Jews," aside from the spoken ones of "snippy and obnoxious." It ruled out the possibility of any of "them" escaping those attributes, and of any of "us" relating to "them" or befriending "them." It also inspired me to come to "their"—my—our— defense much more ardently.

My visceral response to hearing Lisa speak about Jews in that way was hurt, and maybe even a little fear. My sense of safety was being threatened. I allowed my emotions to dictate my actions. There was no cognitive process involved; I did not stop to think about how I could respond in a rational manner that would lead her to understand why her statement was an insensitive stereotype that made me feel personally attacked. All that registered was a sick, strained feeling in my stomach, a result of both a deep sense of pride in my religious identity and a concern that her remark represented an anti- Semitic sentiment that would fester and spread if I did not stop it. I instinctively yelled at Lisa that it was wrong for her to characterize Jews in that manner. I tried to insult and degrade her by targeting her character so she would feel the way I did. She eventually cried and left the lunchroom, and we never spoke again.

For two years following this incident, as middle school crept by, Lisa and her friends berated me when I passed them in the hallway with taunts of JAP (Jewish American Princess). I have always felt that my reaction to her ignorant remark allowed her to justify to herself the negative qualities she associated with Jews. If I knew then what I know now, I may not have reacted so impulsively. At the time, it did not occur to me that Lisa was probably repeating something she had heard at home, and that I had a chance to help her question that way of thinking. Of course, if I had been prepared and able to calmly challenge her statement rather than assaulting her personally and closing lines of communication, my effort may still not have changed her thinking or future behavior, but that scenario would have afforded an opportunity for change. The path I took was almost certain to be ineffective.

As I grew up, my family was not very religious, yet much of my life was structured by Jewish cultural and spiritual customs in which I loved to participate. I lived in a town with a significantly sized, prominent Jewish population, and I now realize this allowed me to cultivate a sense of pride in Judaism and a feeling of connection to the community at large and to other Jewish individuals. Without this grounding, I may not have had the impetus to respond to Lisa's comment. I was not just moved to stand up for myself; I was inspired to stand up on behalf of all Jews. I now realize how relevant this respect for my own identity was in understanding the importance of social justice education.

The incident that marked the end of a friendship symbolized the beginning of my awakening to stereotypic and prejudicial attitudes and actions.

During my senior year in high school, I participated in The March of the Living, an international education program. Each year Jewish teenagers from around the world come together with adult mentors to travel to Poland and tour four former Nazi concentration camps as well as the remnants of pre–World War II Jewish Polish life. The goal of this physical and emotional journey is to teach today's youth the lessons learned, and to encourage them to commit to preventing history from repeating itself.

Although I have no known history of family members who were victims of the Nazi atrocities, I felt an intense need to go on this trip. My interaction with Lisa and other confrontations with anti-Semitism throughout my adolescence were the catalysts driving me. Because I was raised with an acute awareness of the history of persecution that has plagued the Jewish people, I saw from a young age the connection between a sixth-grade classmate's stereotypical remark and a catastrophic event like the Holocaust. This history was an integral part of my synagogue's religious school curriculum, as is true for many Jewish children, and it supplemented my public school education from which I learned very little about these horrific events. I can still vividly remember images of skeletons heaped on top of each other from films we watched in religious school. The purpose of viewing them was not to make children afraid to be Jewish, or to teach us victimhood. Rather, it was to make us understand that if we did not remember what led to the Holocaust—how stereotypical beliefs about the inherent nature of Jews led to their scapegoating—then it would be possible for another Holocaust to occur. At that time, the prejudice spiraled from blame for Germany's collapsed economy, to laws that slowly took away rights from German and then other European Jews, to ghettos, and finally to the death camps. That connection was frighteningly real to me, and I believed as a teenager that the prevention of another Holocaust must be my life's mission.

As an adolescent and young adult I would learn that other genocides, born of Nazi-like ideologies, have occurred and continue to take place in countries around the globe, and I would begin to develop a more realistic perspective on my own limitations to change the world. As a teenager, however, I took very seriously my own role in working to prevent it. Part of what motivated me was the notion that I alone was working toward interrupting a snowballing sequence of events that could lead to a Holocaust. I began to discover through activities such as the March of the Living that countless others believe in the fundamental right of humans to live free from attacks on the basis of their identity and are working toward making this a reality. My outlook on dedicating myself to this mission has evolved into an understanding that, although I am not really working alone, I must act as though the future of social justice depends on me. I believe that if I want to see change occur, it is my responsibility to make it happen.

The strategy I chose to interrupt the cycle of prejudice was education. Having walked through the gas chambers at Auschwitz, I felt that people might be willing to listen to me. As a teenager, I began giving slide presentations about my trip and the events of the Holocaust to synagogues and Jewish organizations, youth groups, and senior communities. One of the concerns driving me was the reality that the generation of survivors was growing older and smaller in number; I felt it my duty as a Jew to tell their stories. As Holocaust survivor, author, and activist Simon Wiesenthal expressed so eloquently in his autobiography, *Justice Not Vengeance*, "I want to be their mouthpiece, I want to keep their memory alive."[3] Wiesenthal was speaking from his experiences as a survivor, a very different perspective than my own as a young activist and educator who grew up in a country where Jews can live openly and practice our religion freely, yet I felt an intuitive connection to his sentiment.

During my presentations, especially while reading poetry written by survivors, I tried to communicate a life lesson I had absorbed as I toured the camps and learned about Nazi tactics: digesting information in terms of sheer numbers (the murder of 6 million Jews and 12 million people in total) can cause us to forget that those statistics comprise individuals like ourselves, who once lived, laughed, learned, loved, and had faces and personalities. This revelation crystallized for me as I walked through the Nazi death camp Majdanek in Lublin, Poland. There were three barracks in Majdanek filled with shoes taken from prisoners who entered the camp, most of whom were killed there. Those three barracks held 840,000 pairs of shoes, but it was the individual shoes that had a powerful effect on me. I saw a red pump, a worker's boot, a baby's shoe, and many others of all shapes, colors, and sizes. I thought of my own shoes and how much they could tell about my life. My shoes facilitate my daily routines and my favorite activities; they know where I have been in the world. The shoes of Majdanek's victims belonged to individuals with lives similar to my own; they each had unique routines, life experiences, and plans for the future. At that moment I felt able to compare myself to any person in the world, in any generation, who wears shoes. This realization, that there are core feelings and experiences shared among those from very diverse backgrounds, continues to reverberate through my life and work as a social justice educator. This experience translated literally for me into an understanding of one of the central goals and admittedly clichéd messages of social justice education—trying to imagine what it might be like to walk in someone else's shoes.

It was through my coursework as a women's studies major in college that I was first able to articulate the idea that I experience life distinctly as a white, Jewish, middle-class, educated, suburban-raised female. These aspects of my identity have shaped my thoughts and perspectives, along with my interactions. I see through a set of lenses that have been colored by the cross-section of experiences I have had as a member of these groups. This idea—that we all have biases because we have been deeply affected on an unconscious level by societal messages and values—is fundamental to social justice education work. It is central to understanding others and ourselves. Yet many people, primarily white Euro-Americans, tend to forget that they themselves are the products of a culture. Many translate culture to mean race or ethnicity, and many Caucasians whose families have lived in the United States for multiple generations do not think of themselves as having either. White people have been taught—through the U.S. media, government, education system, and other institutions—that (nonwhite) "others" belong to racial groups, and that they are the standard to which these groups are compared. Thus they often find it difficult to use themselves and their experiences as a frame of reference for understanding and relating to the experiences of others.[4]

These concepts were central to my undergraduate studies and helped guide my further education and work in the field of diversity and social justice education. Based on confrontations with anti-Semitism throughout my youth, I came to believe that fostering children's connection to their social identities and arming them with tools to productively confront prejudice are two important elements of social justice education. These should occur in schools, where children spend the majority of their time and are socialized by educators, peers, curriculum, and policies. If children are to learn social justice principles, educators and administrators must engage in a critical examination of these values first. Social justice and antibias educational efforts include both preventive and curative approaches to recognizing and rejecting prejudice and discrimination in thought and action, both reactively (when either is witnessed or perpetrated) and proactively (when practicing or teaching others an antibias credo). The goal of this movement is to improve intergroup relations and individuals' rights and quality of life, resulting in the "full and equal participation of all groups in a society that is mutually shaped to meet their needs."[5]

One organization offering social justice education in schools is the Anti-Defamation League (ADL), a 95-year old organization working around the world to blow the whistle on discrimination and hate and defend civil rights.[6] For four years after my graduation from college, I was the assistant director and education coordinator of the New Jersey regional office of the ADL, running the New Jersey project of A WORLD OF DIFFERENCE Institute, an antibias training program, in K–12 school districts. I continue to serve as a facilitator of these workshops, which give educators and students a forum for discussing the impact of the "isms" on their lives, schools, and communities, and for brainstorming effective and realistic responses to incidents in which they or someone else is the target of prejudicial thinking or discriminatory actions.

I was twenty-two years old when I started working at the ADL. It was my first job out of college—the position I had been dreaming of and working for throughout my four years as an undergraduate. I was both terrified and over-confident when I started. On the one hand, I could not believe I was hired and was worried that my job performance would not impress people as much as my resume had. On the other hand, I had attended a women's college for the past four years and was a women's studies major and an alumna of the Institute for Women's Leadership Scholars Program. The combination of these experiences at Douglass College was transformative for me. It was in the women-led, women-centered spaces purposefully created by faculty at the college that I was able to recognize that many of my beliefs and values were feminist, and it was in these spaces that I was able to cultivate my ability to enact those beliefs and values. I found and learned how to use my true voice and potential as a leader in that community.

In college I had been surrounded by inspiring women peers and mentors and had come to believe that my potential as a young woman was limitless. I was high on feminism. When I began working, I was filled with the spirit of the feminist activist culture in which I had been immersed, especially the audacious belief in my own abilities to envision and create change. I joined a small staff at the New Jersey ADL office and was the youngest employee by twenty years. I remember the first time one of my colleagues, now a close friend, told me she considered me unusually mature for my age. I met with this same reaction from many others who I worked with over the years I was with the ADL, but when I heard this for the first time, I thought, "I wish you could meet the women from the IWL Scholars Program!"—women like me who are also mature, professional, and driven.

The reactions of others to my youth became a major theme that shaped my journey as a young woman beginning my career. My colleagues' attention to my age, especially because of my relatively responsible position in the organization, at times made me feel self-conscious about revealing a youthful side of myself, or discussing topics that would remind others that I was still in my early twenties. I was occasionally confronted with the assumption that my age was a sign of my lack of experience (which was sometimes true, and some-times not). This spotlight on my years, and the fact that my professionalism defied stereotypes about young people, intensified the pressure I felt to prove I could succeed. This both overwhelmed and motivated me. Internally, I began to experience a phenomenon common among women described as the "impostor syndrome." Although some men experience concerns about inadequacy or worry that they are not good enough to have earned their accomplishments, women especially struggle with this feeling, believing that it is only a matter of time before their shortcomings will be discovered in spite of all their achievements.[7] However, I did legitimately earn my position, and I believe I made important contributions in my years at the ADL. And of course—as is true of anyone starting a new job—I also had a lot to learn.

While neither my age nor my gender impeded my ability to succeed in the job, I knew that both affected the way others saw me. Just as I had been awakened as an adolescent to the potential of social justice education to address stereotypic and prejudicial attitudes about religion and race, I now began to consider the ways it could tackle sexism. Adjusting to my new work schedule and not having access to the abundant array of organized events I had become so accustomed to during my college years, I took to watching a good amount of nighttime television. This was 2000; pop stars like Britney Spears and Christina Aguilera were all the rage, and reality television shows were rapidly multiplying. This was not my generation's media. I was struck by what seemed a startling change in adolescent programming, especially the representation of young female celebrities in the music and entertainment industries. Girls and young women in the media, those promoted as role models to adolescents and pre-adolescents, were being hyper-sexualized. Their clothing, body language, song lyrics, and personas emphasized sexuality as their essence and ticket to success, and they were only teenagers. I had long been accustomed to the objectification of women in popular culture, which I spent a fair amount of time analyzing during college. But now girls were being targeted.

Meanwhile, I worked with groups of high school students in ADL peer leadership programs. In my experience, such opportunities disproportionately attract girls, with a small number of boys participating. I noticed that the females, even though they made up the majority, were shyer about contributing than the males. The small group of teenage boys often dominated the discussion. In my observations, many of the girls participated less because they were paying so much attention to their physical selves. Even when the meetings were held during the winter months, many of them came dressed for summer, wearing tank tops that, along with low-rise jeans, bared their midriffs, or short skirts, sometimes with no tights for keeping their legs warm. The kinds of clothing they wore reflected those worn by media figures; they were more sexy and revealing than the styles when I was a teenager. Another nonverbal cue was their body language. The girls often sat or stood in ways that intentionally drew attention to their bodies—slumped in their chairs accentuating their curves or exposing skin, or slowly tying their hair back so their midsections were uncovered.

I could not isolate my observations of girls in public schools from their larger social context. Their sexualization felt like a backlash against feminism, both the gains made by women of my mother's generation and those being made by third-wave activists like myself. It was the intertwining of this feeling and my watching adolescent females both in real life and the media that led me to wonder about girls' conceptions of their physical selves in relationship to their intellectual selves, and about how much these are influenced by the pervasive reinforcement of a one-dimensional, delimiting portrayal of girlhood and young womanhood. I had found another avenue for my work as a social justice educator.

I became increasingly concerned that adolescent girls are learning that the primary means for them to gain attention—and thus validation and confidence—is through their bodies instead of their minds and voices. In a socially just society, "individuals are . . . self-determining (able to develop their full capacities)."[8] When a stereotype is pervasive, it informs our expectations and thus our treatment of others, which in turn can influence individuals' self-concepts. The repetitive, invasive message that girls are primarily sexual beings can hamper their ability to be self-determining and suggests that others are in control of who girls are and can be. These concerns became so intense for me that I decided to return to school to study this. I earned a master's degree in education and am now pursuing a Ph.D. in child development focusing on adolescent girls, gender roles, and equity in schools. My current work is rooted at the intersection of social justice education and feminism.

I did not always think of myself as a change agent, although in hindsight I know that I have been attempting to instigate social change since my adolescence. I was simply doing what I believed was right and what led me to feel self-pride. Somewhere along the way, my motivations grew from a desire to feel good and just in my actions to a feeling of obligation and life purpose. This commitment has not detracted from my personal satisfaction in making change; rather, it has deeply enhanced it. I strive to make all of my actions reflect my visions. The personal and the political are inseparable for me.

Attempting to make change is not always a satisfying, feel-good experience. It is often a bumpy, uncomfortable road, and there are sacrifices to be made. People sometimes judge being antiracist and antisexist as not having a sense of humor or being the "PC police." Standing your ground may mean compromising relationships with family members, friends, or colleagues and can be awkward, difficult, and painful. I have often found myself torn between wanting to be liked and knowing it was not worth compromising my beliefs. Over time, I have learned different approaches for challenging people that may lessen the sting or the conflict potentially caused by the confrontation. It does not necessarily get easier; I still feel a lump rise in my throat when caught unexpectedly by an offensive remark or an action guided by assumptions about particular groups of people. The moments when I stand alone to defend my beliefs are the most challenging but also very rewarding. However difficult it is to get out the words, and however uncomfortable the silence or hostility that follows, in the end I try to remember that the result I am working toward is greater than the uneasiness.

When I was a college student, former New Jersey governor Christine Todd Whitman, in her presentation of leadership awards to young women, quoted me as saying, "All I want to do is change the world." Understandably, this elicited a chuckle from the audience. Naïve as it may sound, this idealistic goal still drives me to do the work that I do. Through life experiences, academic and career endeavors, I have come to see myself as an actor rather than a bystander. I believe that all of us can be empowered to become change makers once we realize that we are all shareholders, willing or not, in the outcome.

NOTES

1. Real name has been changed.
2. Gordon Allport, *The Nature of Prejudice* (New York: Addison-Wesley Publishing Company, 1979).
3. Simon Wiesenthal, *Justice Not Vengeance* (New York: Grove Weidenfeld, 1989).
4. See Peggy McIntosh, "White Privilege: Unpacking the Invisible Knapsack," in *Beyond Heroes and Holidays: A Practical Guide to K–12 Anti-Racist, Multicultural Education and Staff Development*, eds. Enid Lee, Deborah Menkart, and Margo Okazawa-Rey, 79–82 (Washington, DC: Teaching for Change, 1998).
5. Maurianne Adams, Lee Anne Bell, and Pat Griffin, *Teaching for Diversity and Social Justice* (New York: Routledge, 1997), 3.
6. For further information on the Anti-Defamation League and its programs, see their Web site: http://www.adl.org/.
7. Lee Ann Bell, "The Gifted Woman as Impostor," *Advanced Development Journal* 2 (January 1990): 55–64.
8. Adams et al., *Teaching*, 3.

PART TWO

Reimagining Leadership

New Models

8

Storybooks and Fairytales from Rural Teso

Leadership as Local Problem Solving

SIVAN YOSEF

You are mesmerized by the beauty of this country. You are grateful to these warm people. But when you stand in front of a classroom of rural Kenyan kids, you face frustration.

To your left is a makeshift wall of bricks constructed by the village boys, holes chiseled out for windows, the hot, dry air slowly drifting in from the neighboring lands. To your right a piece of thin board five feet high is strictly a symbolic border between this class and the next, the voice of the teacher next door bellowing through your precious space. Behind you is another brick wall, this one brushed with black paint to qualify as a chalkboard, yellowed papers fastened with an old piece of tape. A class schedule: history is at 9:50 and agriculture, 12:20. A list of tasks: Papai scrubs the latrines on Tuesdays; Fred sweeps the staff room on Fridays. And in front of you are sixteen four-teen-year olds. They are dressed in crisp school uniforms. Their shirts are white and their faces are black. They sit three to a desk. They smile at your white face, giggle at your melodramatic Western gestures. And they ask questions.

But you spoiled American college kid—you remain disturbed. Not at the makeshift walls or the sixteen pairs of eyes watching the every move of their funny *mzungu* ("white person"). Rather, the problem—your problem—is the English grammar book your hands nervously clutch. As sixteen fourteen-year-olds struggle to differentiate between countable and uncountable nouns, you struggle to understand what possible use countable and uncountable nouns are to rural Kenyan kids. Most will never go to secondary school, let alone leave rural Kenya. And that is when frustration sets in.

I cannot write a definitive essay on "Kenyan culture." I was not there long enough, and anyway, when you are in a country, that "thing" called culture

becomes a myriad of names, bursting personalities, and intricate family histories. Objective accounts seem objectifying. You are there trying to grasp the
bigger meaning of an experience that has become too close, too personal, to
be big.

What I do know is that Kenya has been in my mind for most of my college
life. It was a vision for me far before I even had the tools to engage that vision.
My professors gave these to me. Professors are a special brand of people; they
are married to theory, staunch in their belief that it can teach us how to think.
The problem is that nowadays most people balk at the idea of theory. They are
disenchanted with preparation. They say, "Talk is cheap . . . let's see some
action!" When I think of this raging conflict, the image that comes to my mind
is an uncomfortable dinner meeting: the realist seated on one side, and the
theorist on the other.

When I began college, I met a professor of Swahili and, together with a few
others, we started an organization called the Global Literacy Project (GLP). GLP
rescues books headed for dumpsters and ships them to rural schools and
libraries in impoverished areas around the world. The roots of the organization began with a small campus book drive for Kenya. We eventually got the
idea of calling libraries in the area for help; when we contacted the first one,
they were about to dump six thousand books. We shipped seventeen thousand
books that first year, and seventy thousand the second. By 2003, we were collecting three hundred thousand books and shipping them to other parts of
Africa and the Caribbean.

In my junior year of college, something dawned on me. With this incredible volume of books being shipped around the world, what actually happens
to them upon arrival? Who organizes and maintains them? In rural villages
across the world that can only provide one book for every forty people, the
outlook is not good. This kind of realization is a difficult one. It pokes holes in
your mission. It also pokes holes in your notion of a child receiving a book and
suddenly, miraculously, having a better life.

Books do not hold a sacred enough place in the United States. We have all
undergone the rigorous library education of primary school years, when the
value of books was drilled into our heads, along with the importance of the
Golden Rule and the "bathroom buddy" rule. Yet the majority of Americans do
not read frequently. In a country where books are used to steady rickety tables,
we take for granted the real meaning of self-education. For most of the world,
and in fact many parts of the United States, self-education is not supplemental or a choice: it is the only alternative for a failed educational system.

In October of 2002, I began writing a plan for a service-learning program.
Its aim was to send a group of students to rural Kenya for the summer to
organize the thousands of GLP books already there, create a library manual,
and teach kids how to engage with books, not just stare at them on the

bookshelves. I named my program "GOYA in Kenya." GOYA is an acronym borrowed from a volunteer organization I co-founded at Rutgers University, and it stands for Get Off Yer Ass. It is meant to be said with a southern twang.

With the curriculum and logistics confirmed for a six-week summer service-learning program in Kenya, I set out to recruit some brave participants. I held meetings in the university student center. The first week, five people came; the second week, eight. The third week, we were down to five again. People got excited about the idea, then nervous, then excited again. Over the next semester, we trained ourselves on the Dewey Decimal Classification system and the ideal conditions for a library: good sunlight, clear rules, and a lot of space. We made fundraising presentations and bought ten thousand index cards for a card catalogue. And then, in June of 2003, we set out for Kenya. Our group was composed of Jaymie, Eva, and Amina—three young, beautiful, educated, and tough women—and myself. Their excitement excited me, and their nervousness tripled my own.

Kenya is the eighteenth poorest country in the world. It is bordered by Somalia, Ethiopia, Uganda, and Tanzania. Its capital is a city of contrasts. Mansions and broken-down shacks silently face each other on the same street. The poor face a three-hour walk to work as the rich speed by in their SUVs. Nairobi is home to Kibera, one of the largest slums on the continent, where thirty people share a room and take turns sleeping. The country's banks charge residents monthly checking account fees that are equivalent to forty percent of the average monthly salary.

We spent our first week in Nairobi in a process termed "acclimation," which involves coming to the bewildering realization that all the things you assumed would be the same are different, and all the things you assumed would be different are, in fact, the same. When this was done, we set out for Teso, home of our future library, an agricultural area nestled on the border of Kenya and Uganda. In an even more forgotten part of Kenya, the area does not have a strong history of missionaries. The tobacco companies arrived in the 1970s to convince all the local farmers to grow tobacco plants, a process that is devastating to the environment. They made their profits and bolted, leaving behind a barren agricultural landscape. Trucks plastered with the word AIDS drive around the village but no one has any idea what they do. Residents commonly die from malaria and diarrhea, completely treatable conditions.

As the city faded in the background, the pollution cleared and brick buildings became circular mud huts. On the eighth hour, our jeep maneuvered around the final gigantic pothole and we had arrived. We carefully peered out the window. Women dressed in beautiful *kangas* effortlessly balanced water pots on their heads as the men sped by on their bikes. As our SUV slowly advanced, bringing up a cloud of dust all around, our new hosts turned toward us in an intense stare of disbelief. Teso is not a tourist attraction.

We waved. They slowly waved back, still in shock but starting to smile—welcomingly? The girls giggled and the boys hollered.

We moved into our new home, a Western-style house among huts. One of the first people to greet us was Agnes, the community's leader. Agnes was a small woman with a great big smile. Instead of a normal handshake, she gave everyone—regardless of age, sex, or likeability—a loud high five. Agnes had the strongest grip I have ever witnessed, or felt, even stronger than that of my tiny mother, who is known for being able to beat most men in hand-wrestling competitions. Agnes seemed as pleased to see us, as we were to see her. Together we made plans to meet with all the women in the community the following week.

And thus began GOYA in Kenya. Every morning, we would walk up the road past the butcher and the mango trees to the two-room schoolhouse. The library, a small room attached to the back of the school, had a hectic assortment of six thousand books I recognized from New Jersey. The schoolchildren energetically jumped into the task of organizing and cataloguing but had some limitations. Never having had physical contact with books, most were not able to differentiate between authors and titles. They also had trouble sorting books into subjects: Is *What Color Is Your Parachute?* a book on sports or art? We had taken much for granted. We set the students on other tasks: the crayons and markers were the first they had ever seen, and they soon embarked on making beautiful signs and posters for the library. The small children in the village slowly started coming in to read every day. Barefooted, each sat with his or her book in the children's section, giggling at its pictures as if they alone shared a special secret.

In the afternoons I taught English. My students were funny and interested. Every day they competed with each other in asking intentionally ridiculous questions about America: "Why do you Americans have such soft hands? Is this fair, do you think?" I similarly tried to make the lessons fun. One day, I gave my students an assignment to create an imaginary country. I asked them to make up a name for their country and write about the appearance of the people, their language, food, and customs. At the bottom of the essay, I instructed, should be a drawing of the national flag of the imaginary country. The students nodded energetically as I explained the assignment. The next day they came in with their make-believe countries. All were named Kenya. The Kenyan people were black. The flags were all Kenyan flags. I took a deep breath and smiled at them. They smiled back. I explained the assignment to them again, slowly. They bravely tried again but the next day brought in similar results: sixteen very accurate profiles of a country named Kenya. We moved on to adjectives.

The day of the meeting with the women from the village finally arrived. We waited for them in one of the classrooms of the school, which had a crude cement floor and brick walls, a skeleton, really, of a functioning classroom. The women came in pairs, nodding shyly at us, and arranged the wooden tables in a classroom setup, putting us in the position, presumably, of teachers. We shot each other nervous looks and tried communicating that we wanted the desks in a circle. The last thing we wanted to promote was the "us versus them" paradigm. This was a collaborative effort. Our pleas went unanswered so we gave up and sat down.

I began a heartfelt speech and soon realized that most of the women did not speak English. Our translator quietly moved to the front of the room. I began again, slowly. I started on the notion of meeting actual needs, instead of imagined needs. We had already had so many misconceptions about what the community needed without even visiting it that we wanted to do it right this time.

"Before we tell you what we can offer you, we would like to hear from each one of you about what the village needs." A simple statement. Silence for a moment. Then a flurry of responses, passionate. "We need clean water." "There are no wells in the area." "We carry dirty water from the river." "Our children get sick."

Voices were getting frantic. "We need doctors. Visiting doctors." It was now loud in the room. "The health clinic does not have supplies." "We cannot afford the medicines." "The AIDS orphans and widows live alone." "The children's secondary school fees are unmanageable." "There is no storage space for crops." "The foreign investors come in and swindle us." "We have no food left at the end of the season."

As I listened to these stories, as I finally realized the starkness of life around me, I felt myself growing pale. Of course: Food. Clean water. Healthcare. I shot suspicious looks at Jaymie and Eva. Was Jaymie secretly an expert on the construction of crop storage facilities? Did Eva have a water well license that she forgot to tell me about? Better yet, do I have fifty thousand dollars that I forgot to tell myself about? The panicked expressions on my peers' faces made my stomach turn.

Then someone from our group whispered, "But our mission . . ." Right. Our mission was education. We were organizing a library. But you cannot eat books or make clean water out of books. You cannot inoculate or irrigate with books. "What are we really doing?" I thought, feeling faint, as expectant looks from around the room settled on me. And worse yet, "what was I thinking?"

Looking back, our first impression of Teso was sentimental. It was Africa with a wistful look. It was cute children running around in used 1980s clothing. It was constantly being on a light-hearted, cultural exchange. But then people get tired of being cultural. Superficial transactions between people become apparent. And it becomes stupid, even irresponsible, to pretend power differences do not exist. Talk is cheap—people want action. And if they put you to the test and you give them your sweet ideals, they will not understand. Their eyes will softly say, "Can you please stop ignoring the differences between us?"

At the close of the day of our meeting with the women, we had settled on buying seeds for them. The seeds would be distributed to each woman, planted, and 10 percent of each woman's harvesting profits would go into a savings account for the eventual construction of a crop storage space. As a prerequisite for the money exchange, we asked each group leader to write a proposal specifying how exactly the seeds would be distributed, how they would be planted (communal or individual plots), and how the money would be collected from group members. We smiled at them. They smiled at us. But when the proposals came back to us, they were only sheets of paper with names of women. We wondered disappointedly about the lack of initiative in the village. "They should be promoting themselves, doing more than just helping their village get by" we secretly thought, and then shut up, feeling guilty for our hint of self-righteousness.

On our last day in the village, we held a library opening celebration. The place looked great. All six thousand books were classified and the card catalogue was finished. The sunlight streamed in to show the library rules colorfully displayed alongside subject signs and bright motivational posters. Student art was hung on the windows. Children ran around, showing off books to each other. The older people sat quietly, reading the local newspaper that was now being delivered daily. A core group of student librarians had emerged who understood the function and importance of the library. They were busy giving tours. In the meantime, I was putting up one of the wall maps that we had brought. It was an enormous glossy depiction of the world, with a strip of all the world flags on the bottom. As with many maps, the size of Africa was shamelessly reduced to make Europe and the United States look bigger. In reality, the United States can fit into Africa four times.

As I embarked on a dramatic struggle with the scotch tape, a group of students gathered around me. They were studying the flags.

"Where is Kenya? Ehhhhh! There it is!"

"Wait—which one is that? China? I like that one!"

"Maybe. But I rather do like Mexico . . ."

"Mexico?!? You are crazy! Look at China!"

As they continued to argue, a small argument all its own started forming in my head. Why exactly were these students so excited? What in fact is so special about just another rundown of the world flags? Was it possible? Was it possible that these kids had never seen a flag other than their own?

Things started coming together. The assignment I had given my students: "Create an imaginary country," I had declared to them, "you could even draw your own imaginary flag!" Isn't imagination what children are best at? If you leave a child alone, won't he just naturally create his own games, his own make-believe land with fairies and spaceships, exotic foods, and strange looking people walking around?

But what are fairies to a child who has never read about magic? What is a spaceship to a child who has never even been in a car? And how could people ever, ever look different when you have never had the chance to leave an agricultural land nestled between the Kenyan and Ugandan borders, a district by the name of Teso?

The first time I learned about the world flags was in sixth grade. After an intense year of social studies, we sat with our yellow-haired teacher amidst a chaotic pool of construction paper, bright oranges and deep blues, and there we each created the flag we liked best in the world. I chose Guatemala, but it was a hard choice—there were so many colors and shapes among the flags. So many designs and patterns. I had a base of knowledge about this, a very strong one at that, all at my disposal.

I was the teacher now and I had given these sixteen students a chaotic pool of construction paper. The only thing that I had forgotten was their knowledge of all the possibilities.

A whirlwind of questions started buzzing in my head. You expect a lowest common denominator to start from, but you cannot even begin to realize how privileged your most basic experiences are. Money and power—those are the obvious ones. But what of your way of engaging the world, of temporarily escaping from the world, of creating an alternate reality and working toward making it a real reality? Creativity is a way of making the mundane exciting, of making possibilities apparent. Creativity is the ability to solve problems with the resources you already have.

The one image that kept rooting itself in my mind was our meeting with the village women. Although these women are leaders, helping their people get by day to day, their leadership is not considered good enough. To Western feminists, it is not good enough because human rights are supposed to be a grandiose and visible struggle toward advocacy and policy change. It is supposed to be capitalized. Human Rights. Never mind that the struggle for the right to be human is inherent in these women's lives, that the small battles, like getting a doctor to make a monthly visit, are just as beneficial as the big ones, like being able to vote. And, in fact, to the women themselves, their tactic of "getting by" is not good enough. Why? Because it almost doesn't get them by.

This is where I am supposed to come in with my theories of good development and sustainability. I am supposed to evaluate Teso's performance through neat, side-by-side comparisons. I am supposed to overlook differences in power and resources as well as that minor historical event called colonialism. In short, I am supposed to use my liberal arts education to apply models created for Western environments to an entirely different context and then berate it for being "mismatched," "inefficient," or "backward": "Somebody should be doing something," or "Why aren't they stepping up to the plate"?

Why does that not work? Because the women of Teso have an incredible wealth of knowledge about their resources, capacities, strengths, and weaknesses, and I do not. I could live in Teso for three months or three years and I still would not have it. Only the Atesos have the localized knowledge of their own community. But without education, without the opportunity to acquire outside knowledge through books, the only reality they can rely on is what they can physically witness. This type of reality does not offer much room for comparison or alternatives. If the village next door received funds for a drinking well, then that must be the only way forward to clean water.

The mission of GLP has always been to improve the lives of others through the dissemination of knowledge. But is knowledge, as the age-old catchphrase declares, indeed power? I posit that knowledge does not directly bring about power. Because power is necessarily a relationship of imbalance between two parties, the Atesos remain powerless with or without knowledge. Instead, I propose that effective knowledge is more complex. That the combination of acquired knowledge, through education and access to books, and localized knowledge, through living, together equal the ability to solve not only theoretical problems but also the everyday problems that matter—every day. Knowledge is the way to effectively deal with the obstacles and heartaches that are immediate and unique to your life—your brand of hunger, your brand of thirst, and your brand of health. In this way, localized knowledge is the reality of the matter while acquired knowledge is the creativity needed to combat the reality. Together not power but self-empowerment—the ability to better oneself and one's situation—can be actualized.

In this way, leadership is local problem solving. If leadership becomes good enough, with time it can even become lofty, but justly so because it has earned its right to loftiness. Leadership is dreams with a basis. This is where Teso is directly headed, beginning with the little children who spend their afternoons in a corner of a library, entranced by discarded storybooks. The fuzzy marriage of theory and practice, for me anyway, has just become apparent. The realist and theorist have split the check.

On a train from the airport on my way home from Kenya, I had a conversation with the train conductor. Looking at my disheveled appearance, a weary but happy traveler, he asked me where I had been. I laughed and quickly explained the project. Although my friends and acquaintances were fully supportive of the project, I had already found that most strangers asked just for the sake of sentimentalizing what I had done rather than engaging in a meaningful way: "Oh! That's so great! You helped out in Africa!" I had almost finished my explanation when the conductor interrupted me, his eyes distant.

"You know what they should do?"

"What?"

"They should make up a program that sends troubled youths to poor countries. That way, the kids can have the experience of travel, be able to see, you know, that the rest of the world might have it worse, but they could also help out."

I agreed. It was a great idea.

"That's a great idea. But who's they?"

He gave me a flabbergasted look. We had an awkward moment. I tried again.

"Look, do you know of any programs that do this already?"

"Well, no."

"So it's your idea, right?"

"Yeah."

"And you like it, right?"

He nodded suspiciously, his hand wavering over his walkie-talkie. He was waiting for me to suggest something outrageously illegal, like starting a covert drug operation in Madagascar.

"So who's they?"

Another awkward silence. He sighed, already bored.

"Look, I don't know. But somebody should do it . . ."

I also sighed and turned to watch the scenery fly by. The tall buildings meshed into one another, underneath the grand American sky of opportunity.

9

Navigating Identity Politics in Activism

Leading Outside of One's Community

ALLISON M. ATTENELLO

"Locate yourself in your writing. Acknowledge that your voice is raced, classed, and gendered. Recognize your privilege." As a feminist researcher and activist, I have claimed these as my mantras. I am trained to articulate my racial, economic, social, and cultural identities and to be critical of how these influence my methods, my findings, and my activist strategies. I resist the temptation to believe that my findings will ever be truly objective or that the events I plan and my understanding of the rights I advocate for are detached in some way from my own identities. Understanding the political implications of this helps me to navigate power dynamics that exist when conducting research as well as when working as an activist and serving in leadership positions.

My entry into identity politics began with an analysis of how race and gender operate in social movements, and with an emerging awareness of my own multiple identities. As a college freshman, I enrolled in several classes on racial politics and activism. I read books about Booker T. Washington, Marcus Garvey, and W.E.B. Du Bois, and dissected speeches by Malcolm X, Martin Luther King Jr., Stokely Carmichael, and Louis Farrakhan. I became incensed by social and structural forms of racism that I had previously not recognized in the world around me. These courses were my first formal introduction into the ways that identity and power intersect to privilege some and marginalize others.

Halfway through my first semester, I became aware of a striking gender imbalance in both the authors and the focus of my readings. It was primarily men who wrote these texts, and without exception, all of the literature highlighted male leadership. Women's roles in organizing in past and current movements were not mentioned. Did the absence of women from these sources mirror their scarcity in organizing? Did Stokely Carmichael's joke that "the position of women in SNCC is prone" reflect some kind of truth? I demanded to know: Where are the women?

Unwilling to wait until the last week of the semester to see women inserted into the discussion, I went in search of an academic community and body of literature that considered women's organizing roles as central to social change. With the guidance of professors, I discovered the writings of Patricia Hill Collins, bell hooks, Gloria Anzaldúa, and Toni Morrison. Enraged, confused, and empowered, I embraced feminism.

By the time I declared my major in women's and gender studies as a sophomore, I was obsessed with identity politics, by the idea that a diverse group of people could be bound together by a set of shared experiences and that these experiences could produce a particular sense of identity. I was intrigued that identity could catalyze collective political action and could even lead to the formation of exclusive or separatist groups. As an activist committed to combating gender-based violence, I was working with several organizations on campus at the time and learning firsthand how common experiences and commitments could forge bonds and create sites for collective action for women and men from different racial, ethnic, political, and economic backgrounds.

As a feminist, I was particularly concerned with the relationship between identity and power in activist spaces. Did men assert themselves in ways that marginalized the voices of women? Did white females design antiviolence campaigns without including the voices and experiences of women of color? The relationship between power and identity became the lens through which I evaluated political ideas and strategies as well as legitimated my own participation in social change organizations. Considering identity politics could help me navigate power dynamics, avoid asserting myself in ways that disempowered others, and respond when colleagues used their positions to marginalize my own voice.

In 2003 I joined a community group that represented the needs of Mexican immigrants in New Brunswick, New Jersey. While working with them, I became increasingly trapped and paralyzed by my own analysis of power and identity. Whereas my ideas about this had previously been useful, now they became a roadblock to action. This dramatically altered my use of this concept as an analytic framework. I began to explore the following questions: How can an activist be aware of identity politics without allowing the examination of it to render her powerless? If activists do not belong to a particular community, should they join and play leadership roles in an organization that represents that constituency? This essay will argue that identity politics can be a valuable critical lens; however, it often has a narrow scope. To engage productively with this concept, activists must define identity broadly and recognize how our own defining characteristics can be resources in activist spaces. We must also understand the integral link between leadership and empowerment.

The Context for Organizing

Located in Central New Jersey, New Brunswick is an economically and racially fragmented city. According to the U.S. Census Bureau, of the city's 48,573 residents, 48.8 percent of the population identifies itself as racially white, 23 percent as African American, and 39.9 percent as having Hispanic or Latino origin. The average household income in 1999 was reported at $36,080 with 27 percent of the population living below the poverty line.[1] Beyond the issues of race and class, New Brunswick also struggles to manage illegal immigration as the undocumented population in the city continues to grow. New Brunswick is also home to Rutgers University and its forty thousand students. The presence of Rutgers University creates other types of divisions between temporary and permanent residents and between a population that belongs to the university community and one that does not. Arguably, the two most visible communities in New Brunswick are the Rutgers student body and the Latino immigrant community, composed of both legal and illegal residents. These divisions are significant and visible. Despite living in the same city, these populations have limited and superficial interaction and effectively operate in separate spheres.

In 2003 the *Home News Tribune* printed these headlines: "City Rapes Total 10 in 21 Months: Police Release Details on Possible Serial Case," and "Rapist Shadow of Fear Covers New Brunswick." The articles stated that between September 2001 and June 2003, twelve rapes were reported in New Brunswick, five of which were tied by DNA evidence. A serial rapist was attacking women in the city. Significantly, the rapist ignored the separate spheres that Rutgers women and Latina immigrants occupied; he traversed these spaces and attacked women from both communities.

Despite the threat to both of these groups, police and city officials emphasized student safety, implemented student-directed solutions, and publicized the experiences of student victims. The experiences of Latina immigrants and the specific protections this community required from the police department were marginalized. Consider the following excerpts:

> In the past two years, 11 women and a 14-year-old girl have been raped in New Brunswick. Four of the victims have been Rutgers students. Another woman, grabbed as she stood on the front porch of her home, is the wife of a graduate student, authorities said.[2]

> Police say [the attacker] has stalked young white and Hispanic women walking alone in the late night and early morning hours. He pulls them off city streets at knifepoint and rapes them in alleys and other secluded spots. Police say he is responsible for attacks on two of the Rutgers women.[3]

The charges stemmed from an ongoing investigation into at least a dozen sexual assaults, six of them involving Rutgers University students, that have occurred in New Brunswick, Edison, North Brunswick, Highland Park and Franklin since 2002.[4]

These excerpts highlight how the attacks were categorized: there were attacks against Rutgers women, which were worthy of special attention, and attacks against Latina women, which warranted brief, if any, mention. To protest the marginalization of Latina rape victims, women from the Mexican community in New Brunswick organized a march in July 2003. Tomasa Guadalupe Nelson (Lupe), an active member of the city's Mexican community, spearheaded the organizing effort. Thirty people marched from the corner of Louis and French streets, the site of the most recent attack, to City Hall. Marchers, predominantly Latinas, held signs demanding "¡Justicia Ahora!" and chanting, "¡Aquí estamos, y no nos vamos!"[5] After a twenty-minute march, the group arrived at the steps of City Hall where Lupe read a statement demanding that the police increase their responses to the attacks. She spoke about the stigma of rape, stating that women in the Mexican community were afraid to report their attacks. She remarked that she knew two other women who had recently been raped.

> They don't trust the newspapers, she said. They don't trust the police. They don't trust anybody. They're afraid everybody is going to look at them—look, that's the woman who was raped. They don't want anyone to know. When they call their families in Mexico, they say they are sick, like the flu. They don't want their families to know what happened, and that is very sad.[6]

Lupe discussed women's vulnerability while walking alone to the bus early in the morning or late at night. Women in her community recognized the danger but did not have safe alternative travel means.

A friend introduced me to Lupe at the march. I explained that I was an activist working to combat violence against women and suggested we share information for future collaborative work. Lupe agreed, and we exchanged phone numbers. During the week following the march, I thought a great deal about Lupe's point that women understood the risks of walking by themselves at odd hours but that they did not have alternative transportation to reach their jobs. I wondered: could Rutgers women with access to cars offer volunteer taxi services for Latina immigrants? My idea lacked strategy and details but I felt it had merit and told Lupe about it. She agreed it warranted further discussion and invited me to her next meeting to share my thoughts with her group.

Unidad de New Brunswick

At the meeting, I expected to find an organization with clear objectives and projects, an anticipation based on the fact that Lupe's group had been working together for over a month and had successfully planned the recent march. I also assumed that members identified as activists and feminists, a presumption based on the fact that they were working to combat rape and to address Latina immigrants' invisibility and lack of resources. I imagined that if they showed interest in my proposal I would serve as a liaison between her organization and a feminist collective I was active within at my university. My hope was to facilitate resource sharing between college women and Latina immigrants. By working with Lupe's group, I sought to understand the needs in her community and to work collaboratively to design a transportation service that would meet them. I assumed her organization had formed in response to the serial rapes and that combating violence against women was central to its mission. During that first meeting I learned that each of these assumptions was incorrect.

Eight people attended the meeting—four women and four men, all of who were Mexican. The conversation was conducted in Spanish and Lupe's son, a Rutgers student, acted as a translator for me. After a series of introductions, the group looked to Lupe to begin. To my surprise, she turned to me and asked, "Where should we start?" I believe Lupe's decision to ask me for direction signaled that I had some degree of organizing experience, perhaps expertise. The act repositioned me in the meeting and subsequently in the group. Whereas I entered as a guest, prepared only to present an idea, I now assumed the responsibilities of a leader. I was unprepared to moderate or suggest agenda items. As an Italian American, middle-class university student, what did I know about the needs of this group? Reluctant to speak as an authority and eager to begin a dialogue, I asked: "What do you think are the major issues facing your community?" And then I listened. I had never considered the problems discussed: the lack of photo identification for immigrants; children who needed transportation to and from day care when their parents left for work earlier than school began; and children of illegal immigrants who needed Medicaid. Eventually I asked about the issue of violence against women and whether this was a pressing issue for their community. The group agreed that, overall, they felt safe: gender-based violence was not a primary concern.

This final piece of information shocked me. I connected with Lupe because of her antiviolence initiative and believed that her group was committed to this issue. *¡Aquí estamos y no nos vamos!* We're here and we're not leaving! Where were those voices now? Learning that the group was not focused on combating gender-based violence made me feel like an interloper. What right did I have to be here? Beyond what I had read about immigration and racial and ethnic politics, I knew nothing about the issues placed on the table. I hardly even spoke Spanish. Without shared experiences and concerns what would bind me to this community? What could I contribute to those with such different identities from my own?

Despite my reservations, I discussed organizational logistics: the group needed a name, a mission statement, and a constitution. They should delegate responsibilities, decide how often and where to meet, and determine the leadership structure. What part of the Mexican immigrant community did they want to focus on—women, men, children, or illegal immigrants? A community's needs are boundless. Were there specific issues the organization cared most about? In part, the undefined nature of the group explained why Lupe was seeking help with its direction.

The meeting was a challenging experience. Despite my outsider position and lack of knowledge about the needs of Mexican immigrants in New Brunswick, I was asked to help guide the direction of a group that represented those priorities. Yet at the same time, I was excited about the new space I entered and the ideas I heard. Would I ever be invited to enter a location so different from my own and to engage with issues or people I knew so little about? What would I learn by organizing with Mexican immigrants in New Brunswick? What could I contribute?

Ultimately, I joined Lupe and her fledgling organization. I did not initially discuss with anyone my concern that I was trespassing because I lacked Mexican identity. Instead I attended the next meeting and confirmed the assumption that I was a member. Importantly, I had not reconciled the tension that I believed existed between my identities and that of the group; rather I made these concerns secondary to the task of understanding and engaging in the needs of the Mexican community. During the next four months, I served as the elected vice president of Unidad de New Brunswick (Unity of New Brunswick), a community group representing and responding to the needs of Mexican immigrants in New Brunswick.

Organizing Outside One's Own Community

As a student, I took for granted the time and resources my university life permitted for activism. As a member of Unidad de New Brunswick, both of these were a constant challenge. Although Unidad de New Brunswick had regularly scheduled meetings, attendance was difficult for group members, many of who worked unpredictable shifts as day laborers and long hours in jobs that required travel. Both men and women often worked six or seven days a week for low wages, leaving little time for family and relaxation. Leisure to attend meetings was a resource few members regularly had. In addition, several of the participants were illegal immigrants who were reluctant to host meetings in their homes for fear that organizing activities might increase their visibility and lead to deportation. As a result, finding a regular meeting space was another challenge.

As a college student, I was also accustomed to working with experienced activists. As a member of Unidad de New Brunswick, I learned to work with inexperienced activists. Beyond Lupe and myself, no one in the group had previously participated in such initiatives. This forced the two of us to assume the bulk of planning, execution, and project management responsibilities. As a student organizer working on campus, I had the luxury of being results oriented. As a member of Unidad de New Brunswick, I learned to be process oriented.

Working with Unidad de New Brunswick allowed me to cross a divide that exists between university students and Latino immigrants in New Brunswick. Straddling this gulf introduced me to a new political space and deepened my understanding of activism. I experienced challenges and engaged with problems that were previously invisible to me. Beyond this, I gained invaluable insights to use in coalition work. Understanding that time, space, and experience are resources that not all communities have access to changed my approach to projects and events that are organized by a coalition. I am more sensitive now to the life constraints of fellow activists and more willing to discuss the process leading up to action rather than focusing immediately on the operation itself. The opportunity to work as a member in Unidad de New Brunswick made me a more thoughtful, open-minded, and effective activist.

Serving as a Leader Outside One's Own Community

Working with Unidad de New Brunswick also forced me to struggle with another question related to activism and representation: if activists do not belong to a particular community, should they play a leadership role in an organization that represents that population? After four uncomfortable months as vice president of Unidad de New Brunswick, I determined that my leadership role was detrimental to the group and enabled rather than empowered its members.

As I stated earlier, Unidad de New Brunswick was made up of a small number of inexperienced people whose participation was often compromised by time constraints. The group's decision to elect me as vice president was undoubtedly tied to my experience with activism as well as to the free time I had available for organizing. For instance, I had time to submit park permit applications so that Unidad de New Brunswick could host a bake sale fundraiser, and I had time to attend City Hall meetings and represent the organization during the application process. I also had the English language skills necessary to communicate with City Hall officials. Certainly I had resources and knowledge that other group members lacked, which made me a pragmatic choice for this position. Also, because Lupe was the president and clear figurehead of the organization, one could argue that my being an outsider was not important. As long as Lupe continued to run the group, it was clear that Unidad de New Brunswick represented the Mexican community. My presence at meetings and events never changed the fact that the organization had formed to serve the needs of the Mexican community. That I was not Mexican may have been strange, or even inappropriate, but it did not produce an identity shift in the group—the group identity could not be undone so easily.

An effective leader must have a deep understanding of the group she represents. When I joined Unidad de New Brunswick, I knew virtually nothing about the Mexican community in New Brunswick. What types of jobs did these community members have? Why had they immigrated to the United States? Were they living here legally or illegally? Did they understand their protections under the U.S. Constitution? Could they communicate with police or local government representatives? Significantly, I could not seek the answers to these questions without the assistance of a translator—my Spanish-language skills were too weak. Ultimately, I represented a group that I did not know and could not communicate with directly.

In addition, my playing a central role in Unidad de New Brunswick prevented others from assuming this position and developing leadership skills. For many of the members, the opportunity to represent their community could have been an incredibly empowering experience. Those who felt unsure of their English language abilities could have had the opportunity to speak at City Hall meetings and gather with residents to talk about their needs and frustrations. By fostering leadership among inexperienced members, Unidad de New Brunswick could strengthen over time.

Ultimately, I arrived at the decision that it was improper and unproductive to play a leadership role in an organization that represented a group to which I did not belong. Because it had formed to meet the desires of the Mexican community and I had no shared experiences to connect me to those needs, I was unfit to serve as a leader in Unidad de New Brunswick. If I had shared race, ethnicity, language, class, citizenship, residential status, or education level with the members of this group, we may have found a set of common experiences upon which a leadership role could be justified. Without these shared identities, however, I was an illegitimate leader.

Evaluating Oneself as a Resource

Prior to working with Unidad de New Brunswick, I used identity politics as a tool to help me see and navigate power dynamics that exist in organizing spaces. Working with Unidad de New Brunswick changed my relationship to identity politics. I could not comfortably navigate the new location I had entered, one in which I felt I was intruding. I worried obsessively that by representing the Mexican community in New Brunswick, I was reproducing exploitative power structures by acting as a white, educated authority speaking for a minority group. These fears paralyzed my ability to contribute. Could I be conscious of identity politics without allowing this awareness to arrest my activism? In my final month with the organization, I discovered a useful set of questions that helped me reconsider my position. These new questions continue to guide my activism many years after leaving Unidad de New Brunswick.

After three months with the group, I approached Lupe and discussed my concerns. I explained my discomfort in representing an association whose needs I did not necessarily understand; articulated the necessity for other members to assume greater responsibilities and develop skills; and stated that, as a leader, I enabled rather than empowered the group. Lupe did not feel that my race, class, and education level affected the members; however, she respected my concerns. In part, my decision to leave also related to my own activist interests—I still wanted to work on antiviolence initiatives. During the previous months, it became clear that combating violence against women was not a priority for Unidad de New Brunswick. I would not impose my agenda on the group; however, I wanted to return full-time to organizing on this issue.

In my last month with Unidad de New Brunswick I tried to renegotiate my position. I discovered that I defined identity in a limited way, focusing on my white race, my Italian ethnicity, my middle-class background, my American citizenship, and my college education as though these five elements were all-encompassing. I also defined Unidad de New Brunswick by the race, ethnicity, class, citizenship, and education levels of its members, and I determined that because my characteristics did not match those of the group's, problematic power asymmetries would emerge. According to this analysis, the only way I could serve them would be to leave.

Importantly, Unidad de New Brunswick members did not use the same analytic tool that I did. The identities that produced so much anxiety for me were unproblematic to them. Lupe made it clear that she respected my point of view, but she did not agree that my leaving would benefit the group. Was there another lens I should use to rethink my position in the organization? Was there a role for me in this group?

Still thinking about identity, I explored a new set of questions: Could my race, class, skills, and student status be resources to help Unidad de New Brunswick achieve its objectives? Their main objective was to address the needs of the Mexican community. What tools did I have to help them attain this goal? The answers to these questions reenergized me. I realized that as an experienced organizer, I had skills that could serve this young organization. I discussed with Lupe the option of offering instruction, and she agreed that this could be useful. Hoping to empower the group by improving their organizing abilities, I attempted to move into a short-term trainer role. My idea was to teach them about basic abilities related to activism, such as organizing fundraisers, networking with other community-based organizations, and learning city policies in order to host events. I did not have the expertise to represent this group as a leader, but I could contribute to the body's mission by sharing organizing and leadership skills.

In the end, I transitioned out of Unidad de New Brunswick without conducting a formal skills training with the group. Although Lupe and I tried to organize this, time constraints and lack of interest deflated the initiative. Despite this, Lupe and I talked frequently about strategies and skills, and we shared many of our own organizing experiences and challenges. Overall, the greatest exchange that took place occurred between Lupe and me—each of us learning about the other's organizing experiences and activist spaces.

Conclusion

My work with Unidad de New Brunswick challenged and strengthened my understanding of identity politics and activism. The narrow analytic lens I had used to understand identity and power helped me realize that it is important to participate in organizations that do not represent our own communities, but at the same time, taking leadership in these organizations can be inappropriate and even detrimental. I learned to recognize that particular parts of my identity did afford me certain resources, such as time, money, and language skills, that I could share with others.

Years later I am still engaged in activist work and applying the lessons I learned while organizing with Unidad de New Brunswick. My interest in violence against women and my desire to become bilingual led me to Costa Rica where I spent several years immersing myself in the language, studying, and working. For my first few months in the country, I worked with a rural women's group on an economic development initiative, and I interned at a peace center researching the potential social, political, and economic impacts of the Central American Free Trade Agreement. In both of these internships, I examined the relationship between economic empowerment and violence against women. I finished my M.S. degree in global affairs in Costa Rica and accepted a position developing gender-focused graduate curricula at the University for Peace there.

As a white American researcher and activist working in Costa Rica, I often struggled with uncomfortable power dynamics that mirrored those I dealt with in Unidad de New Brunswick. In rural Costa Rica, my education level was equated with expertise. Members of the women's group I interned with made the familiar assumption that I knew and understood their unique situations and community struggles. In addition, the fact that I was a well-educated, bilingual American living abroad gave me a degree of authority in certain contexts that was incongruent with my actual level of knowledge. Despite these problematic assumptions and power dynamics, I did not become paralyzed by an analysis of identity politics while in Costa Rica. Rather than interpreting my American identity as evidence of trespassing, I recognized that in certain instances this could be useful to those with whom I worked. For instance, as a graduate student with access to research materials in the United States and Costa Rica, I was able to obtain sources on domestic violence and women's health for the rural women's group I worked with. I drew on the lessons I learned during my time with Unidad de New Brunswick and navigated power and identity-related tensions while remaining engaged in initiatives to end violence against women and girls.

As activists we are constant negotiators. We will negotiate our identities and those of our colleagues and fellow activists; we will struggle with personalities and power dynamics, seeking to avoid—but sometimes reproducing—differences that marginalize those we seek to enable. We will also navigate our positions as leaders. At times we will be visible leaders, experts, or figureheads; at other times we will quietly serve communities different from our own, providing resources for their own vigor and authority. Empowerment is both an act of leadership and a way to create sustained and informed direction for future generations. It can help us see beyond narrow analytic frameworks and remain engaged in activist pursuits. When we commit to developing others, we act as informed, compassionate, and effective feminists and activists who are dedicated to sustainable social change.

NOTES

1. U.S. Census Bureau, "State and County Quick Facts," U.S. Census Bureau, http://quickfacts.census.gov/qfd/states/34/3451210.html (accessed August 15, 2008).
2. Jim O'Neill, "Serial Rapes Putting Collegians on Alert," *Star Ledger*, August 31, 2003. See also "Rapist's Shadow of Fear Covers New Brunswick," *Home News Tribune*, July 5, 2003, A09.
3. Jim O'Neill, "Serial Rapes."
4. Ken Serrano, "Man Charged in Another Rape," *Home News Tribune*, August 27, 2005, A01.
5. "Justice Now!" and "We are here and we are not going!"
6. Sharon Waters, "Marchers Want Rapist Arrested," *Home News Tribune*, July 26, 2003, A2. See also Sharon Waters, "March Set to Protest City Rapes: Latinas Organizing in New Brunswick," *Home News Tribune*, July 23, 2003, B01.

10

Finding the Face in Public Health Policy

Leadership Learning through Outreach

COURTNEY S. TURNER

The youngest of three and the only girl in a competitive athletic family, I was raised in the socially and economically progressive town of Columbia, Maryland. A highly sought-after planned community developed and founded by Jim Rouse, Columbia is known as a "social euphoria," which I have found to be true. At a time when race relations in the United States were horrifying, Rouse thought that all people could live together equally and happily regardless of differences. More importantly, he believed that race, gender, and political beliefs should not push communities apart but should be the catalysts that bring people together.

Products of the segregated South, as children and young adults my parents witnessed atrocities that influenced their values and strongly influenced their choice to rear their family in Columbia. My father, raised in the foothills of the Blue Ridge Mountains, saw his cousins murdered in the "Martinsville Seven," the notorious 1949 court case in which seven African American men were convicted to death by an all-white jury for sexually assaulting a white woman in Martinsville, Virginia. This and other painful experiences in the tiny countryside town of Fieldale, Virginia, made him resolve to leave the rural life and work hard to become the first in his family to graduate from college, which he achieved. Growing up, whenever I was down or frustrated in my athletic or academic endeavors, my dad always reminded me that life could be worse—because he had lived it. Despite his thunderous silence (which I have inherited), one look served to remind me that hard work and persistence will help you attain your goals. Without it you will not succeed: therefore, for me, failure was never an option.

To understand our future and identity as blacks living in the United States, my brothers and I had to learn from our past. My mother, an identical twin and the sixth of eight children, was raised in the Baptist faith by educated social activists that W.E.B. Du Bois would have considered part of his "talented tenth." The daughter of a woman with a Ph.D. and the granddaughter of college professors, my mother is a brilliant woman with a phenomenal gift for writing and public speaking. Like her parents and grandparents before her, racial and social activism is part of her daily mantra. At a young age, she and her twin sister sat at lunch counters in Norfolk, Virginia, in support of college students fighting to integrate the restaurants there. This was the beginning of her belief that one should never compromise when trying to make a difference. In adulthood, she and my father worked on voter registration drives; she was the president of our local NAACP chapter as well as of the black mothers' group "Tots 'n Teens." She was committed to establishing racial pride and identity in her children: my brothers and I attended what I called "black history class" every Wednesday for seven years, from the first through eighth grades. Through her activism I have gained an understanding of African American history and struggle, which I will pass along to my own children.

Unlike my brothers, I took to social activism—but in a different way than my parents had. My brothers were my closest friends and fellow athletes. Despite the fact that I was seven years younger, I could run and swim as fast and hit as hard as they could, and I could outsmart many of their friends. I grew up to "think male" on the playground, a pattern of thought that is still with me. This created much conflict in my childhood home, especially because my southern parents—who supported my athleticism and activism— also believed I must perform household duties because I was a girl. I rebelled against housecleaning because I felt that if I had to do it, my brothers ought to as well. As a result of my outspoken insistence that cleaning was "oppressive," my mother often said to my father, "Jimmy, we have a feminist." Their reference to "feminist" was not good, from what I could tell. And they would never inform me what they meant by it. But as I grew up and began to find myself in the world, I developed my own definition of the term, which is now an important part of my identity; happily, I have taught my parents a thing or two about feminism. My early socialization with boys and my parents' beliefs taught me that being a leader is a strength, one I could apply wherever I saw fit. All of this is relevant to my chosen work in public health policy, and to my advocacy for the legalization of needle exchange, which I turn to now.

The field of public health strives to improve the well-being of a population by implementing health promotion and disease prevention strategies. Through this approach, public health experts aim to ensure conditions in which people can achieve healthy lifestyles both physically and mentally. In my experiences as a federal health policy analyst and a former harm reduction outreach worker, I have learned that public health also presents the opportunity to create social change through the empowerment and support of all individual life choices. My personal mission as a public health professional began with advo-cating the legalization of needle exchange, and has developed into ensuring that health care is accessible and equitable for everyone who desires to achieve healthy lifestyles. This focus has helped guide me toward becoming a young female leader and has challenged me to develop the awareness and sophistication to maneuver through management styles that are resistant to social empowerment. I seek to find the face of public health policy through this advocacy.

As an undergraduate, I learned from my mentor what it means to "be" in the field of public health. Kim Evans, the former executive director of the New Jersey Women and AIDS Network (NJWAN), was the epitome of HIV/AIDS lead-ership in the state. NJWAN is at the forefront in identifying issues facing women with HIV/AIDS and is the only female-centered AIDS service organiza-tion in New Jersey.[1] NJWAN is a small agency that uses volunteers to further its programs and services. Evans not only directed the organization, she was immersed in every aspect of its operations inside and outside of the offices. She was always enthusiastic about including her volunteers/interns in any function the agency was participating in or coordinating. When anyone observed NJWAN, they saw Kim and her staff (all six of them) and their impressive dedication and commitment. She was the spirit behind the organi-zation's operation, and this was reflected in her training of each intern and volunteer. As a result of her mentorship, almost all of us either majored in public health or went on to pursue careers in the field. As a mentor, she remains for me a role model of a young female leader who exemplifies public health because she wanted me, as her intern, to have the full experience of seeing, hearing, touching, and interacting with diverse populations. This practical knowledge gave me an interconnecting perspective of who is served by public health, how programs deliver services, and where public health fails to create and implement policies that adequately address the needs of a target population. Through this philosophy, Kim introduced me to HIV/AIDs advo-cacy, outreach, and policy; she is the catalyst to my public health activism sup-porting the legalization of needle exchange in the United States.

As an undergraduate at Johns Hopkins University, Kim did not have the opportunity to work for a needle exchange program (NEP), but she recom-mended that I intern with the Baltimore City Needle Exchange Program because Baltimore was only twenty minutes north of my home in Columbia, Maryland. On my first day as an intern with the Baltimore City Health Department during the summer of 2001, my supervisor asked me what I wanted to do, and I said, "Anything needle exchange." Over the next few months I had a powerful experience that taught me a great deal about collab-orative leadership and the need for policies that are rooted in the lives of those who are affected. I realized that public health fails to adequately evaluate and address stigmatized populations such as drug users. As a result, programs have neglected to address the social, physical, and mental concerns of clients seeking services. Most importantly, health services often lack the ability to foster the development and support of programs needed to facilitate healthy behavior practices and lifestyle changes among a high-risk population.

NEPs (also known as harm reduction programs) are public health programs that are often publicly ridiculed and stigmatized for increasing drug use and spreading HIV and hepatitis, and are associated with high-risk behavior practices such as prostitution. In reality, needle exchange promotes the use of sterile needles and injection equipment to prevent the spread of HIV/AIDs and hepatitis while advocating safe sexual behavior among users and their partners through the distribution of condoms and sexual health outreach programs. Mirroring the clients they serve, NEP workers come from a variety of backgrounds that include former sex workers, former drug users, lawyers, physicians, social workers, and undergraduate and graduate students. In this environment, leadership is defined as a collaborative effort because of the strong dependence on resource sharing. Without this cohesiveness, most programs would cease to exist; consequently, personal ambition is not prevalent.

Through my internship with the Baltimore City NEP, I learned the value of collaborative leadership and its strength to facilitate positive change. As a result of mutual efforts, clients reconnected with their self-pride. Through the care, support, and encouragement received from program staff, clients accessed many resources that aided them in their ability to enter drug rehabilitation. For example, the program works in collaboration with the Baltimore Substance Abuse System (BSAS) in facilitating client entry into drug treatment. When clients request drug treatment, they come to the van, which is a small, family-sized Winnebago that has been redesigned as a traveling clinic. Stocked with harm reduction supplies such as needles, condoms, cotton, and various injection tools, the van is the center for needle exchange, new client intake, substance/HIV counseling, testing, and treatment referral. Because the NEP program is guaranteed a limited number of drug treatment spots, staff members urge clients to enroll in addiction treatment as soon as possible. From there clients enter a drug rehabilitation program to receive substance abuse care and treatment services. These services continue after departure from the program.

Working with the Baltimore City NEP, and later with Atlanta NEP, I gained exposure to the principles of public health leadership that Kim wanted me to experience. For example, NEPs openly employ former drug users as their outreach staff because their experiences contribute a wealth of knowledge to the practice, and their presence maintains the organization's connection to the population and establishes the seeds of dignity, self-pride, and accomplishment in the former addicts. NEPs served as an influential medium for me to embrace the program ethics and a leadership style that rewarded individuals for small personal gains. This exposure reshaped my own personal leadership and influenced my growth. As a perfectionist who measures any achievement only through full success (remembering the childhood message from my father that hard work and persistence will help you attain your goals), I often fail to see that the smallest advancement is a step toward a broader level of success. However, when I began working with NEPs, I was introduced to the concept that reminded me that not everyone strives for success in the same manner and that success comes in different forms.

During my internship with the Baltimore City Department of Health, I designed and implemented a study to evaluate behavioral adherence of injection drug users (IDUs) to the HIV drug therapy called highly active anti-retroviral therapy (HAART). The purpose of the study was to evaluate the need to create a direct observed therapy (DOT) program to administer HIV medications to high-risk populations. Originally established for the treatment of tuberculosis, the idea of the DOT program is, if you bring the medicine to the population, they will adhere to their treatment plans. The Baltimore program was created to provide on-site dispensation of HIV medicine for clients being treated.

Similar in design to needle exchange, the DOT program (which is now operational) would work alongside select needle exchange vans and distribute HIV medication to HIV-positive IDUs, sex workers, and others who did not have access to medications. Data collected from the study were later used in a grant proposal to receive funding for the program. This project provided me with valuable direct experience in research, subject interviewing, policy analysis, and the opportunity to provide policy recommendations related to a major city's public health program.

One of the challenges I encountered working with a government agency was due to my age. As a twenty-one year old woman working in this internship, I was forced to fight for the integrity of my project. If I had not, the significance of my assignment and its goal of influencing policy to benefit a socially disadvantaged group would have been compromised. Upon the initial planning, I encountered harsh criticisms of the NEP and its clients from everyone but the health commissioner. City health department staff members referred to program clients as indigent and incompetent. They were viewed, for example, as having no ability to obtain advanced degrees. Comments such as "these people don't have college degrees" and "they won't speak to you just because you are black" were strong, frustrating statements that sadly displayed the public health insensitivity of these professionals. The more I was inundated with such statements, the greater my drive became to see the project through and to exceed the objectives of the project and what was expected of me. As my mother had taught me, I believed that one should never compromise when trying to make a difference.

Meetings held with the NEP staff were remarkably different. They were a collaborative, embracing experience. I was encouraged to wear comfortable clothing and to present myself to clients as part of the staff on the van. The staff explained to me with honesty and neutrality what I would experience while working on the program van. I was told that I could encounter territorial behavior from women clients and would interact with aggressive, shaky patrons who were dealing with the affects of withdrawal. Some female clients would be resistant to speaking with me and sharing their HIV status and drug behavior because of their own insecurities as women speaking to a younger woman. Others (mostly the men) behaved similarly to hyperactive children who needed a behavior-modifying medication.

To assist in recruiting clients to participate in the study, the staff screened interviewees before they were sent to me to help decrease the stress of interaction and to maintain the confidentiality of their HIV status. In a strange sense, this group treated me like a sibling; they provided the truth when necessary and worked to protect the project to ensure its success. With the support of program staff, I interviewed twenty-two clients in a week's time (most health department staff thought I would not be able to find more than ten), the majority of whom were men. Four of the interviewees confirmed having college degrees.

The first day of my week stay on the program van, I interviewed a woman who was forty-eight years old and had been a known "positive" since 1986. She was mourning the recent death of her husband, a heroin addict who died of AIDS two weeks before we met. He was the source of her infection. During our interview she expressed her sincere feelings for her husband and her pain because his death symbolized the reality of her own mortality. In her reflection she said, "He was actually positive in the late seventies but wasn't diagnosed until 1981 and since I wasn't a user at that time, we figured I couldn't be infected. So when I was diagnosed as positive, we figured we would live this out together. But, now that he's gone, I am alone and must care for myself, alone. It's hard to realize, I am now alone and will probably end my life that way."

My interviewee was diagnosed with HIV in 1986, long before the Centers for Disease Control and Prevention deemed heterosexual women susceptible (only gay men were originally considered at risk for AIDS). Her original treatment regimen thus reflected the absence of women in policies addressing HIV infection, a common theme among all the women I interviewed who were diagnosed before 1991. At the time of the interview, she willingly opened her pillbox to demonstrate the complexity of her daily regimen and her commitment to live. I found myself crying with her as she discussed her story as an HIV positive woman, the loss of her husband, and the hopelessness she felt in being able to seek the resources she needed to survive on a daily basis. In that moment I forgot that she was a drug user and HIV positive: she was an individual searching for a means to remain healthy, but felt hopeless because the means weren't always readily available to her.

From that moment on I became immersed in my project and openly embraced these personal interactions in the field. This woman's emotion became my emotion, and her face was permanently etched into my vision of public health reality. Three days later I had an interview with a male client who, through tears, openly discussed his drug abuse, his disease status, and his strained relationship with his wife (also an addict and HIV positive). Through him I realized that empowerment and leadership were needed not only for the rights of women but for the rights of men as well. This one man's vulnerability as an individual fostered the same compassion and awareness of his life circumstances that my earlier interview had. I felt complete in my view of how I would express my own leadership and feminism in my field. I would empower all those who were seeking to embrace something greater. I would be there to provide the unbiased support and encouragement to facilitate this change among a highly stigmatized population.

Therefore, when I am in the field and a client asks for help, I do not judge. I ask, "What is it that you need?" and "What can I do to help you?" In a world filled with bias, stigma, and skepticism, the last thing anyone needs is to be judged. I believe my greatest asset as an individual and a professional is the ability to listen, learn, and talk through a problem. Through this method, I truly hear the stories of my clients: I learn what life has brought them, and in turn I take the time to work with them on a process of change that is best for them. At the end of the day, as a public health professional, it is not about me and the choices I make, it is about what is best for the clients and the choices they need to achieve change.

As small as I perceived myself in this study, I soon noticed that I was a source of encouragement simply because I was there working to solve a problem. Through efforts to work with clients to define their realities, I (and others) empowered them to acknowledge that they could change their lives. In turn, they enlightened and encouraged me to continue on my path of training by teaching me lessons on life by communicating their realities and their hardships. This shaped my development as a young leader. Clients openly allowed me to ask questions outside of the required survey, and I openly responded to their inquiries about health services. It was through these interviews that I understood the meaning of personal ownership. I realize now, as I did then, how fortunate I was to have had an experience like this as a twenty-one year old. Experiences such as this are rare occurrences and poorly appreciated in a generation like mine that, in comparison to our parents' cohort, was raised with an enormous level of social and economic security.

I never expected to feel that I could contribute to the field of public health. I had thought that my upbringing in a socially secure, middle-class environment would circumscribe my assessment of public health programs. Yet my parents had taught me that discrimination is the purest form of hatred, and my family's history of social and racial activism is part of who I am. Prejudice disempowers individuals and their functioning in society, creating a fragmented sense of self. I wanted to transform this understanding into a path for my future in public health. To do this, I began to embrace the idea that empowerment is nondiscriminatory. To be an empowering person in public health you must be a facilitator at the right moment when the client has made the decision for a life change. Through my experience, I understood one should be available to provide support, encouragement, and the strength to help reach that goal regardless of the patient's race, age, gender, economic status, and life experience. All empowerment should be fostered equally: this defines my view of feminism and leadership as a public health professional. Working in needle exchange taught me that survival must be the focus and compromise cannot be tolerated. The Baltimore workers were unyielding toward their clients because concession would have meant failure or death. They were unwavering in their support but held fast to the idea that without some type of struggle, there can be no progress.

Throughout all of my encounters in the van that summer in Baltimore, each interviewee expressed a shared frustration that was derived from pain and sorrow. Each lived a life filled with the stress of balancing a substance abuse inflicted relationship along with social fears of being ostracized for their disease. Most interviewees said, "You are from the Health Department? You are doing a study? No one from there [the Health Department] ever comes here [the van] to ask us questions and listens to us." And, "You are so young to care so much about *us*." I finally understood why public health policy is a failure for the disadvantaged because it does not consider their stories, their faces, and their realities. This is often because the "reality" reflected in policy is crafted by a privileged few who never interact with those affected by the policies.

I decided that to have an impact on the policies, stigma, and lack of resources associated with substance abuse and HIV, I would attend a top-ten school of public health to earn a master's degree in health policy. I would receive the training necessary to offer the disadvantaged and poor the ability to obtain resources that would enable them to exercise power to change the direction of their lives. However, the program did not meet those expectations completely.

To supplement my classroom's deficiency and to reestablish the realism that was lost, I volunteered as an outreach worker in Atlanta every Friday and Saturday. A close friend of mine called it "witnessing," which is exactly what I did. I witnessed the flow and disconnect of public health through observing where policy was lacking in the connection between theory and the reality of its implementation. My community outreach activities were a foreign concept in my department, and I often resorted to loosely calling myself a radical. In her essay "Let Us All Rise Together: Racial Perspectives on Empowerment for Afro-American Women," Angela Davis defined the word radical to simply mean "grasping things by the root."[2]

My experience studying needle exchange as an undergraduate student and working directly with clients as a graduate student in Atlanta were viewed as radical by most of my graduate school colleagues. However, working in the field and learning about the lives and struggles of those actually affected by public health policy made real for me the need to connect theory and practice, research and action. I was given the valuable opportunity to understand the importance of learning more about the "root" cause of social problems that negatively affect health. Working directly with individuals such as these made clear to me the distance between the privileged policy makers and those that their work affected. I appreciated the chance to help those who were willing to teach me the shortcomings of social policy.

Experiences such as teaching a "working girl" how to use a female condom with her steady male partner and providing her with the opportunity to take control of a situation in which she felt helpless were satisfying for me and empowering for her. The exchange of smiles and the conversations shared taught me that, although I was young, I had the ability to relate and inquire into the reality of others. I also realized that one day I would have the resources to transform the life lessons these clients taught me into health care policies that could address their needs as human beings and, most importantly, as individuals. This was a great feeling.

When I arrived in Atlanta in the fall of 2002, I was ready to make a difference, eager to change the world of needle exchange and HIV. When I left two years later and unpacked my sixty-thousand-dollar degree, it appeared as empty as the education I received in the classroom. The most promising part of my education was what I challenged myself to learn outside of the classroom. Still, I hoped that my degree, the institution from which I earned it, and Atlanta's acclaim for being the "Public Health Capitol of the World" would be the gateway for me to have an impact in public health. From working as an outreach worker and as an intern in Baltimore City, I have gained appreciation for the lives and personalities of others. This has significantly contributed to my development as a woman whose leadership skills and views are constructed around the idea that empowerment comes from the heart, and mastery of the field is only done through immersing yourself in it. I have learned in this field that you cannot fight every battle confronting you in life. But you can help facilitate change and plant seeds of empowerment in others by showing that you are involved and that you care.

Now, at twenty-eight, I find myself at a place in life where I am comfortable with who I am and where I am. I continue to be a twenty-something relishing the moments of what life may bring from day to day, but I also strategically plan what I would like to happen tomorrow. I continue to remain content in my work environment, but I search for new opportunities that can develop my growth as a young leader in the field of public health.

I have come to understand feminism as a foundation of my identity that I express in my life by exploring the concept of individual strengths and articulating those strengths in a way that will contribute to individual and societal progress. My father taught me the importance of identity and of the individual; my mother gave me the grace to want to improve society, no matter what my identity might be. Although my work environment has tried to pigeonhole me according to my race and gender, as a feminist I am uncompromising in my demand for respect. I expect even those who are oppressive to respect me as a woman who happens to be black. Feminism has taught me that when you are firm in your convictions of who you are and what your purpose is in life, you make no excuses or compromises.

I seek to make changes in the health care system because I can never forget the staff and program clients from needle exchange who helped create that connection for me. In my short career as a federal civil servant, I have learned that collaboration, and not individual ambition, is what accomplishes any goal. I hope to have the opportunity to impact health care policy at the national level in the future. Now a doctoral student in health and social policy, I continue to advocate for policy that ensures that health care is a right, and not a privilege, and I firmly believe that public health should be rooted in the lives of those affected. If I am successful in connecting a face with the policies that are created, I optimistically believe that policy can be recreated with the recognition that access to effective and affordable health care is a precious resource, and having a healthy life will be seen in the United States as a universal right for all, not a privilege.

NOTES

1. For more information, see the Web site of the New Jersey Women and AIDS Network: http://www.njwan.org.
2. Angela Davis, "Let Us All Rise Together: Racial Perspectives on Empowerment for Afro-American Women," in *Women, Culture & Politics* (New York: First Vantage Books, 1990), 14.

11

Eating with a Spoon

Learning from Women at the Grass Roots of Society

DAHLIA GOLDENBERG

Over eighteen months in 1999 and 2000, I lived and conducted research in Ecuador on a Fulbright grant. It was a second visit for me. After having spent a semester in 1998 in the capital city of Quito in a college study-abroad program, I returned after graduation to deepen my experience. For most of the time since my return to the United States in 2001, I have been working for GROOTS International and the Huairou Commission, two global networks that support grassroots women's organizations to organize globally.[1] The lessons I learned, which I discuss in this essay, continue to influence my work, and my current relationships with women around the world still test the attitudes, behaviors, and privileges that I discuss here.

Grassroots women leaders in Ecuador taught me, challenged me, and learned from me. My Fulbright grant supported me to study the work of women's grassroots community organizations. I was interested in women who worked on issues that they themselves faced in their own communities. Also called community-based organizations, these groups often form in neighborhoods or villages to confront a collective need. I attended meetings, led discussions, volunteered at day care centers, spent time in their homes, created an audio compilation of their stories, and researched their leadership tendencies, all with the objective of learning from the experiences of women in grassroots organizations. In total, I visited fifteen neighborhood groups and fifteen rural groups. I also met with national-level networks of grassroots organizations and with supporters from more "professional" organizations known as nongovernmental organizations (NGOs). I wanted to learn how poor women lived, organized in their communities, and analyzed gender relations in the context of a developing country. My work was concentrated in marginalized neighborhoods of Quito, with several visits to indigenous and mestiza communities in the rural highlands, and to towns and rural neighborhoods of the Amazon region.

I went to Ecuador with a philosophy of not wanting to demonstrate knowledge or provide help for others but to learn from the insights and community development work of women living in poor communities there. I struggled with an internal tension between my fascination with our differences (I was excited to see how they lived), and my sensitivity about not wanting to treat them as exotic people and communities to be explored. I attempt here to grapple honestly with that tension, and the experiences cited or the essay itself may at times reflect the very attitudes I hoped to avoid.

I hope to remind feminist academics, practitioners, and activists of the importance of seeking challenging, sometimes uncomfortable experiences and reflecting critically on our positions, mostly in relation to Third World communities. Through my own efforts to do so, I learned lessons about differences in consumption and labor between the United States and Ecuador, and I experienced important challenges in my relationships with the women I met. I also reflect here on the ways my privileges distanced me from the grassroots women to whom I wanted to relate, and I explore the tensions and challenges of treating people as "others" in ways that reproduce old and problematic approaches of anthropology and colonialism.[2]

My undergraduate studies helped to shape my attitude when I went to Ecuador to learn with grassroots women's groups. On my first trip to Ecuador on a semester abroad, we read about anthropology and ethnography, and writings by authors who were highly critical of the field of international development. At Rutgers University, I studied feminist views of global development and First World and Third World identity issues. These studies left me believing that I should not go to Ecuador with the goal of bringing or teaching something to people. The work I hoped to do would support the knowledge, capacities, and activities of low-income women themselves.

A small South American country of 12.6 million people, Ecuador is geographically and ethnically diverse. Like most of the world, Ecuador suffers high economic gaps among the population, which makes it important for U.S. students to learn about both sides of the class divide.[3] Approximately 46 percent of Ecuadorians live below the poverty line.[4]

In response to various needs, women have united in small community organizations throughout Ecuador. While some groups have sprung up to fight for basic services such as potable water, electricity, or day care centers in their neighborhoods, others began meeting to confront their economic necessities together, sharing small loans for communal stores or chicken-raising projects, for example. For example, in the Federation of Women of Sucumbíos, one of the organizations I observed, women with only elementary school educations met and compared their experiences in their homes and communities, discussing issues such as domestic violence or sexual and reproductive health. They also spent many hours pressuring local officials, obtaining information, and organizing neighbors to contribute their labor for the acquisition of water and sanitation, health clinics, or schools in their communities. Now these women have a network of fifty women's groups in communities across their province. Their federation allows them to participate in politics at the local and provincial levels. They also develop skills and gain support for income-generating projects, such as knitting or the opening of market stalls. In addition to meeting their practical needs for resources such as water, schools, and incomes, grassroots women acquired the knowledge and confidence to transform their relationships with others and to develop a political consciousness.[5] Groups like these often unite with other organizations in larger social and political movements.

In this essay, I will use "Third World" not as an independent, literal description but as a constructed notion based on political, social, and economic differences. I believe the term has some value in comparing communities, countries, or people with vastly different socioeconomic experiences. In this way, "Third World" considers poor communities in the north to be "Third World," and it considers upper-class, elite communities in the south as pertaining to the "First World." Applying the term with this understanding categorizes women by class across national boundaries and recognizes those from middle and upper classes in developing countries as belonging more to the category of "First World."[6] I will draw on "Third World" to describe the mainstream of Ecuador, but not the elite communities there. I will also use this term to illustrate some generalizations between First World and Third World communities.

Contrasting Ways of Learning

Many American students, most of them white and middle to upper class, come to Ecuador for the first time with college study-abroad programs. Largely protected from the poverty that is endemic in the Third World, such trips do not often encourage authentic interactions with local people, community organizations, or political activities. Instead, universities, their related host families, and tourism opportunities cushion young visitors from the harsher realities of life in the developing world. For most students, just the experience of being in a different culture, speaking a new language, and tasting snippets of life in another country can be a rich and overwhelming learning experience. However, being harder on ourselves and pushing our boundaries of comfort teaches us important lessons about how the rest of the world lives, lessons that no foreigner ought to leave Ecuador without learning.

Returning to Ecuador after my initial introduction, I found it possible to burrow more deeply into the ways ordinary people live—a different way of learning than what was available on my previous visit. Through my interviews, participation in organizational activities, daily life in Ecuador, and the time I spent in women's homes in poor neighborhoods and communities, I learned about how women organized and improved their lives despite enormous obstacles, and what steps they must take to be heard by the government, to acquire basic services, or to convince their husbands to be allies to them (rather than enemies) in their housework and community work. I also learned about how household consumption and labor function in a Third World country and about my own challenges in reconciling my privileges and connecting with people in ethical and mutually beneficial ways.

On my first visit to Ecuador, in 1998, I lived with an upper-middle-class family in the north of Quito. A live-in domestic employee my age cooked, cleaned, and did my laundry. Every morning I took a bus to the most expensive university in Ecuador, where the children of wealthy families, U.S. exchange students, and a few indigenous students on scholarships study. There was an implicit expectation that we would behave respectfully with our host families, despite the injustice they displayed to their domestic employees or the racist comments some of us heard from them. We were also warned to stay away from the more dangerous central and southern parts of town. My host family rarely ate traditional Ecuadorian food; they served Westernized foods like Rice Krispies or beef stroganoff. And we lived with most of the luxuries that a North American might expect—reliable hot water and electricity, wall-to-wall carpeting, a telephone, and washing machine. In my particular study-abroad program, we each volunteered regularly at a different charitable agency and then studied the socioeconomic and political issues that arose there. Although we worked with low-income people for a few hours each week, we still lived and studied with the upper echelon of society—far removed from the life of average Ecuadorians.[7] Our volunteer service provided a brief glimpse at the problems Ecuadorians confront, but our observations and analysis came mostly from our university classes and relationships with our host families.

Reflections on Consumption

By choosing to live and associate with people in a different way when I returned to Ecuador independently on my Fulbright grant, I learned many things about the way most Ecuadorians live that had been obscured during my previous, more closely monitored visit. These details are important because they help people like me to gain more understanding of life for the poor, to realize that it is possible to get by with less than what we have, and to appreciate that people have different concepts of poverty and want. For example, in participatory studies, people living in poverty have defined "social inferiority, physical weakness . . . social isolation, powerlessness and humiliation" as critical indicators of well-being, far different from the common indicators of how much a household consumes.[8]

After my first trip, I had returned home with the observation that Ecuadorians have "proper" table manners, always leaving their forks and knives neatly angled out to the right side of the plate at the end of a meal. My new understanding of daily routines was more reflective of most people's lives in Ecuador and characteristic of some general differences between First World and Third World communities. Many people eat with soup spoons or their fingers—not forks and knives. Food tastes good when it has been simmering in a pot on the corner of a busy intersection all day, and getting sick a few times probably won't kill you. It is common and sometimes fun to sleep a few people to a bed. Even in the city, most people raise at least a few chickens, if not guinea pigs and pigs—all for household consumption. Homes usually range from those with plain, concrete floors to cheap tile, parquet, or pieces of threadbare carpet, and walls rarely have fresh paint. Things that your typical middle-class North American would consider necessary—an abundance of soft toilet paper stored in the closet; a reliable source of running water (both hot and cold); electricity; and a big, squishy sofa in the living room—are not found in most homes in Quito, let alone the rest of the country. While these details all surprised me a bit at first, I eventually came to take them as given. In the following diary entry, I considered the socioeconomic class and living standards that I observed.

> "Kar's" [a friend from a small town in the Amazon region] house is nice.
> When I first came in, I thought it was really bare and ugly and therefore
> poor. But then again, in Anita and Caroline's houses in Atuntaqui (a
> small town North of Quito), things were also kinda yucky. Old, worn out
> furniture and walls that haven't been painted in years. So I guess that's
> just normal for above average, yet not quite "middle class" homes in
> small towns. In the house here at night, there are humongous cock-
> roaches everywhere.

Not only do women perform two thirds of the world's work but developing countries generally use much less energy and create less waste than developed countries. I saw women waking at 5:00 a.m. to cook breakfast for their families (which did not come prepared in a cardboard box), knitting late into the night, and scrubbing laundry on Sunday afternoons. Both women and men carried heavy sacks or furniture on their backs instead of using carts. They stood gathered by street vendors, quickly eating their lunches out of bowls, with spoons, on break from their jobs. They carry out tiring, time-consuming work that most North Americans avoid by buying processed products or using household appliances or other machines. Our privilege to consume more energy depends on their ability to consume less and work harder.

In some rural areas, men used to be responsible for hunting and fishing; environmental destruction has made this impossible as a daily means of subsistence. While women carry out the jobs of cooking, cleaning, farming, and raising animals, often with babies strapped to their backs and other children needing their attention, under these circumstances the men spend much of their time drunk, most likely a response to feeling lost with the shift in roles at home. NGOs bring in development projects to raise chickens and create fish ponds, adding even more jobs to the women's burdens such as cleaning and feeding the animals. This work may contribute positively to women's lives and to the economic well-being of their communities, but using women as instruments for development without also supporting them to overcome subordination was one of the widely recognized mistakes of the "women in development" agenda of the 1970s and 1980s.[9]

Women in Ecuador and other Third World societies can teach First World women much about survival. How would your average North American man or woman get by without washing machines, hot running water, soft toilet paper, or spatulas? People in industrialized countries are not going to reject this level of consumption because we like living comfortably and do not want to be forced to change our lifestyles, but the realities of climate change and disproportionately high consumption of energy and emission of carbon from the First World requires some degree of lifestyle adaptation.

Struggling with Privilege and Otherness

How I lived in Ecuador was one of my biggest personal quandaries. On my second visit, I had a better chance to look at life from the point of view of grassroots women. I came to Ecuador with many privileges—financial, educational, and racial—that I knew I would confront. If putting all of my beliefs into practice proved impossible, I at least achieved a healthy questioning of my privileges, which I believe is a necessary part of a Third World learning experience for someone of my background.

As a young, white woman from the United States with a generous grant, how I appeared to others and how much I should conform to the lifestyle of Ecuadorians tormented me constantly, but these questions are common for people doing community work as outsiders. Social reformer Jane Addams reflects on her own experiences of privilege and self-criticism in *Twenty Years at Hull-House*, an account of her settlement house work in Chicago's slums in the early twentieth century. Of her visits to destitute homes one harsh winter, she writes, "I was constantly shadowed by a certain sense of shame that I should be comfortable in the midst of such distress."[10] She worried that her work and living arrangements at Hull-House only weakly accomplished her idea of residing in solidarity with the poor. She met Russian writer and social critic Leo Tolstoy, whose philosophy of solidarity with the common laborer included living with the poor and working alongside peasants. "Tolstoy, standing by clad in his peasant garb, listened gravely but, glancing distrustfully at the sleeves of my traveling gown which unfortunately at that season were monstrous in size, took hold of an edge and pulling out one sleeve to an interminable breadth, said quite simply that 'there was enough stuff on one arm to make a frock for a little girl,' and asked me directly if I did not find 'such a dress' a 'barrier to the people.'"[11] This anecdote really hit home for me. Like Addams, I felt a sense of shame and fear that my sleeves were too long, or at least appeared too long. Dressing in the morning before heading off to a poor neighborhood, I dashed back and forth between the closet and the mirror. I did not want to stand out as either an unkempt, disrespectful foreigner or a rich, privileged person with money for nice clothes. As I changed between shirts that looked too nice and those that were not nice enough, I often wished I never owned so much unnecessary, high-quality clothing in the first place.

I wanted to live with Ecuadorian roommates or a family in a neighborhood of Quito that would not necessarily be poor but at the very least would be located outside of the Northern, wealthier, privileged sector. I found Ecuadorian roommates, and we rented a nice but simple apartment in a working- and middle-class neighborhood near the central zone of the city. Later I moved with another U.S. Fulbright Fellow to a similar apartment. Our floors were parquet, and the apartment was far larger than either of us required— nicer than anything we could afford during our college years. Our electric shower provided warm water, although it did not compare with a typical American shower. Even though the apartment exceeded our needs, our grants provided us with living allowances that would have enabled us to live in a much more expensive, furnished, luxury apartment. In a mass e-mail letter to friends and family in the United States, I wrote:

> Another issue that faces me every day in many ways is money. I feel like I have way too much, and I'm not sure what to do with it or how to hide the fact from my friends and coworkers here. The Fulbright Commission gives us enough to live like very comfortable foreigners here. . . . Even though I'm trying not to live that way, it means that I'm saving a lot of money on things like rent and food and I end up having the luxury of not having to worry about money at all and being able to spend a lot when I need to. It has become very difficult, especially with my [Ecuadorian] roommates.

My supervisor from the NGO where I interned showed her irritation at my financial and educational privilege one day when we confronted difficulties in our working relationship. As I recorded in my diary: "She [my supervisor] had

some very unrealistic expectations of me . . . she goes, 'And you have a degree
from a university in a developed country, so *you* should practically be teaching *us*, not the other way around. . . . Also, you're making twice, almost three
times as much money as we are here [in the NGO]!' (I had never personally
told her how much money I receive, and it wasn't her business.)" My eyes
welled up with tears. I told her she had touched on a very sensitive topic—that
I wasn't the one who decided how much my grant allowance would be in relation to the salaries of people around me. At that moment, all of my frustrations with the research project I was struggling to carry out under her
supervision surfaced, in addition to the discomforts I had with my privilege.
Although I agree with the mission and function of the Fulbright program, the
economic privilege it gave me added to my other privileges, forming "a barrier
to the people." My background and privileges sometimes irritated those who
had a strong consciousness about such inequalities, as it did with my supervisor in the NGO, and occasionally reinforced the acceptance of such disparities
by people with less consciousness. For example, Ecuadorian women were
sometimes excited to have me as an acquaintance just because I was from the
United States, showing me off to their friends. Male bus and taxi drivers
stopped for me with more care than they did for an elderly man. Standing out
as something special, I unfortunately become the exotic, desirable "Other"
(which in this case equals "better") in a context where I had worried about
objectifying Others! The experience of having to reconcile my differences and
privileges with the people and the issues of poverty I was trying to learn about
are things that will exist as long as I work with people in poor communities
and have been an important part of my learning process.

Balancing Tensions

I experienced two simultaneous tensions that I tried to reconcile internally.
First, I had to balance conformity and respect of the Ecuadorian culture with
being and showing my full (American, white, Jewish, feminist, middle-class)
self with the people I met. Second, I needed to balance the tendency to think
of some of the women as homogeneous "Others" with learning about their
experiences in order to be able to contribute to their work. At times this felt
like a delicate balancing act.

I tried to enter communities, organizations, and homes conscious of how
I acted, sounded, ate, and conversed. It was an effort that I was proud of when
it worked. One successful example was with María, a member of a women's
group that worked to raise awareness about domestic violence. She struggled
for years to acquire basic services in her neighborhood. She once invited me
to her home even though she had not asked other women she knew through
her organization because she was embarrassed that her house revealed her

poverty. Over lunch, she told me that I was more humble than some of the other foreigners she had met because, for example, I did not complain and was not picky about food. What she did not know was that I often pretended to enjoy food that I really disliked, or I ate until my stomach hurt for the sake of developing good relationships.

This approach, striving to conform to the "cultural" norms of the people about whom I wanted to learn, gave me the chance to see how other people lived more closely than if I acted in ways that made our differences more obvious. Yet we both learned more when, after building trust through my "conformity," I broke loose and showed my nonconforming side. Then I would share my differing views about family relationships, sexuality, religion, or food choices. I might admit that I found it difficult to eat everything served to me or protest that it was not necessary for them to feed me when I visited, resulting in more revealing thoughts on the matter from both of us. If I were to simply blend in and take notes, afraid to engage in critical analysis with people about our differing lives and outlooks, I would not have exposed the women I talked with to all of the interesting differences between us. We would both have lost the opportunity for analyzing and learning together, which occurred when I shared my thoughts with them and they shared their thoughts with me. Did my experiences in Ecuador only serve to help me acquire knowledge about my privileges and how I should live and consume differently? Or did they teach me something that will be useful in supporting grassroots women in advancing their work? Did the grassroots women I met learn something in the process, or was I the only student?

Uma Narayan observes that some First World women use Third World women as "mirrors" for self-discovery: "Many such 'Western-focused' works on colonialism leave me, despite their merits, with a sinking feeling of watching the West coming back to a focus on itself, this time perhaps with more critical self-awareness, but nevertheless with a self-awareness that remains devoted to only understanding itself, even if refracted through the critical lens of its encounters with its 'Others.'"[12]

In my work as a Fulbright Fellow in Ecuador and in my reflections in this essay I have, as Narayan suggests, sometimes used Third World women as mirrors to allow me to reflect on myself—my privileges, my interests, my views of consumption and poverty. However, I hope that by sharing my own experiences, criticisms, and observations with the Ecuadorian women I met, I gave them a chance to tell me their observations and ideas that they developed since meeting me. Just as Othering can work both ways, the mirror can be double-sided. This reflection on one another's situations and on our own can lead to what is most important—action for social change.

When a Western feminist treats any group of Third World women as objectified, homogeneous Others, she assumes herself and her culture to be the norm and the authority. When I refer to the grassroots women leaders in Ecuador, I sometimes lump them together in this manner as well. This attitude can reproduce the very colonialist relationships that feminist efforts seek to oppose.[13] As a different journal entry reveals, despite my goal of social change, I struggled at times against an impulse to treat grassroots Ecuadorian women as Others, or to glorify my experiences with some of them as something "exotic" and adventurous.

> Their stories about their family and about getting by financially and their experiences in their organizations fascinate me. Seeing, hearing and sharing a bit of their lifestyles intrigues and excites me, and I have conflict with this "desire" of the "Other." I want to see, hear and share this "other" life, this poor life, this life in conflict, and I can't deny my sense of desire that treats other people as a commodity, that treats the experience as something to acquire. This interest exists in me. When I return home from visiting a friend at her house, or getting involved in a very personal conversation with a woman, I feel all giddy and happy from the experience—also full of motivation to continue working with the women, and to continue fighting for a better quality of life for low-income women. On the one hand, this could be considered an exotification of the Other and a selfish interest in the more "primitive" life—especially in the few instances where I visited indigenous communities in rural areas. However, the desire, the interest, and the craving are justifiable, and in addition to fulfilling my personal desire of the Other they are worthy means to a worthy end.

Some of my interest lay in the rickety outhouses or old furniture in people's homes—in the kitschy trinkets and decorations—pop art for me—or in their rural ways of life. (My life-long wish to milk a cow finally came true!) My motives may have involved the search for a more primitive life, or the allure of "the exotic" that contemporary anthropology tries to overcome, and of which I certainly am not proud. bell hooks' work on the subject lends context to my experience. She writes that modern "mass culture" has turned the idea of the Other into a "commodity," popularizing the interest in racial difference—"a contemporary revival of an interest in the 'primitive,' with a distinctly postmodern slant."[14] She discusses how this contemporary fascination, much like my own, is often propagated by the media and is motivated by the need to fill a void, particularly for young, white people in the United States who are dissatisfied with their identity and place in a postcolonial world. She points out that this desire smacks of white supremacy rather than questioning limited ways of viewing other cultures. My interest and opportunity to learn with curiosity about how other people live reflected a privileged position because I am part of a dominant, white, northern society. In addition, I realized that I could leave Ecuador at the end of my fellowship, while the grassroots women with whom I interacted did not have that option—their poverty was real and would continue long after I had returned to the United States.

Despite these problems in the way I sometimes thought of my experiences or in the way that I described them, recognizing that much of what interested me about the women's ways of life was in fact a reflection of poverty seems to me of great consequence. Yes, I was curious to see what it was like to carry water from a beautiful river to one's house, but I was also keenly and uncomfortably aware of the physical pain, time required, and other burdens that women suffer as a result. hooks does acknowledge that this reaching out by whites can have "revolutionary" intentions—as mine might have. I wanted to learn enough that I could understand how to work in support of grassroots women's organizations like theirs in the future. I hoped they would see that I was there because their knowledge and advocacy was valuable and worth learning from. hooks' argument seems a plausible explanation for the contradictions I experienced, and although she questions whether anything radical can come out of a viewpoint such as mine, she does conclude that open reflection on it can lead to change for the better.

Conclusion

Through my research and experiences in Ecuador, I learned important lessons about how others live and work that related to how I viewed them and how I live my own life. I gained knowledge about self-reflection and I analyzed how I relate to others. Understanding more about the work people carry out to survive in poorer communities forced me to confront the wasteful, extravagant lives we lead in the United States. My discomfort with privilege and the disparities I recognized helped me rethink what I need materially to live and survive. Looking back now, as someone working for a global movement of grassroots women's groups, I know that what I learned about myself, about consumption in the world, and about how women have organized to improve their communities have enabled me to work for social change and to support the leadership of grassroots women while developing as a leader myself. The experience helped me to choose to dedicate myself to this career, to make financial sacrifices for it, and to base my efforts on ethical principles to support grassroots women's leadership.

It is important for feminists, academics, and practitioners working on international issues or doing development work to have a clear understanding of the lives and circumstances of the people they intend to help. Digging deeper by opening up to people, or pushing one's boundaries to see and experience the difficulties poor women face is an important component of learning. While part of my motivation to learn about other people in Ecuador may have stemmed from problematic social constructs, in the end such inner struggles may not have heavily affected my learning experience or my ability to interact and contribute respectfully with the women I met. They may have remained as personal conflicts that I dealt with internally and that rarely reflected in my work. With honest reflection on our experiences, I believe mutually beneficial and liberating relationships among women of vastly different life experience can develop. Together we can work more effectively for change.

NOTES

1. For more information on GROOTS International and the Huairou Commission, see our Web site: http://www.GROOTS.org.
2. bell hooks, "Eating the Other: Desire and Resistance," in *Media and Cultural Studies: Key Works*, eds. Meenakshi Gigi Durham and Douglas M. Kellner, 424–438 (Malden, MA: Blackwell Publishers, 2001); and Uma Narayan, *Dislocating Cultures: Identities, Traditions, and Third World Feminism* (New York: Routledge, 1997).
3. See data on Ecuador in Millennium Development Goals Indicators: http://mdgs .un.org/unsd/mdg/Data.aspx?cr=218 (accessed October 3, 2008).
4. World Bank, "World Bank Development Indicators: Poverty Data, A Supplement to World Development Indicators, 2008" (Washington, D.C.: World Bank, 2008). The United Nations Development Programme Human Development Report of 1996 reveals that the income ratio of the economically richest 20 percent and poorest 20 percent of the world increased from a ratio of 30:1 in 1960, to 61:1 in 1991, to 74:1 in 1997. See Lola J. Vázques and Napoléon G. Stalos, *Ecuador: Su realidad* (Quito: Fundación José Peralta, 1999), 27.
5. See Caroline Moser, *Gender Planning and Development: Theory, Practice, and Training* (New York: Routledge, 1993), 39–41.
6. See Uma Narayan, *Dislocating Cultures*; and Caren Grown and Gita Sen, *Development, Crises, and Alternative Visions: Third World Women's Perspectives* (New York: Monthly Review Press, 1987).
7. These programs provide sheltered learning experiences for students, and the income gained benefits the privileged classes of the country. The elite universities reap the financial benefits of foreign students. Host families receive approximately three times an average worker's salary for each student, and they rarely share the benefits with their female domestic employees, who take on an added work burden.
8. See Robert Chambers, *Whose Reality Counts? Putting the First Last* (Warwickshire, UK: ITDG, 1997), 45.
9. Moser, *Gender Planning and Development*, 2–3.
10. Jane Addams, *Twenty Years at Hull-House* (New York Signet Classic, 1981), 187–192.
11. Ibid.
12. Narayan, *Dislocating Cultures*, 137–138.
13. Chandra Mohanty, "Under Western Eyes: Feminist Scholarship and Colonial Discourse," in *Third World Women and the Politics of Feminism*, eds. Chandra Talpade Mohanty, Ann Russo, and Lourdes Torres, 51–80 (Bloomington: Indiana University Press, 1991).
14. hooks, "Eating the Other," 424.

12

Giving Voice to the Unheard

Writing with Women in Trenton

KRISTEN LYONS MARAVI

I AM

I am an American
I want to feel like a soldier
I am powerful
But I want to be strong
I am willing
But I want to be fulfilling
I am alive
But sometimes I want to be dead
I am tormented on the inside
But I want to be important
And realized
I am a mother
But I want to be better than she was to me.[1]

—Velvet Brown

When I was growing up in affluent Morris County, I thought I was poor because my family didn't go on weeklong vacations like the rest of my friends. I knew that we were money conscious because we bought the Shop Rite brand of most products when we went food shopping. Thanks to my parents, I was an expert in checking unit prices of goods at the grocery store at a young age. What I did not realize was that a few miles away from my nice, middle-class house in the northwestern suburbs of New Jersey, there were kids living in challenged cities such as Trenton who had little to eat and would have loved some Shop Rite cold cuts.[2] I grew up ignorant about the lives of the poor, and mainly in fear of poverty. I did not know how people became or stayed poor, but I felt afraid whenever I was in an area where poor people lived. I was more interested in avoiding poor communities than in investigating the circumstances that created and perpetuated them.

As I got older, I learned more about what it meant to be poor. But it was not until going to college and living in a community with low-income people that the reality of class differences began to bother me. As a student living in New Brunswick, I saw poor people on a daily basis in the downtown area.[3] Riding the bus along George Street, I was shocked by the disparity between the affluent college students who had so much and their neighbors who had so little. I had been to New York City, where the occasional homeless person is on the street asking for money, but I considered that an anomaly. My experience in New Brunswick taught me that there are in fact many poor people living in the United States who might not be sleeping on the sidewalks but who are living on barely enough to support themselves and their families. This realization of the injustice of economic inequality inspired me to choose poverty, women's poverty in particular, as an academic area of interest in college.

As a scholar at the Institute for Women's Leadership (IWL), I landed an internship at a Trenton-based community development corporation that allowed me to learn firsthand about some of the difficulties facing low-income people in New Jersey.[4] First as an intern and later a part-time associate, I worked for Management Interventions, Inc. (MII), an urban issues consulting firm that addresses community redevelopment, public housing, and welfare reform.[5] I assisted the president, Wanda Webster Stansbury, in writing grant proposals for faith-based organizations that were doing good work in the city, such as establishing food banks and after-school programs. Although this experience did not give me the opportunity to work directly with low-income people, I learned about issues that affect their lives, such as the 1996 legislation that established Temporary Assistance for Needy Families (TANF) and the challenges that individuals and families faced as they transitioned from welfare to work.

At about the same time in 2002, Maya Angelou came to campus to speak. As a lover of literature and poetry in particular, I was already familiar with Angelou's writing. Seeing her in person, however, was a whole different story. As she read her work to the large audience, the beauty of the words came alive for me as they never had before. I was reminded of the reason I became an English major; I love language and the power it has to transform. I began to think about creating a project that would connect my concerns about women's poverty with my attraction to literature and my belief in the power of writing. I decided I would design a series of writing classes, sponsored by the IWL, for low-income women in Trenton. By teaching the workshops and providing the participants with a stipend, I hoped to give underprivileged women an opportunity to make time for writing in their lives.

With the help of my supervisor and her staff at the urban issues consulting firm, I recruited a small group of women for the writing workshops.

All of them had been previously enlisted by MII as part of a construction trades training program aimed at helping minorities and women of Trenton obtain membership in local trade unions. Although I mailed many letters publicizing the classes, only five women responded and four actually participated in the sixteen-week session.

I hoped to compile and then publish the participants' writings, as a small step toward bridging the gap of class that separates poor women from their more affluent sisters. Because income levels often determine where we live, work, and with whom we associate, it is typical for most of us to interact almost exclusively with people of the same economic background. Opinions about those in other income brackets are therefore usually based on stereotypes. By publishing the writing produced in the workshops, I aimed to establish a preliminary form of communication between people of different economic backgrounds. While theorizing this goal, I had to reconcile the conflict I felt in my own mind between these disadvantaged women and myself. The small amount of coverage the media gives to the poor portrays them as a threat to society, and this was largely the view I had absorbed growing up.

On the first day of the Urban Storytellers writing workshops I was filled with anticipation. My train ride and walk to the office passed by unusually quickly that day. For months I had been planning this project, but you can only prepare so much and then you just have to try something. I was definitely ready to put my ideas into action and was hoping my pilot would work. I was encouraged by the fact that I was not walking into the workshop alone. That day, I had Maya Angelou's poetry by my side. I knew the words of one of my favorite Angelou poems, "Still I Rise," could inspire the women to write.[6]

I was nervous on that first day, and I think the participants were as well. Marianne Brittingham was the first to arrive to the small conference room in the MII office: she was in her early fifties and had no children. She was a little more reticent about writing than the others were, yet she was eager to offer advice about dealing with frustrating situations that participants faced and to share her stories aloud.

> I am in a Room with No lights.
> A cry for peace runs in the Room.
> A worker is in need,
> My soul is in need of help.
> Joy and happiness rings out
> When you find yourself.
>
> —Marianne Brittingham

Velvet Brown was next to join us. She had already written poetry on her own and was in the process of submitting some pieces to a Web site. She was close to my own age, in her early twenties, with one child.

To my Poets/Readers:
My name is Velvet. I am from Trenton, New Jersey. I am a single mother
and my goal is to become a computer analyst/construction worker.
Velvet Brown

Only two women, Marianne and Velvet, came that first day. We began by
reading Angelou's poem, and writing a response. There was some hesitation
in the beginning, but as we went along, we shared more easily. Velvet was
especially motivated, saying she liked to write and already knew the poem. She
added that unfortunately, she often could not find the time to write. As a
result, she said her thoughts stay in her head "driving me crazy." This idea of
women needing time to write was one of the driving forces behind the
workshop.

Two other women, Asia Lynch and Ebony Williams, also took part in the
writing series. Like Marianne, Asia did not consider herself to be "a writer"
before the workshops, but by the end of the four-session program she had
gained much confidence. She was another young mother, with one child.

To all Poets, Writers, and Readers:
Hi, I'm Asia M. Lynch and I'm a 20 year old single mother from Trenton,
New Jersey. I'm fighting the "when's" and "if's" of every life's situation.
Although I consider myself lucky enough not to have had a nervous
breakdown, there are still nerve wrecking ordeals surrounding my
come up.
Thank You,
Asia Lynch

Like Velvet, Ebony had also tried her hand at creative writing. Ebony was the
most outspoken of the group, yet all of the women were there to write and to
communicate with one another.

To all my Fellow Poets and Readers:
My name is Ebony Williams. I reside in Trenton, New Jersey. I am
20 years of age with a daughter that's six years of age. She and also my
past experiences are what inspired me to write and gather up these
other types of feelings in my poetry. I hope as you read it can heal you
in the way it healed me. So enjoy, if you would.
Peace,
Ebony Williams

Asia, Ebony and Velvet were all a year younger than I was, while Marianne was
several decades older. I felt young or naïve in comparison to the group, yet
some participants thought I was older than twenty-one. I was the only white
woman in the group of black women.

I am a girl who wants to be a woman.
I am a writer.
I am a potential poet, in hiding.
I am a student.
I am learning.
I am hoping to succeed,
Hoping to love,
Hoping to have children who love.
I want to be an inspiration.
Kristen Lyons
Editor

As we shared the time in the workshops together, we realized our similarities as women, and that helped us recount our stories and relate to each other. At the same time, our different perspectives allowed us to give advice to one another. This fostered the "woman communication" which Ebony cited in her evaluation as one of the most enjoyable parts of the workshops. This sense of community was exactly what I had hoped to establish. I wanted participants to feel comfortable sharing their voices with each other and then with a larger audience as well.

Reflecting on the time I spent writing with the women, there were moments when I felt no distance between us at all. We could write about love, dreams, and memories in much the same way. I can relate, for example, to Marianne Brittingham's poem "Rocking Chair."

ROCKING CHAIR

Living in Trenton back in the sixties,
My mother's mother had a red rocking chair in our backyard.
As children we played house in the backyard.
Her rocking chair and a table from a box
We had a house.
We had a peach tree and a pear tree in the back yard
So the dolls had food.
The dolls we pretended to be friends and neighbors.
Cooking breakfast for the dolls and rocking them to sleep
In grandmother's red rocking chair.
Covering them with a blanket we made from paper,
Oh the fun we had.

Now the sun is going down
Time to come in the house
For grandmother will read you a story before bed.

Tomorrow the dolls will cook for us, my cousin said.
Oh the fun we had,
In the little red rocking chair.

—Marianne Brittingham

At other moments, our differences in life experience and language seemed insurmountable. Asia Lynch's poem "SCREAM!" described emotions that were far from my own comfortable reality.

SCREAM!

I am filled with frustration, aggravation, agitation, I just want to
SCREAM. . . .
Please God lead me in a righteous direction,
if not I'll SCREAM
I know God got my back, but still I want to SCREAM,
Feel like my world is crumbling,
I can see myself tumbling, tumbling
For that I SCREAM.
Financially, spiritually, mentally, physically and willingly
I'm at a disadvantage
I feel I need to SCREAM. . . .
Love is knocking, I answer with a SCREAM
Powered with the ability to adapt, why bother
I reform and SCREAM
What I need to be screaming for is Peace.

—Asia Lynch

As noted in my journal entry below, I felt more distance from the four participants after the third workshop session:

Crazy. Two different worlds. They talk about fightin' in school—fightin' and cursin' and eatin.' A different language, a different rhythm. . . . They talk about the "niggas" in their lives—the ones they love, the ones that disrespect them. . . . One [participant] broke her arm, one wants to have nine kids, one praises God, one stays focused and keeps us focused. . . . And I write about planting flowers with my father.

Through compiling and distributing the writing produced in the Urban Storytellers workshop I hoped to reveal the often silent voices of poor women in society. Tillie Olsen describes in her book *Silences* the disturbing phenomenon that there are silences in literature, that the voices of certain groups of people are not represented as often as others are. She focuses on the lack of women writers, especially those who are mothers, working-class, or poor: "Almost no mothers—almost no part-time, part-self persons—have created enduring literature . . . so far."[7]

Listening to the actual voices of low-income women is the first step in designing any policy that might seek to help them. While conceptualizing my project, I thought about the connection between public policy and the experiences of poor women after reading an article, "Work, Politics, and Coalition Building: Hmong Women's Activism in a Central California Town."[8] The author, Sharon Bays, focuses on activism among refugee women in a California town and stresses the importance of uncovering the historically hidden voices of minority groups to better serve their needs through public policy. In relation to the community of Hmong women in particular, "there was a mythology that explained women's and girls' lives [that] was widely repeated and thus easily believed by social worker, school administrator, and refugee coordinator alike."[9] The people and organizations trying to help this group of poor women were unknowingly misled and perpetuating that misinformation. An ideal system would focus on addressing the specific needs of the poor from the poor person's perspective, as opposed to implementing a predetermined racist and classist solution. This will only happen when the "voices of women [are] incorporated into the information that shapes government-funded employment projects."[10]

Other women writers have articulated this same disconcerting trend, that the voices of low-income women talking about their own lives have been masked by the dissemination of biased, "official" stories about the poor. In her fine book *From Good Ma to Welfare Queen*, Vivyan Adair, a poor woman writer, highlights this tendency:

> Headline-grabbing stories about welfare women and their allegedly malicious behaviors . . . safely orchestrate my story as one of chaos, pathology, promiscuity, illogic and sloth, juxtaposed always against order, progress, and decency of deserving citizen. They write the official story of who I am, but they are not, and will never be, me.[11]

Such representations have led many Americans to dismiss poor women as "undeserving" and burdens on society.

In her poem "The System," Ebony Williams, one of the women in the writing workshop, describes the difficulty of being a single mother on welfare.

THE SYSTEM

I'm trying to do the best that I can
And you still won't let me live even if I had a man
Thinking your money would just be enough

When all that I need is support when my timing gets tough
But you push me aside as though you don't care,
And give me a hassle every time that I'm there
I'm always trying to be cool
But when you talk it's like you're cursing me out
When all I'm trying to do is tell you what it's about.
But you're stuck in your world
Your extra money
You don't care to mention
That's why I'm so tired of this fucked up system.

—Ebony Williams

Poverty is at odds with the image many have of the United States as the land of opportunity. As Adair writes, "the American public ha[s] difficulty reconciling the images of poverty that surround them on a daily basis with maxims of upward mobility, social progress, and individual worth that they ha[ve] internalized as part of the narrative of the 'American Dream.'"[12] The financial crisis of 2008, which some have compared to the Great Depression of the 1930s, may cause Americans to rethink these narratives of class permeability, but they have had a strong impact on ideas about American culture and society. In light of the hierarchical class structure of U.S. society, poor women such as Ebony are falsely condemned for causing their own poverty. People blame women on welfare for being poor rather than listening to their stories and discovering the reasons they became poor. To fight "the feminization of poverty" in the United States, we must "shift blame" from the poor people to the welfare system, family policy, and other structural inadequacies of our economic and political system.[13]

Many poor women remain hopeful, however, that they will be able to achieve their dreams despite frustration in the face of a flawed welfare system and social, racial, and class prejudice. The aspirations of these women have not yet been—and hopefully never will be—crushed. As Ebony Williams writes in her poem "The Walk," despite the poverty into which she was born and the fact that she was "headed in someone's tomb," (line 4) she is "reborn to assume [her] position" (6). Her old life is dead to her now because "hopes and dreams came for me to stop it" (22) and it was "time to change the cycle" of poverty and death that she was living (23).

Velvet Brown's moving poem below also demonstrates her hope and appreciation of beauty despite the adversity she faces.

Therefore life is not easy It's what you make it
Everybody says life is hard, life is boring, I wish I was younger. Life
should be cherished whether or not you live in a criminal or violent

neighborhood. Just to be able to breathe, walk, talk and eat is enough for me. Just to get up in the morning and see that the sun has already risen, just to watch the waves in the water, even the sunlight of the water after a day of hard work, and taking care of the kids, last but not least, paying the bills. Life is beautiful, like I said, it's what you make it.

—Velvet Brown

Giving people (and women in particular) time to write is beneficial to them. In her introductory comments to the *Urban Storytellers* collection, Ebony mentioned how her writing has "healed" her. In my own experience facilitating, I noticed on several days the women came into the workshops agitated about a particular problem in their lives. Talking and then writing in a small group helped them diffuse their frustrations and even laugh about their hardships. By writing with the women, I gained information and some understanding about their daily lives, as they did about mine. By taking time out of our regular schedules to write together, we creatively shared and talked; in the process, my own ideas about poor women moved from stereotype closer to reality.

When I flip through the pictures taken on one of the last days of the workshop, I am struck by the group shots. I see smiling faces, some still looking a bit timid while others show wide grins. I feel confident that, even if only temporarily, one of my main goals of increasing the self-esteem and sense of community among the women was reached. My other objective was to share the collection of writing (titled *Urban Storytellers*) created during the workshop series. Although I did not distribute the *Urban Storytellers* collection to a wide audience, I did write a senior honors thesis, "The Inherited Dreams of America's Poor Women," which incorporated the writing in *Urban Storytellers*.[14] In this way I was able to simulate an otherwise impossible "conversation" between the writers in the Trenton workshops and published women writers from a variety of backgrounds as they addressed similar themes.

Through my work in Trenton, I grew in self-understanding and leadership. Earlier I had been afraid of poverty and accepted what Vivyan Adair refers to as the "stigma of poverty"—the negative stereotypes associated with being poor that are propagated by society. Before I interned at Management Interventions, Inc. and met the women in the writing workshop, I had an invisible barrier of difference in my own mind, which kept me from feeling that I could interact meaningfully with low-income people. Through these experiences, I was able to bridge the gap, at least temporarily, between the poor women of the Trenton community and myself. I changed from a girl living in the suburbs of New Jersey who thought she was poor to a woman working in Trenton where the sadness of poverty is an everyday reality.

The Institute for Women's Leadership helped to bring me face to face with what I feared; I learned in the process that fear is no excuse for complacence. As Ebony Williams wrote in her poem "The Walk," "Seems as though I've been here before/Scared and torn . . . But/Reborn to assume my position/Reborn in a soul that once was a wish carried in a heart."

NOTES

1. All excerpts are from the collection of writing that I compiled and edited, and are used here by permission of the authors. Kristen Lyons, ed., *Urban Storytellers: Women of Trenton Tell Their Stories* (New Brunswick, NJ: IWL, Rutgers University, Fall 2002).

2. According to the 2000 U.S. Census, Morris County, New Jersey, has 470,000 residents—87 percent white, 7.8 percent Hispanic or Latino, 6.3 percent Asian, and 2.8 percent African American. The median household income is $77, 340, and 3.9 percent of the population is living below the poverty line.

3. According to the 2000 U.S. Census, New Brunswick, New Jersey, has 48,600 residents—49 percent white, 39 percent Hispanic or Latino, and 23 percent African American. Median household income is $36,074, and 27 percent of the population is living below the poverty line.

4. According to the 2000 U.S. Census, Trenton, New Jersey, has 85,400 residents—52 percent African American, 33 percent white, and 22 percent Hispanic or Latino. Median household income is $31,074, and 21 percent of the population lives below the poverty line.

5. For more information, see the Web site of Management Interventions, Inc.: http://managementinterventions.com/.

6. Maya Angelou, "Still I Rise," in *And Still I Rise* (New York: Random House, Inc., 1978), 41–42.

7. Tillie Olsen, *Silences* (New York: Delacorte Press/Seymour Lawrence, 1965), 19.

8. Sharon Bays, "Work, Politics, and Coalition Building: Hmong Women's Activism in a Central California Town," in *Community Activism and Feminist Politics: Organizing across Race, Class, and Gender*, ed. Nancy Naples, 301–325 (New York: Routledge, 1998).

9. Ibid., 307.

10. Ibid.

11. Vivyan Adair, *From Good Ma to Welfare Queen: A Genealogy of the Poor Woman in American Literature, Photography, and Culture* (New York: Garland Publishing, Inc., 2000), x–xi.

12. Ibid., 29.

13. Ibid., 16. See also Diana Pearce, "The Feminization of Poverty: Women, Work, and Welfare," *Urban and Social Change Review* 11 (1978): 28–36.

14. Kristen Lyons, "The Inherited Dream of America's Poor Women," undergraduate honors thesis, Department of English, Rutgers University, May 2003.

13

Moving through Message

Feminist Counternarratives for Social Change

LIZA BRICE

To borrow bell hooks' terminology, my life can be defined as a long-term effort to move from "margin to center."[1] This endeavor began when I was quite young, growing up fractured by class and gender violence, both within my family and by virtue of our place in the community. The pain of hierarchy is one of my earliest memories. My childhood experiences produced an environment where I felt inequality, isolation, and trauma. But somehow, at the same time, I was able to see through these forces and recognize them as part of a larger system of injustice. I wanted most as a young girl to move beyond class and gender oppression. Fortunately, I learned that another world was possible.

What saved me as a teenager was music. The female rock musicians I listened to contradicted the social messages that made me feel inferior and alone in personal struggle. When I was a kid finding my way out of oppressive conditions, the music of Patti Smith, Bikini Kill, Ani DiFranco, and others created a place for me to transform. DiFranco's song "Fuel" sticks out in my mind as one of the first political songs that was transformative in my growth as an activist; she describes how the messages of the media and popular culture are all the same. This became an anthem for me as a teenager, before I consciously and fully understood the complex dynamics of corporate consolidation of the mass media.

When I entered seventh grade, with my body kicking into full gear and becoming that of a woman, I stopped eating. Classically, I could not control the devastation of my family life, but I could be in command of my body (or so I thought). Sculpting a thin, "perfect body" was a way for me to compete in a social world where I had limited means. I can now see my lifelong struggle with body image as a symptom of living in a misogynistic society.

The feminism that came to me through music is what turned my internalized violence into a political issue. For the first time I understood that I was not alone in my experience; what was happening to me belonged to a larger system of judgment of and control over women's bodies. This was the beginning of my shift from the personal to the political, and it gave me new power.

Finding a Frame: Politicizing in My College Years

After leaving the Long Island town where I grew up, I began to find more of the things I treasured in Ani DiFranco's music: critical thought, political consciousness, queer identity. Looking at the ways women are represented in the media and popular culture was one of the first conversations that drew me into women's and gender studies as a college student. I could immediately relate to this issue. Discussions about the objectification of women's bodies, eating disorders, racism, sexual violence and their relationship to TV shows, magazine covers, and movies was interesting and felt relevant. I realized that humans are impressionable, and that media has a powerful impact on the ways we see and understand the world. I began to think about media as a tool and a means to interpret and express different sides of feminism. I also began to consider more seriously gender and the role of women in the media, the ways in which sexism and patriarchy function through media, and the need for a radical change where women and other underrepresented peoples become the media-makers. My studies broadened from sociology and women's and gender studies to include communications and media.

I found a flyer in my mailbox at school for a program devoted to women's leadership and social change. Instantly engaged, I read further to find out that this institute offered internships for female students in women's leadership, human rights, antipoverty work, and the media: I knew this was it. As scholars at the Institute for Women's Leadership (IWL), we were required to select a policy area of concentration, such as women and poverty, women and law, women and human rights. I found it difficult to pick a single focus because they all seemed interconnected to me. Through my involvement with the Leadership Scholars Program, I began to think of media as a lens into a wide range of political and feminist topics.

Consciousness-raising, which is a tool from second-wave feminism that involves the naming of things, the sharing of ideas, and the birth of analysis, informed my evolving thoughts on media and social change. In *The Feminine Mystique*, Betty Friedan recognized the power of language in her description of "the problem that has no name."[2] In considering the oppression of silence and the act of creating narratives from the margins, I began to turn my attention to existing vehicles of representation—film, television, radio, the Internet—that could be leveraged on a mass scale to advocate for social change. The ways that music reflected my own set of identities (being female, queer, working class) had so profoundly affected my survival that I became inspired to understand the role that art, media, and communications have not just on individuals but on society at large.

Class readings and discussions when I learned about other people's lives and evaluated them in relation to my own were another crucial point of learning for me. I discovered how to see my own experience in larger contexts. Coming to know terms such as "patriarchy," "class struggle," and "capitalist exploitation" took my personal experience out of the closet and put it in a broader social context. Being political in college meant understanding that I certainly was not alone in the experience of class and gender violence. The participatory, feminist pedagogy practiced in the department of Women's and Gender Studies was central to my growth. Drawing upon and valuing the personal, sharing ideas, and connecting these to the production of theory showed me the power of academic inquiry, communications, and language in a very intimate way. The IWL took this to the next level in teaching me about action.

As an undergraduate, I looked for the connection between theory and practice and for ways to apply the ideas we discussed in the classroom. During seminars my mind would race ahead, wondering urgently, "What can we do? How can we change this? How can we take this from a niche area of academic study to actually eradicate racism, sexism, and classism?" I began to think about ways to bring people together across distances, both physical and conceptual, to form the basis for a collective movement. This was my second reason for studying media for social change.

Learning not only about social justice issues but also about how to actually make social change was a higher level of engagement for me. Instead of just studying the problems, we came up with plans to address them. Through internships and a capstone social action project, I learned the meaning of leadership, I learned the difference between thinking and doing, and I learned how to do both together. Leadership involves taking action. Leadership is not simply a radical thought on its own—leaders in power in general are "in action"; the unique approach the institute fosters is to transform power through reinventing who the actors should be (women and those at the social margins, along with men).

I came out of childhood with a strong yearning for liberation and justice. I believe that my personal experiences allow me to relate to an environment in struggle, to people who are not free, and to recognize injustice on all levels—community, state, and geopolitical. In addition to being able to empathize, wanting to be a social change agent also includes a shift from living solely for self-preservation to working for the preservation of the community as we grow to see these as inextricable from one another. One doesn't need to be victimized to work with those who are, but the kind of wisdom and strength that can be born out of oppression is powerful and can fuel social change organizing. This understanding furthered my movement from the personal to the political. As I studied at the IWL in seminars where we read works by women of color, and we discussed racism in the feminist movement with students from diverse racial and class backgrounds, I learned how complex leadership for social change is—and must be; as Audre Lorde has taught me, "the master's tools will never dismantle the master's house."[3] What is most important is to create new ways to live and act—new ways to lead.

One of our first assignments at the IWL was to conduct an interview with a woman leader in our policy area of interest. My professor suggested that I interview someone at Women Make Movies (WMM), a nonprofit media arts organization established in 1972, during the second wave. WMM distributes films made by and about women, and it supports women filmmakers in realizing their projects.[4] I remember calling the organization and asking to interview the executive director, Debra Zimmerman, but her assistant kindly informed me that she was out of the country on business but that I could still talk to another female leader. I interviewed Christie George, the sales and broadcast manager, and nervously recorded our telephone conversation with a semifunctioning tape recorder borrowed from a friend. I had never conducted a formal interview before, and George was intelligent, quick, and sharp—"so New York" I thought, and I wondered whether I would be able to keep up. We discussed her current publicity work for *Señorita Extraviada*, a film about the mass murder "disappearances" of women in Ciudad Juárez, Mexico. When the call was over I felt immense relief that I had gotten through the interview and was able to facilitate an engaging conversation, and I was in awe of the work Christie was doing at WMM. I had asked her about what advice she had for young women like myself, who were studying leadership for social change. What has stayed with me is her call for young women to push through social boundaries to achieve greatness, whether those were barriers of race, class, gender, or any other kind of difference. Today I sit at literally the same desk at Women Make Movies where Christie George sat five years ago when I interviewed her.

Inside-Out and Outside-In Strategies

As one leaves adolescence and enters adulthood, society asks us directly what we want to do, as a reflection of who we are. I recall discussions at the IWL about the best ways to enact leadership for social change, from reshaping existing social institutions by entering and eventually transforming them (the "inside-out" approach) versus creating change outside of the mainstream (the "outside-in" method). The multiple voices in our discussions reflected a diverse group of women with varying ideas on leadership and gender. When I think about these two different methods for creating social change—transforming traditional institutions or working in alternative organizations—I find myself vacillating between both kinds of approaches. I have spent much time in "outsider" groups, focused on personal transformation and community action, with the assumption that the only thing one can change is what is in one's own backyard. I have also gone beyond the local and worked on international levels at WBAI Radio and Democracy Now! as an intern, and I spent time as a freelancer at a politically minded nonprofit book publisher called The New Press.

I am still early in my career, learning how I can best contribute to social justice movements. My work at Women Make Movies, along with my other experiences, has given me hope in change from both inside-out and outside-in strategies; I feel that using both kinds of approaches throughout my future will yield the strongest results.

One inside-out way of creating change is making sure that women are in decision-making, leadership positions in organizations, including those in the arts and media. Women Make Movies focuses on films by and about women because, despite the fact that some claim the feminist movement has eradicated sexism and patriarchy, women are still starkly underrepresented in senior positions in the film world. Of the top 250 domestic grossing films released in 2007, 21 percent employed no women directors, executive producers, writers, cinematographers, or editors.[5] In addition, women only accounted for 10 percent of the writers of these films. It is important for viewers to know who is writing the stories they hear, and to consider the effect this has on our culture. Media has a deep impact on our lives and consciousness; it is dangerous when half of the world's population is left out of the discussion—still. Every day when I arrive at my desk at WMM, I work to help create a feminist counternarrative that includes the films and interpretations of women from all across the world.

My job involves everything I care most about: feminism, independent media, and the arts used as a vehicle for social change. My position as the online marketing and outreach coordinator puts me at the center of challenging and exciting projects; my focus is on bringing our public relations tools up to date with the most current communication technologies, including social networking sites, video integration into our marketing materials, the launch of an official YouTube channel, and integration of RSS (Rich Site Summary) feeds, a format for delivering regularly changing Web content from other sites into our Web site. The issues our films describe include urgent political needs in the world today: rape and the human rights crisis in the Democratic Republic of Congo, queer partnership and civil rights, the epidemic and underreported murders of indigenous women in British Columbia, Canada, to name a few.[6] I am grateful every day for the opportunity to harness the power of these communication tools to educate the public about such important feminist and human rights issues. Creating a film and distributing it effectively is a way to take action. By raising the public consciousness about pressing political and social issues, films can inspire collective action, which can drive the direction of social movements.

Leadership is the use of one's agency to create social change. Women Make Movies is a leadership organization because the films we distribute both educate and make an impact. One of our biggest releases of 2008, *The Greatest Silence: Rape in the Congo*, a documentary about the mass rape of women in the civil war–torn Democratic Republic of Congo, has led to changing political definitions of rape. After screening the film, Amb. Zalmay Khalilzad of the United Nations Security Council brought this issue before the council and argued that rape should be considered not just a war crime but also a weapon of war.[7] On behalf of the filmmaker Lisa F. Jackson and all others involved in making the film, I believe this is what leadership for social change looks like. As a core member of a relatively small staff at WMM, I am part of a team of leadership.

The Power of Media for Social Change

Social change occurs as we bring ourselves from margin to center in all our differences—whether these are race, gender, class, sexual orientation, ability, language, nationality, or age. bell hooks warns feminists against reinstating patriarchal structures. Feminist leadership must be transformative and must create new, liberating structures that support our lives rather than constrain them. Creating new ways to live and act includes thinking about the most effective methods for implementing social change. Each of us must decide for ourselves if the best way to reshape social institutions is by entering and eventually transforming them (the "inside-out" approach), or by creating change outside of the mainstream (the "outside-in" method), or by some combination of the two.

As my academics, work in independent media, and leadership transform my feminism, I am in a constant state of growth. In the same way that I strove to understand my budding interests in college, I am now on a determined and focused trajectory, reaching for the next stage in my development. It is dutiful and noble work to participate in social movements, but to lead one must bring new ideas and share them effectively. When I think of all the artists and activists who have inspired me, what I see most clearly is the way in which they contribute new concepts, new ways of looking at things, and solutions that inform social justice movements. My next step in leadership development will be toward learning how to best create content through language, media, music, and any and all other forms of communication I can get my hands on.

Through all of my political learning and practice to date, I have realized that working for transformative social change means creating the alternative.

People are already doing this, as I am as I work to make and disseminate alternative media and film. A central goal in the struggle for independent media must be to bring the tools and resources for mass communications to those who are marginalized, to make our personal struggles part of community discourse. We must remember media's powerful impact on the ways we see and understand the world, and we must be part of creating counternarratives. If we as social justice students, activists, and feminist leaders integrate our convictions into our communities and across the world, our common dream for progressive, transformative social change is possible.

NOTES

1. bell hooks, *Feminist Theory: From Margin to Center* (Cambridge, MA: South End Press, 1984 and 2000).

2. Betty Friedan, *The Feminine Mystique* (New York: W. W. Norton & Co., 1963, repr. 2001).

3. Audre Lorde, "The Master's Tools Will Never Dismantle the Master's House," *Sister Outsider: Essays and Speeches*, The Crossing Press Feminist Series (Berkeley, CA: Crossing Press, 1984).

4. For more information on Women Make Movies, see their Web site: http://www .wmm.com/about/general_info.shtml.

5. Martha M. Lauzen, "The Celluloid Ceiling: Behind the Scenes Employment of Women on the Top 250 Films of 2007," http://magazine.women-in-film.com/ Portals/0/Article_Images/lauzen/2007ceiling/2007_Celluloid_Ceiling.pdf.

6. *The Greatest Silence: Rape in the Congo*; *In Sickness and in Health*; *Finding Dawn*. Women Make Movie's list includes more than five hundred titles. See www.wmm.com for a full listing.

7. "Should Rape Be Considered a Weapon?" National Public Radio, http://www .npr.org/templates/story/story.php?storyId=91692457; see also "Rape Victims' Words Help Jolt Congo into Change," *New York Times*, October 18, 2008.

14

The Transformation of a Chrysalis

Becoming a Global Citizen

SASHA TANER

chrys · a · lis (krĭs′ə-lĭs)

n. *pl.* chrys · a · lis · es or chry · sal · i · des (krĭ-sălʹĭ-dēz′)

1. A pupa, especially of a moth or butterfly, enclosed in a firm case or cocoon.
2. A protected stage of development.[1]

Maria Sibylla Merian, the seventeenth-century artist and naturalist, not only studied and illustrated transformation, she epitomized it. As a child who lost her father at the age of three, she cultivated her passion for observing and drawing insects and plants that later led to major contributions in both art and science. Most notably, Merian studied the mysteries of the transformation of the caterpillar into a butterfly. She was a woman leader in many respects: she followed her interests and calling while surviving two divorces, changes of residence spanning different countries, and in her seasoned years undertook a three-month-long, cross-Atlantic journey on a merchant ship to Suriname where she spent two years observing and illustrating changes of the natural world. Merian was a woman with a pioneering spirit who helped transform our understanding of the world.[2] I find her life and career stimulating because her travels, inquisitiveness, and interest in the natural world resonate with my own personal journey of transformation. I emerged as my adult self through my travels, my growing understanding of the interdependence of women's lives around the world, and the "cocoon" of women's education at the Institute for Women's Leadership (IWL).

Important Journeys: Adventures Abroad

With a determination for seeking clarity and direction, I went as a nineteen-year-old community college student to London for a semester abroad. I stepped off the plane knowing I was beginning an important journey, but

I did not realize the extent of the personal growth I would experience, nor did I have any inkling that my travels would stretch across several countries and over a period of six years.

Those years were marked with colorful people, places, and experiences. I made some wonderful friendships while studying in London and—seeking an adventure after my semester there—set out to create a temporary life in Santorini, Greece, with a few of these new friends. I found work in villas carved into the side of a mountain and was enamored by the natural beauty that surrounded me. After five months, I felt it was time to move on, so I took a bus, a ferry, and a train across Greece, through Italy, and landed in the quaint harbor town of Antibes, France, where I cleaned boats and regrouped. I enjoyed meeting people from different backgrounds and cultures, and I thrived on being independent and capable of maneuvering in foreign lands. After a few months, I had saved enough money to travel through Spain and Portugal, and then spent several months in Morocco, an immensely interesting country. I was especially intrigued by the traditions and culture of the Berbers in the mountains. I had many different experiences in Morocco that whet my appetite for living in a predominantly Muslim culture.

After a year of learning how to live abroad on a shoestring budget and navigate myself safely through many different environments, I returned to North America to finish my associate's degree at my community college. My next adventure was heading out on a four-day Greyhound bus trip to Seattle (with a small pup tent) on my way to experience a season of hard, wet work at a fishery in Alaska. What thrilled me about these trips was getting to live a moment in another's shoes, seeing and feeling the beauty of different natural environments, and discovering that I had the ability to create my own reality, whatever limitations or challenges there might be. My rainy summer in Alaska was followed by a wonderful, warm winter working in Hawaii. I rented a room there in a beautiful house set on sacred ground on Maui, and I was swept away by the lush landscape and abundance of tropical fruit growing in my own backyard. After my time in Hawaii, however, I felt that I needed to do more than just get by, that something was missing. Because I was young, this itinerant life was fun and exhilarating, but it also took a massive amount of energy to maintain, and I wanted more stability and substance in my life.

I once again crossed the Atlantic and settled in London for a year while I earned a certificate to teach English as a second language (ESL) and worked in two jobs, one in a deli and another in an art warehouse. I believed ESL certification would be a vehicle for me to continue to spread my wings but at the same time would provide me with more meaningful, dependable work. Upon my completion of the certificate, I applied to several Near East and Middle East countries to teach English. I was eager to expand my horizons again and learn from and live in a predominantly Muslim society, and I found an interested employer in Turkey whose terms were agreeable. When I stepped off that plane in Izmir, a strange sense of coming home overwhelmed me. I walked down the local streets and felt connected to my surroundings in a way I had never before experienced. I attended a wedding the first night of my arrival, and my mother, sharing her perennially upbeat, supportive tone over the telephone, teased me about her premonition of what was to come.

Through these experiences abroad, I changed from a nineteen year old resolved to find my own independent path, to an adult with a commitment to global citizenship. Through my travels and education, I realized that we each have a responsibility to look beyond our individual selves and nationalities to try to see the world in a bigger way. I felt myself move from an inward, personally focused mindset to a global, outward-looking worldview. Travel gave me the physical and mental space I needed to make those connections, yet I was not finished with my adventures. I had more to learn, and the next stage of my development was about to begin.

Work and Love in Turkey

Turkey had a profound effect on me on so many levels, partly because of my immense curiosity and openness to learning. I found that I loved teaching, which was a surprise to me, and I thrived on working with diverse populations of students—from businessmen to journalists, village children to city-dwelling youth taking their exams for entrance into the university. I did not realize just how much I would learn by teaching, and I was hungry for these kinds of interactions. Outside the classroom, I quickly picked up the language and immersed myself in understanding more about the culture, politics, religion, activism, and terrorism that the country faced. I loved speaking with Turkish women in particular, observing both their power and vulnerability, and found myself gravitating toward those in rural and traditional areas who lived in poverty. They not only managed to get by with minimal resources but also experienced joy in their communality as women. They cooked, worked, laughed, and raised families together. An American journalist invited me to accompany her as a translator on an interview with a young Turkish woman, and I seized the opportunity. The heartbreaking story the young mother shared, about the discrimination she faced because she gave birth to a child out of wedlock, was eye opening. I traveled to many villages, talked with hard-working women and girls, and gained a profound feeling of connection. I began to think about the lives of women in a more holistic and global way.

At the same time, I enjoyed a wonderful friendship that turned into a love story, and I felt the sweet bitterness of saying goodbye as my boyfriend embarked on a year and a half of mandatory military service in the high, dangerous Mount Ararat in the northeast corner of Turkey on the Iranian border. Shortly after his departure, I was presented with an opportunity I could not pass up, a chance to work in the capital at the United Nations High Commissioner for Refugees (UNHCR). I worked forty unpaid hours a week while staying at a friend's house and working nights and weekends teaching English to earn money. My work at UNHCR involved helping resettle migrants who had fled to Turkey and been awarded refugee status. Almost 90 percent of these asylum seekers were escaping from the repressive conditions and persecution in Iraq and Iran.

I learned about the internal conditions of these two countries and became radicalized about the plight of asylum-seeking women and their vulnerability due to their gender, as well as the helplessness of their UN lawyers who had quotas and could not assign them refugee status because gender persecution was not a protected category. I made connections with the United Nations staff and at the U.S. Embassy and met representatives of nongovernmental organizations that were trying to address global problems locally in Turkey. I was inspired by their work and tried to learn how I could get more involved in helping find solutions to improve the lives of women for the global good. I began to see the lives of women as interdependent, and to consider my own life as an American in the context of the situations of women from much less affluent parts of the world. It dawned on me that we are not all isolated individuals going through our personal experiences, but many of the events in our lives are commonly informed by our status as women living in patriarchal societies. I was encouraged by my dear friends and mentors to finish my education so that I too could contribute more deeply to social change work.

Upon my boyfriend-turned-fiancé's return from the military, we solidified our partnership in a civil marriage ceremony in the capital and later in a traditional religious Muslim ceremony in the eastern region of Turkey. Since then, long-term visits with my husband's family and relatives have deepened my understanding of women and girls in the Anatolian region of Turkey and have further solidified my desire to help create social change for women. Fueled with inspiration and support, my education was our first priority, so my husband and I moved together to my home in New Jersey so I could apply to Rutgers University and build on my associate's degree by earning a bachelor's degree. For the next few years, I moved back and forth between the United States and Turkey, determined to complete my education and accumulate the credentials and knowledge needed to move myself into a position of service to make a difference.

Making Sense of It All

Back in the United States, I hoped to make sense of all the things I had seen and experienced in my travels. Poverty, oppression, and the subordination of women, minorities and children—these issues cross all intersections of race, class, gender, and ethnicity and happen everywhere. Through my undergraduate education, I deepened my understanding of the inequities that women face as well as other global imbalances in power and resources. The discrimination I had felt as a female foreigner, often mistaken for a trafficked woman due to my appearance, accent, and even my name, furthered my interest in women's issues in Turkey and the Middle East. When I returned home, the first thing I did was sign up to major in Middle Eastern studies at Rutgers; I also took courses in Islam and studied intensive Turkish at Princeton University for my language requirement. I wanted to get to the root of issues about gender, culture, and human rights and to gain a more nuanced understanding of the challenges women face around the world, so I took a course called Women, Culture and Society. It was at this class that a student visited to publicize a women's leadership program for undergraduates interested in social change. Social Change! I was compelled to apply because the idea of women's leadership for social change resonated with me so strongly. To my delight, I was accepted into the program, and another stage in my own transformation was about to begin.

After earning my undergraduate degree, I took a job at an immigration law firm in Manhattan but found that this work lacked the transformative potential I sought in my career. For this reason I began a part-time job at a New Jersey community organization called 180—Turning Lives Around, which is devoted to survivors of domestic violence and sexual assault.[3] A year later, I left the law firm and entered a master's program in global affairs while increasing my hours as a residential advocate at the domestic violence shelter. At 180, I deepened my awareness that violence against women is pervasive and cuts across the entire spectrum of society.[4] My studies reflected what I saw in my work: that the conditions that keep women in abusive circumstances have roots in societal structures such as the legal system, the family, the health care structure, and the workplace. I saw at the domestic violence shelter how encouragement, listening, and sharing knowledge, resources, and support can bring about personal transformation. Creating the conditions for the empowerment of women brought my thoughts back to the Institute for Women's Leadership (IWL) and the strength that women gain from being in single-sex environments that facilitate the sharing of experiences, and the understanding of the ways women's lives connect to larger social structures. The womb-like environment of the IWL was a place for me to change and grow in a new way, using the tools of women's studies curriculum, mentorship, and guidance through an activist project and female peers who were also deeply committed to social change.

The Transformation of a Chrysalis

In 2005 I embarked upon a different kind of journey when I gave birth to a son. The experience of motherhood has deepened my commitment to women's leadership for social change as well as my resolve to address gender inequality, violence against women, and the need for global citizenship. Holding my newborn son in one hand and opening my fresh graduate diploma with the other, I realized that my priorities and perspectives were undergoing a major change. Change is never easy, and growth is not linear.

Now that I have a child, I am inextricably connected to the next generation and feel an intense desire to find solutions for the kinds of social and global problems I have witnessed both in Turkey and in my work at the domestic violence shelter in the United States. I consider the work the IWL does as a model that can contribute to progressive social change. Eight years after graduating from the program, I am now a staff member at the institute myself. I feel that I am on the frontlines of positive transformation, working in a solution-focused, forward-looking, optimistic, and energized environment. I am confident when I see students making their own connections between the personal and the political, the local and the global, that they will continue to tackle the issues they feel strongly about long after they have left the cocoon-like environment of the IWL. As a staff member at the institute, I create space for other young women to have an experience as profound as mine. Young feminists can fill our current leadership void and pave new pathways to lead our societies into better models, based not on competition but on collaboration. I know that working toward increasing power and developing leadership among women and girls is a vital strategy toward creating a more equitable world, one where women and girls can realize their potential and work together for change. Visionary thinker and activist Jean Shinoda Bolen echoes these sentiments that we must "gather the women, [to] save the world."[5]

My expression of leadership these days is to help others succeed and achieve their potential, to create optimum environments for sharing and learning, and to give young women tools to raise their voices and be heard. The young women I know are finding their passions, raising their consciousnesses about women's leadership and contributions to social change, embracing diversity and collaboration, and seeking out and being sought by mentors. Maya Angelou said, "we allow our ignorance to prevail upon us and make us think we can survive alone, alone in patches, alone in groups, alone in races, even alone in genders."[6] To create a society that is supportive of women and girls' issues is to change the fabric of our culture. Educating young women at the IWL is a way for me to contribute to this, and I have full confidence that we can change social norms through feminism because it has the potential "to free us to be who we are—to live lives where we love justice, where we can all live in peace."[7] bell hooks is right: feminism is for everybody.

Feminist leadership is needed today more than ever. In the span of two decades, more than 150 interstate and civil conflicts have transpired, resulting in 35 million displaced people worldwide (of whom 80 percent are women and children), an increase in violence toward women, devastating poverty, and environmental degradation that threatens the future of many species, including our own. As a hyperaggressive version of society plays out its assault on humanity and our life systems, it appears to me that we have come to a crossroads, and it is with these thoughts that I have asked myself how I might help achieve a societal transformation. I believe that encouraging young women's movement from a national to a global perspective and from an individual frame of reference to a collective one—through education—will bring about such a transformation.

Three hundred years after the work and life of Maria Sibylla Merian, young women are demonstrating creative ways to manifest positive social change, and are working toward reinventing society into one that nourishes, supports, and sustains inclusiveness, equity, sustainable peace, and justice. I continue to be inspired by Merian's leadership, adventurous spirit, curiosity, and brilliance in an era when such things were not expected of a woman. My own development into adulthood has been influenced by her vision as well as by the powerful metaphor of the chrysalis enclosed in its cocoon, which eventually emerges as a butterfly.

NOTES

1. *The American Heritage Science Dictionary* (New York: Houghton Mifflin Company, 2002).
2. Merian helped change the way we think about and see our natural world. She created the first drawings and watercolor paintings of insects and plants; http://en.wikipedia.org/wiki/Maria_Sibylla_Merian. See also Kim Todd, *Chrysalis: Maria Sibylla Merian and the Secrets of Metamorphosis* (New York: Harcourt, 2007).
3. For more information on 180—Turning Lives Around, see their Web site: http://www.180nj.org.
4. L. Heise, M. Ellsberg, and M. Gottemoeller, "Ending Violence Against Women," *Population Reports*, Series L, no. 11 (Baltimore: Johns Hopkins University School of Public Health, December 1999).
5. Jean Shinoda Bolen, *Urgent Message from the Mother: Gather the Women, Save the World* (Newburyport, MA: Conari Press, 2008). For more information on Jean S. Bolen, see her Web site: www.jeanbolen.com.
6. Maya Angelou, Address, March 1990, Centenary College of Louisiana. *New York Times*, March 11, 1990.
7. bell hooks, *Feminism is for Everybody: Passionate Politics* (London: Pluto Press, 2000), 118.

PART THREE

Leadership in Practice

Creating Change

15

Changing the Face of Leadership

Legislators at Large for American Women

EDNA ISHAYIK

Election night 2000 was a major disappointment for progressive Americans, but it was especially devastating for me. The Congressional candidate I had worked so hard for lost by one percentage point. To her innumerable supporters, she represented what was hopeful in the world of politics: intelligence, honesty, and dedication to making positive changes. To me, she was proudly carrying a banner that is too often set aside. She was a woman seeking power to make progress and social change not only on behalf of her constituents but in many ways for all women. Her candidacy was rich with the promise of advancement for women's issues in America.

That night, squinting into an army of lights and cameras to deliver her concession speech, she asked the young people who worked for her not to give up hope and to continue fighting for what we believed was important. We knew what she meant; it would be easy to let this defeat us. It would feel justified to talk about how hard we worked and say we tried our best. But to step out of the ring feeling powerless would be a loss greater than the one we experienced that night.

As a young woman attending a women's college, I was just starting to learn that the world was not always fair, particularly for women. When I joined that campaign, I knew my candidate's victory would mean a step forward for all American women. I knew we would send to Congress not just a vanguard but a champion for women's issues. Through the sharp pain of defeat I realized how important it was for my friends and me to carry on and elect others like her. That candidate may have lost, but the meaning of her bid for Congress stayed with me and gave me the passion and dedication to continue to work on campaigns as a career.

Growing up, I was more interested in music, movies, and malls than I was in politics. I was not particularly concerned with women's status in society past a "girls rule, boys drool" mentality. But through Douglass College and my participation in its organizations, I came to realize there was a world past the end of my own nose, and the women in it were not doing as well as they should. This startling realization and the questions it raised prompted me to take classes in women's studies, and classes about women in politics. Throughout my college career, my professors and my peers pushed me to think about the status of women in the world from many perspectives. I learned about gender inequities throughout history. We studied the intersections of gender with race, class, sexuality and anything else gender could intersect with.

I remember reading with deep sadness about welfare moms who struggled to feed their children who were then stereotyped as lazy and used as scapegoats every time there was a budget crunch. I was outraged at the fact that women earn less than men for doing the same work. I thought about what it might mean if access to reproductive health care were scaled back. I worried about all the messages about body image we are bombarded with every day and how these messages make young women see themselves. I was overwhelmed with all the problems that affected the female population in our country.

As the summer before my senior year approached, I began to think about careers I could pursue and paths I might follow. My question was, how could I use my life's work in a way that would begin to untangle the messy knot of women's place in the world? I wondered where my efforts to help would be most effective. With so many issues to be addressed, how could I choose just one?

Like so many things in life, my answer came by chance. I was recruited to take an internship with a Congressional campaign in a neighboring district. The candidate was a woman fighting in a fierce primary battle with a typical "good ole' boy" from New Jersey's Democratic Party machine. I had never worked on a campaign before and was not sure what to expect. After this intense, hands-on experience, all my thoughts about women, leadership, and politics jelled. More women in elected office would mean more attention paid to the women's issues that concerned me. One of the best ways to ensure that these topics were on the national agenda was to campaign for progressive women running for office. So after graduation I continued working on campaigns for other female candidates. Political campaigns became my career and working to elect female legislators became my raison d'être, my way of changing the world for the better.

There are many challenges in this line of work, but I love it so much that the downside is insignificant in comparison to the rewards. Having found my path, I ripped up my LSAT scores, canceled my appointment with career counseling, and did not worry about what color my parachute was. The long, grueling hours of campaigns did not faze me. Nor did the need to uproot my life and move every nine months to pick up a different race. I was unperturbed by the low pay or the lack of health care benefits—I was so swept up in the idea that I could have an impact on issues that were important to me that none of these factors seemed problematic.

When I was on a campaign, I worked twelve to eighteen hours a day, seven days a week, barely able to return a personal phone call. In between campaigns was the opposite: I would either take a few months off to travel or spend the time relaxing and deciding on my next move. To me, this was the most valuable "perk" of the job. I did not mind working my fingers to the bone for nine months partly because I knew I would have three months of free time afterward. Looking back, I wish I had thought more about what it would mean to miss being with friends and family for months at a time—the death of a close friend brought that into focus and led me to work closer to home.

After eight years in campaigns, I have worked for a variety of candidates— women and men, gay and straight—always selecting individuals I believed would bring a fresh perspective to their elected offices. Up and down the ticket and across the Northeast, I supported candidates I thought were interesting, smart, and progressive, including Patti Morrissey for delegate in Virginia and Eliot Spitzer for governor in New York. After Spitzer's victory in November 2006, I became the executive director of New York State's Democratic Party. But the idea of building a career around electing more women continued to drive me.

Lessons from the Campaign Trail

From my experiences in political campaigns, I have learned that female candidates can face unique challenges. Take as an example the single working mom with two young daughters aged eight and ten. After six months on her campaign, it was clear to me why more young women weren't running for office. While working out of the candidate's basement, we encountered outrageous temper tantrums, loud sleepovers, and even the occasional head injury. Balancing work and parenting is difficult enough; adding the full-time stress of a campaign seemed next to impossible.

In addition to the rigors of the campaign, I found myself making peanut butter and jelly sandwiches, driving the girls to soccer practice, and making sure homework was done to free up the candidate for campaigning. I'll grant you that working in electoral politics tends to blur the lines between the personal and the professional to begin with, but when your candidate's child is screaming, "You're taking my mommy away from me" in front of a room full of donors, I would argue that the intermingling of work and family has gone too far. (Luckily, everyone in that room had paid in advance.)

Sexism added to the burdens of juggling campaign, career, and family obligations: the comments about accessories (like the American flag–print scarf one candidate used to wear so often that it caught the attention of the local press), dresses versus pantsuits, and the ultimate negative attention getter—cleavage. There is the constant mistaking of a male staffer for the candidate or elected official. There are jokes about frizzy hair and the resulting weekly, ninety-minute blow outs. I defy anyone to find a comparable male grooming time-suck. These are not necessarily reasons women do not run, and they may not be reasons they lose, but they are things male candidates do not have to deal with (John Edwards' four-hundred-dollar haircut notwithstanding). In the world of politics where time is money *and* votes, these little annoyances can turn into death by one thousand paper cuts. And when publicized, these annoyances unfairly trivialize the woman's candidacy.

Usually sexism surfaces in subtle, insidious, arguably more dangerous ways, but occasionally it hits blatantly, such as the radio ads depicting one of my candidates as a "ditsy" game show contestant who was "confused" about the issues. Studies have shown that voters do not discriminate against women, but that does not stop opponents from doing their best to eke out a percentage point or two by making gender an issue.[1]

Even if we assume that the "iron my shirt" comment shouted out by a male audience member and its reverberations did not cost Democratic presidential candidate Hillary Clinton her nomination in 2008, we should not discount the effects that these kinds of low blows may have had. And although I agree with the opinion that Gov. Sarah Palin was not prepared to run for the vice presidency, calling her "Caribou Barbie" is still not appropriate. There is artifice in people (both men and women) laughing off these remarks. Attempts to categorize them as problematic are shot down as nit-picky or hair-splitting. So embedded and sewn-in is the tendency to want to play down these sexist sentiments that to call them out is characterized as a shrill, whiny, windmill-tilting endeavor. But it can take its toll on a candidate and on her campaign just as it seeps into the psyche of any woman striving to achieve big things in a male-dominated field.

Fundraising can also be more difficult for female candidates (although some of the best fundraisers I have seen have been women). First-time candidates in particular do not like the idea of it; they do not want to make the "asks," and it can become a struggle to get them on the phones. In their study of 3,700 professionals, Jennifer Lawless and Richard Fox found that women in more significant numbers than men find the idea of fundraising repulsive enough to deter them from running for office. Some of these negative feelings filter in even once women do decide to become candidates. When that happens, it can put a stress on the entire campaign that can be difficult to overcome.[2]

Expanding the Definition of Leadership

Despite these and other factors stacked against them, I believe women would run in larger numbers if they were simply asked. Anecdotally, I find it true that they are not encouraged as often as men are, and studies prove this is the case. Party officials and other "gatekeepers" are less likely to identify women as leaders who can win.[3] But "leadership" is one of those loosely defined terms, completely contextual; there can be almost as many definitions of the term as there are people defining it. Must a leader hold a formal position or title within an organization? Must leaders have a staff or a following? Must they produce something quantifiable such as money or laws? Must they be well known? Someone with a traditional conception of leadership might answer "yes" to these questions because, historically, definitions of "leader" conjure up images of military might, business boardrooms, or presidential speeches.

But women have had a difficult time fitting these characterizations. The arenas in which they have historically been allowed to take responsibility—the family, the community, and female-dominated occupations—are not incorporated in the narrow definition that is implied by the word "leadership." Traditional definitions of leadership trump a more inclusive version of the word. When scoping for candidates, for example, nurses and teachers are routinely passed over for lawyers and millionaires. Women have been constrained from participating in the military, their input has rarely been asked for when deciding strategy, they have been discouraged from working outside the home, and they have not been allowed to vote let alone participate in lawmaking until they have fought for it. Only in the most recent decades have women been able to break through to become leaders in some of the historically male roles that the public equates with leadership.

There is also a more nuanced view of what people think leadership looks like: it should not appear that you have studied too diligently for it, worked too hard to get it, or thought too much about it. Amanda Fortini wrote in *New York Magazine* during the heated Democratic primary campaign of 2008: "'Leadership' is more effortless, an *assumed* mantle of authority, confidence that doesn't need a PowerPoint presentation to back it up. But it's difficult to imagine this traditionally male archetype—embodied in [then-presidential candidate Barack] Obama's easy manner and unscripted, often overly general approach—working for a woman in the same way it does for a man."[4] In fact, Hillary Clinton was harangued for trying the same approach early in her campaign. Her tone was interpreted as disingenuous, too forced. She was the smarty-pants in the front row with her hand in the air waiting to be called on. But this may not be fair. Women often combat the subtle sexism (and sometimes the more obvious discrimination) they face by working harder, being better prepared, having all the answers. Traditional leadership looks different on us because women's practicing it is not the norm.

Enough time has passed since the days of strict gender roles that we should be expanding our conceptions and definitions of what it means to be a "leader." Leadership must include social roles that do not involve titles, money, or power. When thinking about women's leadership in particular, the definition must make room for the ways that mothers, sisters, grandmothers, and first ladies have been organizing their families and communities throughout history. We should be able to apply the term to teaching fifth grade classes, balancing the family checkbook, demanding a cross walk at a dangerous school crossing, or increasing profit margins of a corporation. As our definition expands, maybe we will broaden the profile of who is encouraged to run for elective office and how we treat those that do.[5]

"If You Want Something Done . . ."

Women often approach leadership roles, particularly political ones, fueled by a desire for social change—by an obligation to help a community or solve a problem. By virtue of their powerful positions, politicians have the potential to be agents of social change. My hope is that legislatures and executive offices will fill with women committed to enacting social change in general and for women's issues specifically.

Although women candidates gained impressive ground in the 2008 elections, they are still underrepresented in our local and national governments. We are 51 percent of the population and less than 20 percent of the legislatures and executive positions of this nation. Currently 17 percent of the representatives and senators in the U.S. Congress are women. In 2009 there will be eight women governors in our fifty states; women constitute about one-fourth (24.2 percent) of the membership of state legislators on average. We have never had a female president or vice president, and with Hillary Clinton's presidential candidacy behind us and Gov. Sarah Palin back in Alaska, this dreary picture represents the most headway women have made in elective office to date.[6]

In the abstract, this imbalance seems incongruous at best and tragically flawed at worst. On its face it doesn't seem right, but how bad is the reality? Does the male majority in the public offices of the United States suffice to solve the problems that expressly face women? Furthermore, are their decisions better off, better informed, more balanced without the input of women?

A number of national studies reveal that the majority of women who serve in public office believe they have a special responsibility to represent women and their interests. These interests admittedly are broad but include women's health care, family policies, equal pay, children's well-being, gender equity laws, sexual harassment, and reproductive rights, among others. Women representatives from the 103rd and 104th Congresses who were interviewed about their commitment to "women's issues" produced "near universal agreement concerning their responsibility to represent women."[7]

Some examples in a representative's own words include Nydia Velázquez, a Democrat from New York's Lower East Side who said, "Before I came here, I worked for a congressman. And while I worked for him, I saw that women's issues were not part of the national agenda . . . and it is as true today. . . . If we don't force others to focus on women's issues, then it will not be part of the debate."[8]

We hear the same thoughts from the moderates on the Republican side of the aisle: women's issues are not part of the agenda and women representatives find themselves saying, "If you want something done, you've got to do it yourself." This is what former representative Nancy Johnson, a Republican from Connecticut, did when she stated "I know a lot more about the shape of women's lives and the patterns of women's lives, so I need to look and see: how will the public policy affect those patterns? How will they help or hurt?"[9]

These women's words are not just lip service. Ongoing research finds that women in office have a direct and significant effect "not only in the outcomes of the policy process, but in defining the legislative agenda and in framing issues to advance women's needs and interests." Since the mid-seventies, "the role of 'legislator at large for America's women' is being embraced more and more by women in public office."[10]

Elected officials shouldering this responsibility should not be taken for granted—it is no easy task. Serving as a watchdog for America's women requires resources of time, energy, and money—three things that no politician has in abundance. But more women in public office, compared to their male cohorts, are willing to expend those resources. As Del. Eleanor Holmes Norton (D-DC) said, "The kind of concentrated, systematic focus that goes from bill to bill . . . is what I think women mean when they say, 'We represent women.' It means not just on this issue or that issue, but [that we] . . . in addition to everything else we do, keep a watch for women's issues."[11]

In 1964 Margaret Chase Smith demonstrated that one woman among one hundred senators can make historical differences that improve women's situation for generations. Smith was the first female senator in America. Hailing from the Republican state of Maine, she never embraced the term "feminist" or admitted that women's issues were a priority to her. Nevertheless, there were plenty of instances throughout her career as a public servant when she became a bastion for women's liberties and equality. The most impressive of these was her leadership in including gender in Title VII of the Civil Rights Act of 1964, the "closest approximation that women now have to legislation granting them equal rights." The phrase that would outlaw discrimination based on "race, creed, color, and national origin" was enhanced with the word "sex." When the minority leader moved to have that word removed from the bill during a committee meeting, Smith asked, "Do you mean to say that you are going to state on the floor of the Senate that the Republican Policy Committee voted to strike the word 'sex' and have it known around the country that the Republican Party is opposed to women?" The leader rethought his position, the phrase stood as it was, and the lone woman senator changed the course of history for women.[12]

In a more current example, the early nineties debate over funding for breast cancer prevention, the work of a few Democratic women legislators raised funding levels from 72.3 to 100 million dollars. This funding made it easier for low-income women to gain access to health care services to prevent the incidence of breast cancer. As one staff member close to the process observed, "without Rosa DeLauro and the other two [Democratic] women . . . that program would not have seen the increases it saw over the last two years. I don't think there is anyone who would question that."[13]

These examples of women acting on behalf of their gender prompt the question, would men have picked up the slack if those women were not leading the charge? A quote by former Rep. Marge Roukema (R-NJ) leads one to think not: "I didn't really want to be stereotyped as the woman legislator. . . . I wanted to deal with things like banking and finance. But I learned very quickly that if the women like me in Congress were not going to attend to some of these [women's issues] . . . then they weren't going to be attended to. So I quickly shed those biases that I had and said, 'Well nobody else is going to do it; I'm going to do it.'"[14]

Looking at the numbers behind Roukema's "on the ground" assessment, we see that even men in public office who say they support women's issues will rarely do the heavy lifting to work on them. A study conducted by the Center for American Women and Politics at Rutgers University examined the strength of state legislators' declarations of support for women's issues. They wanted to know how often those who say they care about women's issues actually work on relevant legislation. The study concluded that over one-half of women state representatives and nearly two-thirds of women state senators addressed women's issues, compared with just over one-third of their male colleagues.[15]

This same study found that in the upper houses of state legislatures across the nation, nearly 75 percent of Democratic women senators worked on women's rights bills, as did half of Republican women senators. In comparison, 45 percent of Democratic male senators contributed to legislation that would benefit women, as did 33 percent of male Republican senators.[16] The gap in these statistics raises the question, what issues would be ignored if women were not in office to work on them? More disturbingly, what issues continue to suffer because there are not more women around to do that legislative work?

These results are echoed in the words of Former Colorado Rep. Pat Schroeder when she said, "The influx of women in Congress did make a difference for women's issues which would be nowhere otherwise. The men just don't think about them." She cited the fight to get mammograms covered by Medicare: "I don't know how many times we passed that on the floor. It'd come up for a vote and sail through. Then it would come back out of conference, and it was gone. What happened? When it went to conference, there wouldn't be a woman on the committee, and it would be the first thing missing on return!"[17] The sad truth is that these are not isolated incidences. That this is the norm in legislative bodies across the United States is an unnerving problem and exposes the pressing need for more women in public office.

The Women of the 2008 Election and the Road Ahead

Over the past thirty years, the numbers of women in elected office in the United States has increased incrementally—a handful every year. It will be interesting to see if there is a substantial up-tick in female candidates after the 2008 election cycle. One thing is clear about the candidacies of both Senator Clinton and Governor Palin; it will take a generation of pundits and thinkers to unpack all the meanings behind their campaigns and losses and to catalogue the effects they will have moving forward. To what degree was latent, subtle, and subversive sexism a factor? In which ways did their candidacies move the needle forward, and how did they set it back? Every move they made was, and will continue to be, dissected to the most detailed degree by political scientists and the press.

As Amanda Fortini asks in *New York Magazine* with regard to Senator Clinton's campaign, was this a sign of progress for women in politics or the "exception that proves the rule"? Clinton's candidacy might have been a loophole born of her First Lady notoriety, or the self-made success of a women's college graduate and a life-long crusader for women's issues. Was she ultimately defeated by the familiar forces of patriarchy we thought had subsided over the past generation—are we still a nation that is just not ready for a woman at the helm? We have only just begun to sort out the answers.

I am thankful that Senator Clinton's campaign has prompted these questions in the minds of a broader public in a way that has not happened for decades. It goes without saying that she will go down in history as a pioneer. Both her successes and failures brought to the public discourse the awkward clash of adding gender to such a rarefied and traditionally male environment. What ensued was a flurry of discussion as the world watched Hillary Clinton try to determine how a woman should "be" when running for president. The conversation was incessant both on her campaign and in the twenty-four-hour commentary of the media: "She should be more male. . . . Now she's too male. . . . She must be a ruthless bitch; I'd better cross my legs. . . . Likeability tour? Spare us. . . . Wait, she's crying. . . . That's more like it, cut her some slack." The discourse very often strayed from the substantive issues to minutiae of irrelevance that, say, Chris Dodd or John Edwards never encountered.

All of this was heightened by the fact that her opponent was dealing with the same thing on the racial front: "Is he white enough? . . . How about now? . . . Too white? . . . Fist bump? . . . No! Too black!" Between the two of them, the media had a field day scrutinizing every word uttered by every surrogate of each campaign, just waiting—and I think hoping—to catch someone in a gaffe that they could whip into a "newsworthy" conflagration. The primary struggle between Senator Clinton and Senator Obama was rightly celebrated as historic and groundbreaking, but they were also pushed into a downward spiral of divisive identity politics. I think each campaign did an excellent job of keeping the latter to a minimum in the face of so many forces that would have preferred even more of it.

I hope that Senator Clinton's and Governor Palin's (in whatever ways it can) candidacies brought to the fore the need to broaden our understanding of leadership, and to redefine what it looks like, especially when referring to women. As much as I disagree with her politics, I have to admit I enjoyed watching the right-wing pundits celebrate Governor Palin's achievements in the Wasilla, Alaska, PTA. They were forced to defend her résumé and sell her as an acceptable choice to voters. Given her stances on the issues, I strongly suspect she would not have been an advocate for women's issues had she won, and her candidacy was certainly a mixed bag when it came to promoting women in politics. But it did come with some interesting silver linings. One of them was seeing conservative political commentator Pat Buchanan ask *Hardball's* Chris Matthews what his problem was with "strong women." Sadly, Buchanan went on to refer to Governor Palin as "this gal," exposing the shallow nature of his newfound feminist side. If nothing else, Palin's candidacy foisted onto an unlikely and unsuspecting population of American conservatives the idea of seeing a woman at the highest echelons of power.

Senator Clinton's deep command of the issues could not be more in contrast with Governor Palin's breezy colloquialisms like "you betcha" and "gee-whiz," which reminds us of the danger of generalizing about female candidates. Palin was the "Dubaya" of the 2008 election—likeable but of questionable intellect, and perhaps even likeable for that very reason. This presented a problem for the promotion of women in politics. Clinton's mastery of the intricacies of serious policy matters made the sexist remarks lobbed at her seem unfair and irrelevant. But Sarah Palin's tepid understanding of basic issues made some of the insulting remarks made about her plausible. It is not clear that we will be able to discern a net gain for women from Palin's rocky, brief, and rather bizarre campaign, but thanks to her candidacy and most certainly that of Senator Clinton, I am confident that more women will now begin to feel comfortable with the idea of running for office. Clinton's new role as secretary of state in President Barack Obama's cabinet is a nod to both the 18 million votes she won in the primary as well as her formidable intellect and skills.

In the eight years since that first campaign I worked on in 2000, the numbers of women politicians has inched forward at a snail's pace. Hopefully, their ranks will continue to swell and they will bring greater focus to how policy and legislation affect the female population of this country. Women in elected office act as watchdogs for women: they put the problems that affect us high on their lists of legislative priorities, they speak up on our behalf, and—dramatically more than men—they take on the political tasks of passing laws that will improve the quality of our lives in the family, community, workplace, and other social institutions. In the meantime, we will rely heavily on the minority of women sitting in seats of power to bring women's issues forward, to monitor the ways that policies affect women uniquely, and to expand the definition and "the face" of leadership.

Despite the difficulties, young women must take up the task of helping to increase the numbers of women in public office, both by running ourselves and by campaigning for those who do. Just as the women in the 103rd and 104th congresses found they had no one to rely on but themselves when it came to legislating for the female population, young women today have no choice but to shoulder the job of striving to balance the male-dominated halls of power in the U.S. government. If we want to see our issues championed and bring our own insights about leadership to the table, it is up to us. Leading the way in the twenty-first century means taking on this challenge.

NOTES

1. Jennifer Lawless and Richard L. Fox, "Why Are Women Still Not Running for Office?" *Brown Policy Report* (Department of Political Science, Brown University, March 2008), 2.

2. Ibid., 5.

3. Ibid., 6.

4. Amanda Fortini, "The Feminist Reawakening: Hillary Clinton and the Fourth Wave," *New York Magazine* April 13, 2008, http://nymag.com/news/features/46011/.

5. Mary S. Hartman, ed., *Talking Leadership: Conversations with Powerful Women* (New Brunswick, NJ: Rutgers University Press, 1999), 3.

6. Center for the American Women and Politics, Rutgers University, "Women Achieve Record Numbers in State Legislatures, Advance to Statewide Offices; Republican

Women See Setbacks at Both Levels," CAWP Election Watch, November 11, 2008, http://www.cawp.rutgers.edu/press_room/news/documents/PressRelease_11-11-08.pdf; "Record Numbers of Women to Serve in Senate and House," http://www.cawp.rutgers.edu/press_room/news/documents/PressRelease_11-5-08updated.pdf.

7. Mary Hawkesworth, "Legislating By and For Women: A Comparison of the 103rd and 104th Congresses" (Center for American Women and Politics, Rutgers University, November 2001), 4–9; see also Institute for Women's Leadership, "Power For What? Women's Leadership: Why Should You Care?" National Dialogue on Educating Women for Leadership, no. 2 (New Brunswick, NJ: May 2002), 21–27.

8. Hawkesworth, "Legislating By and For Women," 9.

9. Ibid., 11.

10. Ibid., 5–6.

11. Ibid., 6.

12. Susan J. Carroll, *The Impact of Women in Public Office* (Bloomington: Indiana University Press, 2001), 109–110.

13. Hawkesworth, "Legislating By and For Women," 29.

14. Ibid., 6.

15. Carroll, *Impact of Women in Public Office*, 10.

16. Ibid., 12.

17. Hawkesworth, "Legislating By and For Women," 10; Hartman, *Talking Leadership*, 229, 231.

16

Choosing Nursing

A Feminist Odyssey

JAN OOSTING KAMINSKY

"Nursing . . . has faced the paradox of being women's work—invisible, devalued, underpaid—and yet a critical necessity to society."

—Andrist et al., *A History of Nursing Ideas*

For many middle-class women in our mother and grandmother's generations, the question was simply "Will you be a teacher or a nurse?" Young women expected to limit their aspirations to traditionally female careers with the understanding that they would limit or leave work when their children were born. Nursing has traditionally been seen as women's work; therefore, the history of nursing is directly tied to the evolution of the feminist movement. Our generation has been given the gift of choice to expand our possibilities, to embrace careers in the highest echelons of medicine, law, and business. Why, then, would any intelligent young Generation Y woman with these possibilities open to her choose nursing? My father asked me that very question when I told him that I was considering rejecting other career paths in favor of nursing. With the world at our feet, young educated women have choices. However, by the hundreds of thousands, young intelligent women (and men) *are* choosing this expanding occupation.

My road to the nursing profession was definitely nontraditional. During a college study-abroad semester in South Africa, I worked as an intern with a nongovernmental organization (NGO) that distributed health information to women in rural areas. We educated women of all ages about their rights under the relatively new Constitution. We handed out copies of a new women's health handbook that had been developed by NGOs working in the area to answer questions on issues ranging from divorce to reproductive rights and HIV/AIDS prevention and treatment. I began to realize that changing lives through health education and preventative treatment was a perfect match for my activist background and presented the excitement of a challenge.

My experience during this internship was deeply influential in my decision to pursue a career in health care.

I graduated from college in May of 2001 and moved immediately to New York City to start my career as a research assistant at a major health care institution. Just four short months later, our country seismically shifted when terrorism hit home. The events of 9/11 caused many people to reevaluate their lives, and I was no exception. I realized that I had only so much time in my life to define and pursue my goals. As my first few months of independent young adulthood coincided with these horrific events, a new imperative that I had not felt before convinced me that "meaningful work" would need to define my career. At that time, I began to search for a field of work that would give me that chance, along with the job security and opportunities for growth that I knew were important to me.

After surveying several options in health care careers, I, like many of my colleagues, decided on nursing because of my deep interest in helping people get through times when they are less able to care for themselves. I explored my educational options and discovered programs for second-degree students in nursing. I immediately knew that this would be the perfect option for me. I chose the Johns Hopkins University School of Nursing and moved to Baltimore for an intensive accelerated program that would result in a bachelor's of science in nursing. For a little more than a year, I immersed myself in the culture of hospitals and health care, received my degree, and returned to New York to work. The nursing shortage was already in full swing, and I was hard at work at my first nursing job within two weeks of graduation. Because I have always had a rapport with children, a natural place for me seemed to be pediatrics. I accepted a position in a pediatric intensive care unit (ICU) close to my home in Brooklyn.

The most unexpected part of my early career as a novice pediatric ICU nurse was being invited so immediately into the most intimate details of the lives of the families for whom I was caring. As a new graduate, I did not fully understand the sheer humanity of the process. This aspect of nursing was, and continues to be, profoundly moving. Each day that I am at the bedside of a critically ill child with that child's family, I marvel at the strength and love that families are able to show despite the desperation they must feel. I have had the same experience from the other side in several circumstances with recent family illnesses, and I have experienced firsthand the importance of high quality nursing care and evidence-based practice. Having a career where you are so significant in the life experience of a stranger is stressful at times but often exhilarating as patients progress from illness to health.

I have a unique perspective on the nursing profession because my original undergraduate degree was in women's studies and history. Since I began nursing, my professional experience has been colored with those gendered lenses as I explore the connections between women's experiences in American society and within the field of nursing. In many ways, nursing and feminism have been two ships that passed in the night, with nursing still viewed by many traditional feminists as inferior to other fields. However, nursing has been influenced by feminism in ways both large and small, including the change of nursing uniforms from starched white skirts and pinned hats to gender-neutral scrubs in most places. The incursion of female physicians and male nurses has also had an influence as roles traditionally based on gender have evolved to be roles based on other types of hierarchy, which can have both positive and negative implications.

On the positive side, there has been a huge shift in the relationship between physicians and nurses. Gone are the days when (female) nurses would carry charts for (male) physicians or stand when physicians entered a room in the "hospital salute." This is due in part to the technology with which we work. Often a nurse is more familiar with a frequently used piece of equipment and is able to educate the physician. In general, nurses and doctors must work well together to reap the greatest benefit for the patient. It is essential that there be a level playing field on which all health care workers can come together to promote healing. Most health care professionals realize this, and in my experience there has been great professional collaboration, with due respect given for the ideas of all parties.

In the hospital setting, nurses and physicians work together on a minute-to-minute basis, and effective communication is required. Although the number of women physicians is now approaching 50 percent, many hospital-based positions are still filled by male doctors. The interaction between nurses and physicians has changed over the years as gender shifts have occurred. However, the leader–follower structure of the physician giving orders and the nurse carrying them out has a distinctly gendered feeling. In my experience in two different hospitals and seven different units, I have found most physicians to be respectful of the nursing role. The nurse is seen as the essential final link in the chain of care for the patient and is usually treated as such. Of course some physicians do not value the role of nurses and retain the old standards of seeing the nurse as not worthy of participation in the interdisciplinary health care team.

The interconnection of feminism and nursing has also had a complicated history. Since the 1970s, nursing and other female-dominated fields have been denigrated by many feminists who wanted young, educated women to embrace traditionally male-dominated professions. Women were encouraged by the so-called second wave to reject "women's work" and to become doctors, lawyers, and business leaders. They heeded this call in large numbers, causing important societal shifts in perceptions of the value of women's work in general and nursing in particular. Some of the women who would have taken these jobs in the past did not, leaving a gaping generational hole in the nursing profession. At the same time, hospitals were seeing more and sicker patients, and patients were living longer and requiring more nursing care due to improvements in technology, medications, and other therapies. Third-wave feminism has not taken a stance on nursing specifically, but this generation of feminists in general is more inclusive of women making radical or traditional decisions for themselves, including the decision to choose a field of work that is still dominated by women.

Nursing remains a women-centered profession, with men holding 6 percent of nursing jobs. Nursing is one of the few health care fields in which the number of women in academic positions is disproportional to the number of men; women hold greater than 95 percent of academic jobs in nursing. Of the top ten schools of nursing, ranked by the National Institutes of Health (NIH) in order of amount of funding, all ten are led by distinguished women deans. This imbalance should encourage men to come into the nursing profession, but we should also see it as an aspect of nursing to be celebrated. Women are in powerful, decision-making positions in all areas of nursing, and we should see this as empowering.

Nurses have been activists since the origins of the profession, caring for patients whose families refused to or were unable to. Nurse pioneers such as Florence Nightingale, Dorothea Dix, and Margaret Sanger believed that nurses were obligated to improve the lives of individuals and communities through their activism and public health improvements. Nurses were among the most prominent members of the antislavery movement and were active during the Civil War, before formal nursing education appeared in universities and hospitals. Louisa May Alcott, Harriet Tubman, and Sojourner Truth all nursed during the Civil War.[1] Nightingale herself was partially responsible for the evolution of nursing as a job for women. She believed that nursing was nurturing, an extension of women's role in the home, and she discouraged men from filling nursing positions. Unfortunately, her advocacy in this direction may have helped to lower the societal value of nurses as well as the level of compensation.

Since the Civil War, nursing has evolved exponentially. No longer are nurses the handmaidens of physicians; instead we are an integral part of the health care team, making interdisciplinary decisions to improve patient care. Young women and men now come to the nursing profession prepared for a challenging, technology-based, science-oriented curriculum. Every day we care for people being kept alive by machines and medications that were unimaginable even a generation ago. These technologies require caregivers with technological expertise and the ability to recognize subtle changes before they have consequences for the patient. Nurses are challenged scientifically in school, and this continues in the workplace with new technology information every day balanced with patient care and safety.

Many nurses have autonomy now that could only have been dreamt of in previous generations. Nurse practitioners (NPs) now number more than fifty thousand nationwide. In many states, they have full prescription privileges and can even admit patients to the hospital, but NPs have quite limited privileges in other states and must only work under the license of a physician. NPs are becoming a growing trend for many reasons, including the ability for insurance companies to cut costs for well-patient care using this option. Both salaries and malpractice insurance costs are lower for NPs than for physicians. Nurses have autonomy as well in the area of nurse midwifery and, through relationships with physicians and hospitals, offer women alternatives to the soaring cesarean section and epidural rates. There are departments of nursing at many prestigious Ivy League colleges and universities turning out nurses prepared at the master's and doctoral levels, primed for leadership positions at the helms of hospitals, businesses, and universities. Legal nurse consultants advise lawyers on health care–related cases, and nurse anesthetists are used frequently in critical care settings in many states. Nurses are valued across many disciplines for the "in the trenches" knowledge that they possess in the area of patient care and safety.

Nurses are well paid compared with many other entry-level/college graduate positions, with average starting salaries ranging from $45,000 in rural or outlying areas to more than $80,000 in some urban areas. The Bureau of Labor Statistics (BLS) reports the 2007 median wage for registered nurses in New Jersey to be $78,510.00.[2] Nursing offers the prospect of being paid well and treated as a professional while caring for and nurturing others during the most difficult times of their lives. Many nursing jobs offer flexible work schedules, such as working three twelve-hour shifts per week. This can be an extremely convenient schedule when raising children or attending graduate school to further your education. I did not have children when I made the decision to become a nurse, but now that I have two sons I have reaped the benefits of flexible scheduling, shift work, and the ability for work–personal balance that is missing from so many fields. This has been essential in my ability to both work full-time and dedicate to my children the time that they so richly deserve.

Bedside nurses play a central role in the health care structure caring most intimately for individual patients. I have been privileged to be a pediatric intensive care nurse, and I have seen the vital importance of safe staffing levels, a central problem facing our health care system today. Currently there is an acute state and national nursing shortage. In New Jersey alone, it is projected that there will be a shortage of more than 37,000 nurses statewide by the year 2020, the equivalent of 43 percent (out of a total of 100 percent) of needed nurses, according to the Bureau of Health Professions, Health Resources and Services Administration.[3] The Bureau of Labor Statistics estimates that more than one million new nurses must be attracted to the profession by the year 2012 to replace retiring nurses and meet the health care needs of an aging population.[4] According to the BLS, nursing leads all other professions in the projected need for workers in the years to come.

This shortage helps to give nurses a louder voice when advocating for improvements in working conditions and pay. Many states and individual hospital systems have strong nursing unions in place. These groups work to support the nursing role at the hospital and state levels, advocating for safe staffing levels and good salaries and benefits in this demanding career. Nurses have successfully lobbied for causes that affect all of American society, including staff-to-patient ratios, medication administration safety, and nonpunitive reporting of medical errors. Lobbying by organizations such as the American Nurses Association is essential in the improved health care of all Americans.

This year I will be starting in a doctoral program in nursing that I hope will guide me to influence the future of the profession, leading it through the increasing crises of personnel shortages, multiplying health care costs, and spiraling numbers of chronically ill patients. My graduate education will be fully funded by the Jonas Foundation, which has been established by the Jonas family, New York philanthropists who enable young nursing leaders to continue their educations in order to enter nursing academia, where there is a "shortage within a shortage." I have been incredibly fortunate to receive this fellowship, without which I would be unable to pursue an advanced degree. In today's nursing shortage, nurses have become that much more valuable. With increased demand come greater influence and a higher "value" placed on nursing. Nurses are no longer invisible as we reach for higher levels of autonomy and education, and we need to continue to advocate for appropriate wages, safe nurse to patient ratios, and quality health care for all.

In my doctoral research work, I will be studying the impact of domestic violence on children in the home, working with the New York City Mayor's Office to Combat Domestic Violence. I will have many opportunities to interact with people at their most vulnerable, and I have a responsibility to guide them well. This research topic suits me because it connects my women's studies background and nursing work with pediatric populations to advance families and affect public health for a large group of people.

I am fortunate that I became a nurse at the beginning of its current resurgence, when there were empty places to fill in nursing schools. Now large numbers of young women and men are choosing to enter nursing, but hundreds of thousands of qualified students are being turned away every year due to lack of nursing faculty to teach them. Additionally, the number of nurses retiring in the next few years far surpasses the number of new graduates projected to enter the field. To make matters even worse, the number of aging Americans who require more advanced health care is steadily rising, thus increasing the need for qualified nursing staff. Philanthropic and government money is being allocated to help nursing schools meet their needs. My doctoral scholarship will enable me to be trained not only as a researcher but also as a teacher, and I plan to be part of the solution to the problem of the faculty shortage in years to come.

Young women entering nursing will be replacing nurses of the baby boomer generation who are expected to begin to retire in the next few years. Young nurses will have unprecedented opportunities to lead and to steer the field of nursing toward future ports. Some feminists and women leaders have turned away from nursing in the past, seeing it as traditionally women's work. This view undermines nursing and indeed is counterintuitive; nursing should be valued that much more *because* of its history as a women's profession. As more men become involved in nursing, the entire field will benefit as men push for autonomy and competitive salaries alongside women. Feminists and all women should see nursing care for its power to heal physically and emotionally, and as a field in which women have always held sway and will continue to do so. We should embrace women's work as highly valuable when it is the choice of the individual woman to perform it. If the nursing profession is held up as a valued and interesting option for young, intelligent women of my generation, society as a whole will benefit from high-quality care and better health care outcomes.

NOTES

Epigraph: Linda C. Andrist, Patrice K. Nicholas, and Karen A. Wolf, *A History of Nursing Ideas* (Sudbury, MA: Jones & Bartlett Publishers, 2005).

1. Ibid.
2. Bureau of Labor Statistics, "Occupational Employment and Wages, May 2007: 29–IIII Registered Nurses," September 30, 2008. http://www.bls.gov/OES/current/oes29IIII.htm.
3. "National Advisory Council on Nurse Education and Practice: Second Report to the Secretary of Health and Human Services and the Congress," Health Resources and Services Administration, U.S. Department of Health and Human Services. http://bhpr.hrsa.gov/nursing/NACNEP/reports/second/3.htm.
4. Bureau of Labor Statistics.

17

Safe Keepers and Wage Earners

South Asian Working Women in the United States

ANURADHA SHYAM

I always get anxious when I first sense that it is too cold to commute to work in my flip-flops and soon will have to switch to sneakers. It is already October and along with cooler temperatures and fall colors, I realize that the busy audit season is almost upon me: "Busy Season," with its stressful deadlines, late nights, and all meals at my desk for weeks on end comes around every year. During these three or four months, I mysteriously receive no calls from my friends, and I feel fortunate to catch dinner on a few Saturday nights with my husband.

As a recent promote to senior associate at a Big Four accounting firm, I have seen a sharp increase in my workload. I have also come to realize that my responsibilities in this firm will only increase, and I will have to devote more time and commitment to my job as I rise through the ranks. Even in the slower summers, sudden and unplanned business travel leaves me little time to spend with friends or family. I find myself constantly juggling my work schedule and household responsibilities. While I put my "all" into work, I often feel guilty about not being able to properly celebrate the holidays or pursue my other passions in classical Indian dance and music. I am amazed at women who are able to balance their corporate and personal lives and still manage to find the time for their children.

After graduating from college with a business degree and having ambitious goals for the future, I found myself "navigating a new set of dreams within a powerful sea of strong traditions and close-knit families."[1] Like other women, I asked myself many questions: "How should I get ahead? Find job satisfaction? Assert myself? Manage my home life with my career? [Find fulfillment through my volunteer work or leadership activities?] Deal with family expectations?"[2] Thinking about the reasons behind why I feel pulled in several different directions, I realize that my views and expectations of myself are shaped by the milieu of the South Asian society into which I was born. My father is an entrepreneur who owned his own software company and was considered the head of our household. Although my mother was able to exert some influence, he made all the major decisions on issues of finances, health, and our education. As I grew up I remember having all the time in the world to do what I wanted, and I did not help much around the house. My parents took care of everything.

In the India of my childhood, women from economically successful families had the option to be—and generally were—stay-at-home moms. Their career ambitions were usually not factored into any decisions about their futures. Women from middle- and upper-income families in India had a lot of help from working-class men and women to maintain and run their households. They spent quality time with their families and were encouraged to pursue liberal arts courses in college. The goal was self-improvement, not careers. As was customary, these women took care of their in-laws, who would generally live with or near them. Old age homes were rare and not looked upon with favor. Parents focused on getting their daughters married off and "comfortably settled" as soon as was practical. This was my mother's world and the world into which I was born. Growing up in this traditional, sheltered society, I also once believed that men should be the family breadwinners and women should be the homemakers. One of my childhood memories is of a family party where we were discussing what I wanted to be when I grew up. I remember my uncles asking me the question and my answer, without much hesitation was simply, "I want to be just like Amma (Mom). I want to be a housewife." However, my parents, especially my father, had other ideas for me. Although my parents' roles in the household were "traditional," their thoughts around the subject of prescribed gender roles were hardly that conventional. My mother's role as a homemaker evolved more out of lack of financial necessity than from anything else.

When I was twelve, I flew to a totally different world in the United States. To supplement the income from my father's start-up software company, my mother had to get a job. Although she had never worked outside the home, with some encouragement from my father, she gathered enough courage to be trained in computer programming and found a relatively demanding job at a large accounting firm. Suddenly, there was no maid, chauffeur, or even a relative to rely on for help. More importantly, we had not simplified our lives nor had we integrated into the fast-paced life in the United States. My family "retained [our] taste for traditional food, along with [our] values concerning home, family, children, religion and marriage."[3] My mother bore the brunt of the downsizing. She continued to be responsible for all household activities without significant help. She made us breakfast in the morning, packed our lunches, and had a hot meal on the table for dinner. In addition to being a full-time homemaker, she had to handle the pressures of a full-time computer professional's life. In short order, she went from a comfortable, upper-middle-class existence to juggling a full-time job and a family.

With my mother working outside the house during the day and at home in the evenings, my brother and I were expected to help for the first time in our lives. However, our schoolwork and future success were prioritized above all else. In my parents' eyes, it was just as critical for me to achieve as it was for my brother; my ideas were never undermined nor my potential squashed simply because I was a girl. My parents were my biggest advocates, my champions in that very impressionable time in my life. Realizing that I had their unequivocal support, I confidently started making independent decisions; I dreamt big and never felt judged by them for doing so. This was the way I expressed my feminism—even without understanding its meaning. It was only when my high school AP English teacher commented on an autobiographical essay I wrote in her class—"I see a budding feminist in you"—that I started thinking about what feminism meant to me.

In college, while completing my coursework for the Institute for Women's Leadership (IWL), I became interested in South Asian immigrant women in America, along with patriarchy and gender roles in their families. Experiences from my own family as well as my South Asian friends taught me that even though the culture in Indian cities continues to Westernize, immigrant families maintain the same traditions they upheld when they were in South Asia. More importantly, I realized that immigrant women are still pressured to adhere to prescribed gender roles and to uphold "cultural continuity" and family honor.[4] I noticed that South Asian women's employment outside the home hardly ever affected the extent of their household responsibilities. According to Madhulika Khandelwal, "Indian men [in America] balked at the idea of full gender equality and household work remains with women. A system in which the first spouse arriving home starts cooking dinner is too radical a transformation for an average Indian family."[5]

With deeply entrenched cultural norms like these, Shamita Das Dasgupta summarizes the challenges South Asian women face as immigrants in the United States: "A woman's identity in South Asia has never been conceived of in individual terms; rather it has always fused with that of the men in her life: father, brother, husband and son. . . . [This] inordinate dependence on the family is a source of strength as well as vulnerability for the South Asian woman in America."[6]

My exposure and research into these issues caused my ideas about leadership for social change to begin to evolve. I realized that these cultural norms, in the extreme, could be a source of oppression for women. I turned my attention to violence against women, and specifically domestic violence in the South Asian immigrant community, and learned that women who face emotional or physical abuse are often left helpless and alone. Current Indocentric cultural values coupled with a lack of social contacts in an unfamiliar country leave battered women in the United States with few options or resources. With poor English language skills and often lacking visas that permit them to work, they are dependent on their spouses for money and immigration status, and they get trapped in abusive relationships. The taboo nature of domestic violence and the shame and humiliation of divorce offers neither hope nor opportunity for women fleeing mistreatment. As Dasgupta explains, "The violence that women suffer at home is fervently denied much of the time by community members in order to maintain an unblemished image in the eyes of the mainstream world. This disallowance of women's negative experiences is part of the male fantasy of an idyllic family and perfect wife, a family that is affable, conflict free and a wife who is mother, friend, lover, supporter all rolled into one."[7]

In an effort to assist battered South Asian immigrant women, organizations in the United States are attempting to reach out to the community and acknowledge that domestic violence does indeed exist. Manavi is one such organization, founded in New Jersey in 1985 by six South Asian women. One of its long-held goals is to support South Asian women's self-reliance and autonomy. It is the first organization of its kind in the United States to focus on the silence surrounding violence in South Asian families.[8] My majors in accounting and economics as well as my interest in the field of women and work led to my decision to use the social action project required by the Institute for Women's Leadership to shape a program that would provide resources to further financial independence among domestically abused South Asian women. I researched domestic violence and worked as an intern at Manavi where I helped fundraise and attended outreach events. I was also given the chance to meet the women at the transitional home and develop relationships with them and their children. There, I heard many success stories of women acting courageously to leave their abusers while fighting to become financially independent.

After hearing many tragic stories, I realized that these women needed skills such as financial management, résumé writing, and job interviewing. I decided to organize a conference with workshops that would address these needs. I located speakers who were well versed in topics such as financial independence and lawyers who specialized in immigration issues. "Road to Success: A Conference for Financial Independence for South Asian Women" came together and was held in November 2002 at the Institute for Women's Leadership. The workshops taught résumé writing and interviewing, financial management, and continuing education, and a working lunch focused on immigration issues and domestic workers and their rights. The conference was well attended by women from Manavi's clientele as well as the general

South Asian community in central New Jersey. A few months later, a woman attendee called to thank me. She said she had been a victim of emotional abuse for more than twenty-five years but lacked the courage to leave her husband. Most of all, she said that she did not have the skills to support herself financially. After the conference, she gained the strength to leave her husband and find a job. She thanked me for organizing the conference and told me how it had influenced her decision to become independent. With some awe, I realized that I had made a difference in at least one woman's life.

The stories I heard from the survivors while at Manavi and the lessons I learned while planning the conference provided me with greater self-awareness. The women's stories helped me see the multiple perspectives of women facing adversity and how they were able to overcome them. They also made me realize how important it is for every woman to be self-reliant and economically independent; in fact, these experiences strengthened my own decision to remain economically independent throughout my life.

As part of my undergraduate course work, I had the opportunity to meet and interview Shamita Das Dasgupta, one of the founders of Manavi. Hearing her speak about her leadership in the community was a very humbling experience. To my surprise, she did not even consider herself to be a leader. She said that she was simply doing what she was passionate about, and her advice to young students working for social change was just that. I have followed her advice ever since and can say that I am more confident in my decisions than ever before.

Second-Generation South Asian Women, Work, and Families

I had a busy first year after my graduation from college. I joined a Big Four accounting firm, passed my CPA exam, married, and moved to New York City. Needless to say, I was overwhelmed when I first realized that I was responsible for the household duties but that I did not even know how to cook a simple Indian meal. After an initial emotional reaction, I slowly came to the realization that all second-generation South Asian women like me, whether they were born in or came to the United States as children, are faced with the dual pressures of integrating South Asian values while also having to assimilate into American society.

I came to accept that while second-generation South Asian women want and are encouraged to perform well in school and work in challenging careers, we also have to face the responsibility of being the best in other facets of our lives—as daughters, sisters, wives, daughters-in-law, and mothers.

The pressure of working long hours in stressful jobs coupled with home-making responsibilities poses a whole new set of problems for my peers and me. Like our mothers who immigrated to the United States, we continue to be accountable for the household chores while pursuing demanding careers in medicine, law, finance, and accounting. As a 2007 study noted, "Traditional Asian gender roles prescribe for women to place the role of wife and mother above all others; men are expected to be the family breadwinner and spokesperson. Asian cultural values consequently encourage distinct spheres for men (e.g., work) and women (e.g., home) and a gendered division of labor in which the burden of household duties such as housekeeping tasks and childcare rest heavily on women."[9] South Asian traditions add complexity to an already difficult situation for women because we are also expected to preserve the culture and religion for generations to come. As Dasgupta explains, "The practice of making women emblematic of a nation's cultural survival is in the tradition of locating family *izzat* (Urdu for honor) in its female members. In the new country, women not only carry this antiquated responsibility but have also been assigned the role of bearers as well as transmitters, of culture and traditions to the next generation. They alone have been made accountable for the safekeeping of an ancient culture."[10] As a result, we often juggle our careers with the study of music, art, language, and dance so we will be well rounded and respected in our communities. "Deviations from familial expectations, like marrying late (after late 20s) . . . or not bearing children a few years after marriage are considered socially abnormal."[11] Many times, our families and communities expect us to give up our careers when we have children in order to care for them, just as we were cared for when we were growing up. As a South Asian male family friend in his early thirties put it, "My mother stayed home when I was young. . . . I expect my wife to do the same for our kids." Although noticeable changes in the South Asian community are taking place as a result of women studying in American schools and choosing to pursue challenging professions, managing a career and family is extremely complicated. A woman's career needs or wants are usually not given much weight in long-term decisions such as where to settle down or when to have children.

South Asian Women in Corporate America

Many South Asian women have to respond to two conflicting prescriptions in order to have fulfilling family lives and successful careers. It is expected that we behave with deference and modesty at home, but it is imperative that we demonstrate assertiveness and decisiveness in the corporate world. When I got my first "real" job in corporate America, I realized that I was taught as a child to defer to those who were older than me. In contradiction to that value system, I found myself needing to learn how to assert myself as soon as I began working with my firm. South Asian women "face many of the same challenges that all women do at work but with a twist."[12] South Asian women in the workplace, especially in corporate settings, "endure stereotypes unique to Asian women. . . . On the one hand, [we're] considered very intelligent and technically adept. But on the other, [we're] labeled as passive and submissive, unambitious and unassertive. In the business world at least, these perceived qualities can hinder a woman's professional growth."[13]

Immediately after my first week of training, I was assigned specific financial statement areas at a major pharmaceutical client and was expected to perform audits of account balances. My lack of experience or the lack of coaching from my supervisor (or perhaps a combination of the two) suddenly became apparent to me, and I was put in the uncomfortable position of not knowing what I was doing or what I was even supposed to do. In addition to being a new member of the team and making the transition from college to the working world, I had a very fuzzy understanding of the group dynamics, which made it difficult for me to fit in. I had a hard time making decisions with respect to my assigned areas and found myself regularly asking for reassurance from my peers and supervisors. The long hours and lack of flexibility had me wondering if I even belonged there or wanted to continue in the profession. For the first time in my life, I felt as if I had none of the answers and that I was being penalized for not understanding the "big picture." My evaluation from this first engagement came as a surprise because I was never used to being rated "average" compared to the rest of my class. I was told that I needed to "step up," and think more closely about our testing plans. My supervisor believed I had the potential to handle more risky accounting areas but that I had to proactively ask for the opportunity and accept the challenge wholeheartedly.

After this conversation with my boss, I concluded that I was not being assertive enough and not speaking up with my ideas. Realizing that my passivity would only be a detriment to my career, I learned to be more decisive and realized that successful interaction with my teammates as well as my client contacts is imperative. I also learned that my questions were worthwhile and that I should take credit for my successes. Through communication with mentors and managers, I came to appreciate that my contributions were valued. Soon I had the opportunity to engage with executive levels of management at my clients' companies. Although nervous at first, I now have the confidence to speak clearly and at length about accounting issues that arise during our audits, and to provide coaching to newer associates with poise and clarity. I have gained self-assurance in my potential and strengths and am now comfortable with my supervisor's expectations.

I often think about my future in this industry, and although I would like to continue climbing the corporate ladder, either at my firm or elsewhere, I have to accept the sad truth that women represent at least 50 percent of all starting associates but an insignificant percentage of the senior management.

More importantly, I do not even know of one partner in my group who is a South Asian woman. I have noticed that more and more women managers at my firm are quitting or moving into positions with lower stress and more flexibility at the company. As a consequence of rigid attitudes toward work–life balance, fewer women stay on the "fast-track," making the workforce much less diverse in the higher managerial roles. Lisa Singhania captures this when she writes:

> Talk to a group of ambitious female college graduates, and you are likely to find aspiring CEOs, law firm partners and executives. Fast-forward 10 or 15 years, though, and you'll hear a different story. With families and children to consider, many women shift their focus away from professional advancement to careers that allow them the flexibility to take care of a sick child, attend a school play or simply end their workdays before daycare closes.[14]

Many banks, law firms, and accounting firms (including mine) are gradually realizing that reconciling careers and parenthood is important to keep women and mothers working in the executive track and contributing their full potential. Retention is a serious issue, as Singhania notes: "It can mean a brain drain, as corporations watch employees they've invested in walk away, citing the incompatibility of family and professional life."[15]

The business research organization Catalyst has drawn attention to the dwindling numbers of women in the professions at the higher ranks. They report: "In the legal profession, in the accounting profession, women are now 50 percent or more of the talent pool. If by the time you get to the partner level, you're down to 10, 15 or 20 percent women, you know you're leaving a lot of talent on the table."[16] A positive result of this "brain drain" from corporate America is that my firm, like others, has become much more open to flexible work arrangements where women and men work from home one day a week or have reduced schedules. Extended maternity leaves and lactation rooms in the office are also available, and women are taking advantage of these opportunities to simplify their lives and help alleviate the stress of balancing motherhood and fast-paced careers. However, progress is slow and the challenges considerable because the attitudes of management, what a leader looks like, and the corporate culture must change first and become more open to its employees incorporating flexibility into their daily lives.

As I weigh my work, family, and personal priorities and goals on a day-to-day basis, I have realized that while I am steadfast in advancing my career, I am just as committed in the long term to working to empower disenfranchised South Asian women. To this end and much to the distress of some family members, I took a month off from work last summer and traveled to

Nanded, Maharashtra, a remote village in rural India. There I conducted interviews with groups of women who had come together and started small businesses (self-help groups) with seed money from local nongovernmental organizations (NGOs). These women's narratives and stories were truly awe-inspiring. In rural India, where basic necessities such as food and water come at a premium, I learned that girls drop out of school between the ages of eight and ten in favor of contributing to daily chores; they are married off at the tender age of sixteen to men from neighboring villages, never to be seen again by their families. I discovered that for these women, economic independence not only means a greater sense of self-worth but more importantly a reduced likelihood of being trafficked or sold into prostitution against their will. Their eagerness to become self-sufficient and the enthusiasm with which they spoke to me about how they overcame their obstacles left me humbled. The knowledge and sense of fulfillment I have gained from working in this field both presently and during my college days has stayed with me, and I continue to look for my niche in this area.

The questions still remain for me: how can I "have it all?"—close family, a successful career, fulfilling work that fosters women's leadership, a happy married life, and children (someday). I realize that while all of these goals are possible and important to achieve, I do need to prioritize aspects of my life at any given time. More importantly, I believe that managing a career and family is a subtle balancing act and that I should not expect myself to always get it right.

NOTES

1. Martha Lagace, "The No-Sari Zone: South Asian Women at Work," *Harvard Business School Working Knowledge*, March 21, 2005. http://hbswk.hbs.edu/archive/4701.html.

2. Ibid.

3. Shamita Das Dasgupta, "Marching to a Different Drummer? Sex Roles of Asian Indian Women in the United States," *Women and Therapy* 5, nos. 2/3 (1986): 297–311.

4. Margaret Abraham, *Speaking the Unspeakable: Marital Violence among South Asian Women in the United States* (New Brunswick, NJ: Rutgers University Press, 2000), 1–13.

5. Madhulika Khandelwal, *Becoming American, Being Indian* (Ithaca, NY: Cornell University Press, 2002), 133.

6. Shamita Das Dasgupta, ed., *A Patchwork Shawl* (New Brunswick, NJ: Rutgers University Press, 2000), 8.

7. Ibid., 8–9.

8. For more information on Manavi, see their Web site: http://www.manavi.org.

9. Stephanie T. Pituc and Sarah J. Lee, "Asian Women and Work-Family Issues," Sloan Work and Family Research Network, Boston College, 2007, http://wfnetwork.bc.edu/encyclopedia_template.php?id=4442.

10. Dasgupta, *A Patchwork Shawl*, 5–6.

11. Khandelwal, *Becoming American*, 118–124.

12. Lagace, "The No-Sari Zone."

13. Ibid.

14. Lisa Singhania, "A Woman's Role in Corporate America," Associated Press, July 9, 2006. http://www.norfolk.com/node/122661.

15. Ibid.

16. www.Catalystwomen.org.

18

Blurring the Lines That Divide

Social Change through Activism, Politics, and the Space Between

SHIRA LYNN PRUCE

Growing up in suburban New Jersey, I was always taught that young women could do anything they put their minds to. I watched my parents build their careers and shape our community. At the same time, I learned Hebrew, Jewish history, and Zionism, both at home and in school. Looking back, I see that this explosive combination bred my activist energy. But back in the 1980s, no one thought a little girl with attention deficit disorder (ADD) would get into much trouble in the future, which just goes to show how very underestimated the chatty girl child is.

As a young girl and a teen, I began developing my identity as a Jew, as a woman, and as a leader. Whether in my youth group or high school, fundraising, rehearsing for a benefit concert, or planning the prom, I could be found in front of the crowd, shouting instructions, greeting the newest participants and keeping things running smoothly.

A year before entering college, I continued to form my identity by taking a trip to the death camps in Poland. There I bore witness to the near extinction of Jewish religion, nation, and culture—Hitler's World War II regime, during which Jews, homosexuals, people with disabilities, and other nonwhite, nonconformists were gassed, shot, hanged, beaten, burned alive, and starved or worked to death. I took on, with a very real sense of personal responsibility, the task of making sure this could never happen again.

I also recognized that the international community had allowed this persecution and genocide. I suddenly felt responsible for carrying on the Jewish nation. Practically overnight, I became more sensitive to the struggles of persecuted groups and to biases that lead to discrimination. The experience instilled in me a sense of urgency to grow up and change the world.

For the Jewish refugees who survived the Holocaust, the creation of the State of Israel was the light at the end of the tunnel. Israel as a Jewish state ensures that what happened will never happen again, and Zionism (the political movement and ideology that supports a homeland for the Jewish People in the land of Israel) provides a modern-day safety net for Jews.

With this in mind, I spent a year in Israel before going to college; it was a year that changed my life forever. In September 2000, I arrived in Jerusalem to live and study for six months at Hebrew University before moving to a kibbutz in the south. The political climate was in the positive throes of post-Oslo meetings and peace talks.[1] Children were educated toward peace in most public schools, peace was promoted publicly through mass media, and the majority of Israelis felt hopeful. Israeli society as I understood it was trying to live out Prime Minister Yitzhak Rabin's dream of peace before his tragic 1995 assassination.

Then, in the fall of 2000, President Bill Clinton met with Palestinian Authority Chairman Yasser Arafat and Israeli Prime Minister Ehud Barak in his final attempt as American president to solve the Arab–Israeli conflict. Unfortunately, Yasser Arafat rejected the generous "land for peace" offer made by Barak and promptly left the bargaining table. This marked a significant break in the ongoing peace talks and prompted attacks on Israeli settlements in the disputed territories. That same week, controversial Israeli politician (and future prime minister) Ariel Sharon took a stroll on the Temple Mount, a Muslim and Jewish holy site then under Muslim control. These events and the prevalence of influential terrorist groups in the impoverished West Bank and Gaza sparked the Palestinian uprising against Israel that would persist until 2004. What followed this political upheaval would be my pre–9/11 introduction to terrorism.

By the middle of my fall semester, terror attacks were on the rise. Now mundane from overuse, the term "terror attack" simply does not do the act justice. In just a few months, I experienced several close encounters with suicide bombers—in this case Palestinian extremists who strap explosive devices to their bodies and detonate them in the most crowded area possible. The attack leaves one extremist—a hero in the minds of terrorist groups—dead and entire communities paralyzed by loss and fear of "the next one." This form of terrorism is very calculated insofar as science and logistics, but ultimately it is blind; suicide bombers kill everyone in their paths—Jews, Arabs, Muslims, Christians, Israelis, Palestinians, children, adults, foreign workers, and tourists of all nationalities.

Throughout this time of turmoil in Jerusalem, I was experiencing the Arab–Israeli conflict firsthand yet from the perspective of a tourist, an outside observer. This perspective—although one of the most valuable for learning—comes with bias. Even though I was not Israeli, I found it difficult to pity the Palestinian people while physically under attack. And for a time, my anger and fear made it impossible to recognize my own bias. But as I met people and learned more about the world, I began to see my own bias and, more important, to control it and learn from it.

During this time, I also learned the power that leadership holds. A leader can incite hate and violence in a community, as do wealthy terrorist leaders amongst the underprivileged, or a leader can make an injured nation believe in peace, as Rabin did. There are great leaders of grassroots peace efforts on both sides of the divide; by instilling the idea of peace in their children, their work may turn up in twenty or thirty years as the solution for peace in the mind of a young leader. That is power. Because at the end of every day, who is right and who started it are irrelevant if you do not have leaders who seek to end violence and conflict.

Back in the United States, my experience in Israel stayed with me. Every time a door slammed, I jumped ten feet in the air. On the flip side, the bond that I felt with Israel—the war-torn nation, the culture I loved—was one that could not be broken. So, shortly after starting my first semester at Douglass College, when an editorial in the student newspaper called for the total destruction of the State of Israel, it struck a deafening chord inside me.

It was six weeks after 9/11, and the editorial blamed the events of that day on Israel and the "occupation of Palestine." The author called for the total destruction of the Jewish state as the solution to the United States' problems and the conflicts in the Middle East. Rational minds could see that Israel had nothing to do with terrorists striking the United States, and yet this accusation became a new stream of thought in the most "progressive" circles. Ridiculous though the editorialist's argument was, it had the power of penetrating the minds of impressionable students and simultaneously embarrassing and intimidating Jewish and Israeli students on campus. I was amazed by his power and frustrated by the lack of public reaction and outrage from the Jewish community. I looked to Jewish student unions' staff and elected student leaders for guidance, and I found apathy.

The following winter, at a two-week Jewish advocacy and leadership-training seminar in Israel, I had the chance to learn formally from politicians, professors, and experts on Israeli politics. I learned facts, whereas my previous experiences in Israel had been based on emotion. I also met with other activists to brainstorm how to tackle the mounting problems Jewish and Zionist students faced on campus. The most valuable message I took from this program was that instead of looking to staff or other "adults" to lead, I must be the leader. It was the agency I needed to take the next step: changing apathy into action on my campus.

In my early days of student organizing, although I tried to stick to positive programs like "falafel and Israeli music night," I could not ignore the graffiti swastikas turning up on the Jewish student building and the anti-Israel street performers who "portrayed" Israeli soldiers, wearing Jewish stars on their clothing, playing out murderous and terrorizing acts.

Along with friends whose passion for the cause inspired me, I founded an unfunded, unaffiliated Jewish Zionist group, and we planned to take the campus by storm. We enjoyed the freedom of not having to answer to a funding institution while working toward our goal of giving Zionism and Judaism a face, a name, and a local presence. Yet our independent activism made it easier for student newspapers, faculty, and other institutions to label us "fascists" and "right-wing extremists," and eventually to label me as a figurehead. While none of us were extreme in our political views, we were simply unaffiliated, unrestricted—and that scared the authorities and the university.

During the instances of anti-Semitism on campus and personal attacks on my character, my emotions began to get the best of me. My attempts to stay positive were shaken when I was faced with toxic leaders of opposing groups who preferred low, demeaning tactics to peaceful, productive dialogues. The skills I had acquired up to this point and the guts I depended on were no longer enough to deal with the situations I was facing. Apparently there is more to leadership than creative planning, passion, and a quick tongue. I did not know I was about to receive the best gift anyone could have given me: the tools and support to become the leader my community needed.

At the same time I was taking to the streets with my friends, I was also taking my first women's and gender studies course. Topics I had never identified with, like public health, urban issues, education, and lesbian-gay-bisexual-transgender (LGBT) rights, suddenly applied to me as a woman. I began to see the world in a new light; life applied to me more when I looked at it through a gendered lens.

The activist in me immediately recognized the force I had felt working against women for so long: patriarchy, a system of male normativity and control that systematically oppresses women. Before my first course in women's and gender studies, I didn't know I could say out loud that I felt excluded and marginalized. Learning about the patriarchal system validated my suspicions that practiced subordination of women still exists and that sexism permeates every aspect of women's lives. I started seeing the glass ceiling and walls everywhere; armed with that knowledge, I felt I had the power to produce real social change.

I also began to see politics and war in a gendered light. Feminist theory taught me that the same patriarchal forces that use male traits as the default social functions label woman as "other." If we look at "other" as anything that deviates or represents difference from the norm, then we see a bridge between women and minority groups, or any group of marginalized people.

This connection also asserts that women are essential to conflict resolution as peacemakers and mediators. That is not to say that every woman possesses or uses these features, or that men do not; I believe it means that patriarchy can have a positive effect on women as leaders. In recognizing our position in respect to the male norm, women can use commonalities in status to end injustice, violence, and political oppression.

By the end of my first year at college, I had declared my women's studies major and applied to the Institute for Women's Leadership (IWL), two decisions that would change the course of my life. From the very start of the IWL's two-year program, its deliberate planning guided me into owning my leadership. Whether I was learning leadership theory and feminism, being mentored through an internship, writing proposals, or running a funded social action project, I was supported all the time by staff that was simultaneously learning from the young women scholars while we learned from them.

My internship at New Jersey's Division on Women in Trenton, as part of the IWL program, was my first experience with a formal political institution. At the time, my mind was racing with a serious debate: grassroots activism or formal political participation (by which I mean legislative action, political parties, electoral office)—which is more effective? There was no doubt that I felt more passionate about grassroots work. But at the same time, as I researched and wrote for legislation supporting an important women's health initiative, I realized that with the right connections and pressure, bills can be passed that save women's freedoms. I also knew that when political positions are in the "wrong hands," citizen's rights can be curtailed and oppression can be enforced. At the Division on Women, for the first time, political institutions and elective office no longer seemed inaccessible to me. The activist in me, I learned—who was already doing important work in the community—could grow up, clean up her language, and hold political office some day. I was beginning to understand that the dichotomy I had perceived between activism and politics was in my own head. Government representatives in offices and activists on the street are not as distinct as I had once thought, yet society portrays one group as professionals in suits, and the other as trouble-makers in jeans and sometimes handcuffs.

I grew because of this leadership program from a fiery, scrappy yet power-ful activist to a professional, focused, more powerful leader—every bit as passionate, if not more, but disciplined and refined in a way I had not antici-pated. I graduated from IWL a stronger, more confident, and more articulate woman.

As I continued my academic career and the situation in the Middle East became more violent, anti-Semitism raged on in colleges across North America.

When an international anti-Zionist organization threatened to host its annual conference at my university, my friends and I were inspired to gather Jewish students from all over the continent to boost pride and resources for students confronting anti-Semitic violence and intimidation on their campuses.

We organized a series of events under the umbrella movement "Israel Inspires" to combat the negativity surrounding Israel with positive messages of pride, progress, and support. Months of fundraising and speaking engagements with Jewish leadership and community members raised a budget that supported the transformation and education of Rutgers University's Jewish campus life. It was a joint activity of many Jewish organizations and impressive student leaders with five young women sitting on the founding and steering committee. Seven thousand people attended our rally—including New Jersey senators and our governor—and three hundred students attended the conference. We made the front page of the *New York Times*, and I was interviewed by CNN. If the true test of success is longevity, then I can be proud that Israel Inspires now serves as a model for university and advocacy leaders all over North America. My new composure and skills served me well and enabled me to achieve this great accomplishment.

The next semester, I pulled a long-awaited 180-degree turn and broke through the feminist activist barriers on campus. Organizing for women's rights and LGBT rights was always a goal for me, and the upcoming 2006 March for Women's Lives in Washington, D.C., marked my chance to get involved. With a few girlfriends who were as frustrated as I was with the existing women's student groups—mostly stuffy, micromanaged campus chapters of well-known national women's organizations—I organized a campus effort that attracted the attention of the highest ranks of the National Organization of Women (NOW). As our efforts to sell tickets to the largest gathering of women at the White House began to grow, we received a challenge from NOW—to fill ten buses. Not only did we fill ten, we needed more. We brought the largest delegation from a college campus in the nation, and we were loud and proud that day, marching for women's rights to control our bodies and minds.

For me, organizing with women was as gratifying as organizing with Jewish students. No matter what the cause, I always found myself surrounded by strong women. Perhaps I am drawn to them, and they are to me, when looking for a worthy partner—or opponent—in working toward social change. I add opponent because some of the women I organized with for the March for Women's Lives were the very same Palestinian women rallying against Israel on campus. One day my enemies, the next day my friends, there was a sense of awkward respect among us.

There was one young Palestinian woman in particular whom I knew from much less pleasant interactions and then worked with to organize the march. It was a challenge for us to rise above our differences, yet we did. Driving home together after a late meeting, I saw her apartment and realized it looked like any other student apartment—not that I thought it would look different, but I had never given any thought to her life outside of our point of contention. We each have homes, families, classes, and other similarities, which I firmly believe can be used for building bridges. This says a lot about the abilities of women leaders—not necessarily to overcome difference but rather to blur the differences in the face of a common cause.

Taken a step further, if the Palestinian people had the same privileges as most Israelis—economic opportunity; a dependable infrastructure; democracy; and accessible, quality education—these could be the basis on which to build a bridge of understanding. When I worked with this Palestinian woman, we did not talk about politics but we shared a feminist stance. Maybe if we had had more confidence or time together we could have broached the subject that divided us; perhaps, at least, we taught each other a valuable lesson in the potential role of women's leadership in conflict management.

Between Israel Inspires and the March for Women's Lives, this year was seminal for me as an activist, as a leader in my community. My vow to uphold reproductive freedoms for women is as strong as my vow to protect the Jewish people and the state of Israel. I was prepared to exit my comfort zone, to blur boundaries for the sake of these causes, and to encourage those around me to do the same.

I graduated from Douglass College, and my experiences both inside and outside the classroom left me confident to take the boldest step yet. I moved to Israel. After many good-bye parties and promises to keep in touch—which I do—I got on a plane with a two-part plan: (1) Adopt a dog to name Jersey; and (2) Get an internship at the Israeli Knesset (parliament). The first one was easy. The second, I was told, was far-fetched. A man working for an internship placement office looked me square in the eyes and told me to pick a second choice because "Knesset placement is very competitive." I calmly but firmly told him that "I am also quite competitive and I do not have a second choice"; I told him to check my résumé if he doubted my ability to handle the job. This is a great lesson for a young woman moving into the workplace: do not be modest. When you walk into the room, they already have low expectations, and it is your job to raise the bar every step of the way. In proper feminist fashion, I went over the head of this worker straight to the woman in charge. After listening for a few minutes while I described my experience, she told me to list the top five members of Knesset (MKs) that I wished to work with.

My internship with Labor Party MK Yuli Tamir—a strong feminist and champion for education—was short-lived due to the fall of the coalition government and subsequent internal elections. By then I had been in the Knesset long enough to make some acquaintances and learn a few things about work within the government: nothing is certain, what you have today may not be there tomorrow, and never underestimate the power of a friendly smile. Of course, I would be remiss not to admit that as a young, blond American girl, I caught people's eyes in the Knesset. But I had to impress with hard work and intelligence to make that initial notice last.

I had met some people who were working on building a Christian–Jewish coalition lobby in the Knesset, and when my internship with Tamir fell through, they took me on as an intern. Although the idea of working with Christian leaders originally scared my feminist self, I knew it could build an international ally for Israel. As I eased into the work, I found my Christian counterparts to be kind, caring people. The focus was Israel, so the few times that abortion and gay rights came up, I quickly responded that the caucus is reserved only for Israel advocacy. It was another example of my two identities mixing like water and oil—and I had to choose. I am not proud of having been "in the closet" about my feminism with most of my Christian associates but it was the best I could do to work harmoniously with them. What was important to me was that I was helping Israel and, maybe more important, that I was furthering my career. I know I can work with both of my passions, Israel and feminism, to create real social change—but that time will be in the future.

Slowly, I began to take on more responsibility. Eventually, while the "big boss" was away and his assistant took time off to deal with personal problems, I saw my chance to impress. I organized three successful events, and when my boss came back, he saw what an asset I was to this lobby. I had proven to him that I could be his full-time assistant, and after I mustered up the courage to ask for the salary I felt I deserved (and needed!), the job was mine. My salary request and negotiation was well planned and unabashed because we do not need to be embarrassed to ask for the proper pay and benefits for high quality, hard work.

In securing myself that job, I also landed myself a ringside seat to a series of pivotal matches on the Knesset floor—and a struggle between Right and Left in Israel. It was the summer of 2005 when I snuck into the gallery of a closed session of the Knesset and witnessed a very heated debate in which, one by one, Right-wing MKs were removed from the room, according to Knesset procedure, after three warnings for disruptive behavior. The Right-wing MKs were getting themselves removed from the debate on purpose, in protest. I looked on in amazement. This was democracy. This was activism meeting formal political institutions and the legislative process. This was the bridge I had been looking for between passion and procedure.

And yet what that scene lacked was the loud strong voice of a woman, taking control of a room of torn, passionate activists and politicians. In the Israeli
election that followed, even fewer women were elected, just 17 out of 120 MKs.
Once again the party coalition talks excluded women, as none of the top two
seats of any party belonged to females. Few women were included in the negotiations concerning important ministry positions as well as committees on
issues such as finance, foreign affairs, defense, law, and justice. Even though a
central-ish party had emerged in this election, seemingly breaking the polar-
ized Right and Left wings in Israeli politics, there was a frightening lack of
influential women in decision-making positions.

In the summer of 2006, war broke out between Israel and the Hezbollah,
a Lebanon-based terrorist group. After eighty-one days, 44 Israeli citizens, 119
Israeli soldiers and reservists, and more than 1,000 Lebanese citizens had
been killed. When a cease-fire agreement was reached, a date and time were
set for both sides to put down their weapons. Leaders on both sides waged war
until the last moment, as if their battles would be more meaningful if fought
for an extra few minutes. For me, the fact that the cease-fire treaty specified a
certain time, instead of being effective immediately, signified a weakness in
leadership and an utter lack of respect for human life. It also signified a serious lack of women's voices in conflict resolution, a lack of blurring egos and
machismo for the sake of saving one life.

I wished more than ever that some sort of feminist revolution were brew-
ing in Israel and would somehow permeate the government and the military.
I see great work in many women's organizations in Israel, and although I am
impressed by their activities, I am dismayed that they have not yet begun to
translate organization into public action, media attention, or electing more
women to public office. In short, women's voices are barely heard during a crisis, and the 2006 war with Lebanon was a tragic example.

After nearly two years at the Knesset and a short stint working at an
international NGO, I was given the opportunity of a lifetime: coordinating
Jerusalem's March for Pride and Tolerance. At this time, Jerusalem's LGBT
community was still fighting to uphold their civil rights. In 2005, an ultra-
Orthodox Jewish man wielding a knife ran into the crowd at Jerusalem Pride
and stabbed three. In 2006 International World Pride came to Jerusalem and
it was protested violently—by Christian, Muslim, and Jewish extremist groups
alike. The 2006 pride march was cancelled because of the war with Lebanon
and security issues, and an alternate event was held in a stadium. Still, it felt
like a success for the protesters and a loss for the LGBT community.

In 2007 I joined the ranks of a strong community and a committed staff,
and it was crucial that we did march that year. I coordinated logistics and sat
in on negotiations with police and the municipality. The homophobia

I witnessed, not only from the religious opposition but from within the institutions we had to work through to coordinate the march, was shocking. In spite of the red tape, though, and thanks to hard work and a passionate community, we marched in the center of Jerusalem.

I was discovering that grassroots organizing and formal political involvement, my two life passions, intersect much more than I had once thought. Here the politician is a potential activist and the activists are all essentially a part of the political game. I know that two important aspects of social change—activism, which is often undervalued, predominantly female, and volunteer based, and formal political involvement, which is mainly male, highly respected, and well paid—are not the distinct arenas I once thought. I can blur the line between formal political participation and activism to push the boundaries of social change past their current limitations.

At times activism and politics interact in support of each other, and often in opposition to each other. Activists have a strong potential to challenge the political game, to bring change, and to expose truth. Politicians and government officials can chose to embrace activism as a tool, as a friend, or as an enemy. It is a dynamic relationship. As the authors in Nancy Naples's anthology *Community Activism and Feminist Politics* demonstrate, "women translate the consciousness they develop through daily interactions with the state . . . into political action, [and] women's activism challenges traditional and feminist political practices."[2]

Today I continue my work with the LGBT community in Jerusalem, where I've started a leadership school. In our pilot year, we have eight participants, and each of them is launching a social action project to help empower and strengthen the LGBT community. I have been fortunate to help young leaders turn their passion into action. Passing these skills on is the best way for me to preserve what I have learned. My work in leadership training reminds me that without young leaders, none of the movements I have worked for can survive. And without the balance between formal political participation and activism, there will be no real system of checks and balances—no voice for those in political positions and no effective work on the streets.

Blurring the boundaries of formal political involvement and activism is possible in Israel by the very nature of the short history of the state's political infrastructure; its youth provides a certain flexibility and opportunity to penetrate and change the system. If we can achieve peace with our neighbors (a dream that today feels nearly impossible), a lot of good can be done. This holds true for politics, activism, and all the work that lies between. Just as I lived for years in the space between "Zionist fascist" and "renegade feminist," I can live in the space between the important changes that need to be made and the great roadblocks that stand in our way. I hope I will have the opportunity to continue my work in social change, and I know that when I am ready to make the big moves and important decisions, I will make them with the composure, strength, passion, and dedication of the activist-meets-leader I have grown to be.

In looking back at the work I have done and looking into the future, I hope that my experiences and lessons will help focus a few more minds on the trend I suspect we are creating by fostering young women's leadership. Whether formally teaching and organizing leadership programming or simply setting a great example as women leaders, we are rewriting our fate in a world that has us marked from birth as "less than."

Measuring social change can sometimes come immediately, as I found on campus when rallying Jewish students to have pride in their nationality. But it also can be a very slow process as we see in the fight against gender oppression, and we need to remain dedicated and persistent. Women in Israel have a long journey ahead of them, with social, historical, and religious roadblocks to surmount. Change can be measured in the rise in grassroots women's leadership programs and meetings to discuss the future of women in politics. It can be measured in a rumbling of passion in a people just beneath the surface. In Israel and around the world, strong women are getting ready to step up, and in many countries have already been chosen to lead. These are the leaders who will blur the lines that divide to cross boundaries and make change.

NOTES

1. Oslo II was a 1995 agreement between Prime Minister Yitzhak Rabin and Palestinian Authority Chairman Yasser Arafat that included guidelines for security issues; communication between the two governments; prevention of hostile acts, including incitement of hatred between the nations; adherence to human rights; and cooperation; among other decisions.

2. See Nancy A. Naples, ed., "Introduction," *Community Activism and Feminist Politics: Organizing Across Race, Class, and Gender* (New York and London: Routledge, 1998), 17.

19

Practicing Leadership

The Unexpected Plunge into Politics

ALANNA CHAN

From the outside, I am calm and collected, flashing a smile as I am being introduced, but on the inside, I am sweating and feel queasy due to nervousness. No matter how much I prepared for this presentation, my audience of twenty high school females intimidates me. In hindsight, I was being silly; however, it felt like there was a lot at stake at the time. I had forty minutes and had to keep the attention of adolescents who were more interested in after-school plans than what I had to say. In a blur, I captured my audience with an interactive exercise that made them think twice about politics and feminism. Both were taboo topics because high school girls conceive them negatively: politics are a bore, and feminism is about men bashing. Afterward, coming off my delirium of nervousness, I was shocked that a class of twenty high school girls was the toughest audience that I had to face as an active college student leader.

This public-speaking experience was part of my visit to a women's studies class at East Brunswick High School, a suburban high school in central New Jersey thirty miles from New York City. My goal was to provide high school girls throughout the state with skills-building workshops that would facilitate their activism in community service and politics. As the project developed, my passion for introducing politics to young women developed as well. Before I could attempt to carry out this project, I had to learn about women's history, women's struggles, feminism, civic activism, the need for more women in politics, and how that all related to me as an individual, a citizen, and as a woman of color.

A little more than half the U.S. population are women—51 percent, to be exact. Therefore, even by a hair, I am part of a majority. On the other hand, as a Chinese American, I am part of a minority. Even though women make up more than half of the population, they are still considered a minority in all professional fields. There are plenty of women working in various professions, but only a handful of them are in high leadership positions. There is even less leadership opportunity for women of color. Men are the rule makers and have established the archaic yet reliable "old boy's club"—a forceful network that has supported them for thousands of years and a system that women are only beginning to understand, accept, and establish for themselves.

What Politics Used to Mean to Me

If you were to ask me my thoughts on politics when I was a freshman in high school, my answer would have been blunt and pessimistic. If you were to also ask me at that time if I would ever get involved in politics, I would have answered honestly, "no way, that stuff is not for me." Like many of my female peers, I did not relate to politics. We simply could not because we did not see a female figure in the political forefront. There was Hillary Clinton as the First Lady, but most, if not all, coverage of her was negative. The same was true of Monica Lewinsky. Though she was not an elected official, she is an example of how the media negatively exploited and continues to misrepresent women in politics, creating an entirely new and undignified meaning for public service.

In addition to not seeing women in politics, I did not see any women of color, specifically Asian women. I did not see an Asian face associated with American politics at all. In my small world of East Brunswick, New Jersey, politics was not a common career choice among my Asian peers. Most of this was due to parental influence because it was common for my peers to be descendents of immigrant parents. There is something very specific about immigrant families: they are very practical. Considering that they took a chance to uproot themselves from their home countries to move to an entirely new nation with little money, immigrant parents have hopes that even if they cannot seize opportunities in America, their children can.

This was definitely the case with my family. My parents emigrated from Hong Kong to Manhattan during their adolescent years. By the 1960s, both of their families already had several generations of immigrant history.[1] Before they could enjoy a different life in the United States, my grandparents had to struggle to make ends meet. This included working in factories that did not require English proficiency and even creating small businesses for supplemental income. My grandma was not just a seamstress, she was also a landlord. Grandpa was not just a bookkeeper, he was also a cook.

Wearing multiple work hats was also the reality for my parents, even as teenagers. Out of a need for survival, my parents lived chameleon-like lives. During the day, they were students making friends with fellow adolescent immigrants while awkwardly adjusting to American culture. After school, they were laborers to support their parents' businesses while still being immersed in their native culture. In between they had to shift their identities to survive the melting pot streets of the city. They faced the same challenges that typical teenagers face such as peer pressure, parental expectations, racism, and a whole lot of uncertainty.

This was the life that my grandparents and parents lived, and as part of the first generation to be born here, this was a history that I had to come to grips with—whether I wanted to or not. This was history that I did not want to know because it required me to understand my parents. When I was in high school, I was constantly disagreeing with my grandpa who raised me and with my mother and father. Being a teen is hard enough, but being a teen growing up in two contrasting cultures was exhausting in many ways. My sister and I are now experiencing the culture clash that our parents experienced when they were younger, but in reverse—instead of adjusting to American culture, we are adjusting to our Chinese culture. As American-born Chinese (ABCs), we grew up immersed in the American culture that surrounded us, both inside the home through television and outside the home through friends and school. Nonetheless, we were still Chinese, and as children we were constantly reminded of our history, background, values, and customs. These often clashed with what we knew as "native" American values and culture, to the point that it was difficult for us to accept certain aspects of our Chinese culture. Throughout high school, I had a "they don't understand" attitude toward my parents and grandparents. In some cases, my parents truly did not understand; however, it was worse that I did not make any attempt to understand them. This proved to be regretful, and it was not until the death of my grandfather that I realized that family history explains a lot of the present.

The experience that my family had as Chinese immigrants in the United States was not a perfect one. Nonetheless, they persevered so that future generations could have better and even new opportunities. These come in the form of education that leads to professional jobs and good salaries. A high-paying salary is prized and bragged about among Asian parents because it equates to security; as parents get older, they want to be sure that their offspring are capable of taking care of themselves and have the finances to do so. This is why white-collar professional jobs (accounting, anything math related, business, law, medicine) are attractive to Asian parents. They are high-paying careers, not jobs. Although one can have a profession in government or politics, such an option is not appealing because the salary does not compare to that of a career in law or medicine. Government and politics are public service, and with a history of having to depend on one's own hard work to survive, it is difficult for immigrant Asian parents to understand that serving the public is one way to make a living.

Discovering Feminism

Although I did not see how politics affected me, what I did see that influenced me was my race and gender. To me, that was real. Because I grew up in a two-generation household, I was raised more traditionally than other Asian kids. Obeying elders and familial hierarchy were the golden rules of my household, no questions asked. One's seniority (age) was more important than one's gender. Even though my sister and I were not raised to fulfill traditional Chinese gender role expectations, I could not avoid inheriting my parents' hard work ethic and their attitude of delayed gratification. I was always told by my parents to never take anything for granted and never do anything less than your best. As a result, I became an overachieving student and saw that hard work was always rewarded. I never considered my gender and race as hindrances. I was going to work hard to achieve success, regardless.

Teachers found me focused and determined while my classmates thought I was intimidating or too loud. Close friends were used to my blunt opinions and understood them as part of my personality, but others considered my attitude too strong. When some of my peers (mostly males) would try to check my manner, I would return the favor, asking what was the difference between us. Their response? It was because I was a girl; better yet, I was a bitch. Apparently, it was not cool for girls to have strong opinions and voice them confidently. I learned from my classmates that it was OK for a girl to have a brain and take advanced placement courses as long as she did not outshine her male peers. Even though I did not get along with some of the boys in my high school class, I did not let that prevent me from being friends with other guys. It was not until my senior year of high school that I realized that my strong attitude was my expression of feminism. Fortunately, my high school was a progressive one, where the faculty added a women's studies course to the elective curriculum—not called women's studies but Women's History and Law. I took the class because it interested me, and my history teacher encouraged me and fifteen other girls to take it. On the first day of class, she wrote on the board the word that I learned to understand and embrace: FEMINISM.

Mrs. Rose was the epitome of second-wave feminism and wanted everyone to *understand* women's history, not just know it. All of us knew that women had had to gain the right to vote but we did not comprehend that women did not originally have this right because by law they were considered second-class citizens. I noticed that Mrs. Rose was tough on all of her students, but she was more challenging to the females. Some classmates took this personally and found her hypocritical; however, I saw her approach as a form of tough love. It was not Mrs. Rose's intention to pick on her female students: she challenged us to not only absorb her lessons but to understand how they applied to us. Mrs. Rose's class was not intended to be a "girls' club"; it was intended to make change. Her female students would not be considered equals unless they understood the history of women's struggles and saw themselves as agents in the long movement for gender equality. She was the one who taught me the fundamental meaning of feminism—the belief that men and women should be considered equal: financially, professionally, politically, and socially. It was not about male hating; it was about women having the same rights as men. While learning about women's suffrage and about the first- and second-wave feminist movements and how they applied to current events, I found my niche. I realized that I did not have an attitude problem; I just had a different attitude.

First Step into Politics

My newly discovered attitude prepared me to enter Douglass College, then the largest women's college in the nation. I knew I would have a unique experience, different from other undergraduates. Even though I was a student at an all-women's college, I was integrated with students from other colleges within the university, both male and female. Being a Douglass student allowed me to make the most of my college years because of unique programs that provide young women with the skills they need to excel in their professions of choice. Being active in student life was very important to me; as a commuter, I found this to be a healthy challenge because it encouraged me to meet other students by staying on campus longer than my time spent in class. I became more connected to my college and felt more confident to take advantage of new opportunities that came up.

One of those opportunities was a summer internship in Washington, D.C., through the Public Leadership Education Network (PLEN), a national organization of women's colleges that work together to educate women for public leadership. I interned for three months in the D.C. Mayor's Office on Asian and Pacific Islander Affairs (OAPIA), where I experienced local politics first-hand. Even though I am a member of the Asian community, I had no clue what "Asian affairs" meant. It was interesting to work for an office whose purpose was to bring awareness of issues specific to the Asian community. After a couple of weeks on the job, I realized the need for such an office. Asian and Pacific Islanders (API) are the third-largest ethnic group in the District of Columbia and experienced a population increase of 30 percent within the three years prior to my internship.

The recurring problems that the office had to tackle were limited English proficiency in the Asian community and the lack of nonprofit organizations serving the community. With restricted English-language skills, recent immigrants, refugees, and other members of the API community had trouble finding jobs and receiving medical and governmental services. In comparison to the Latino community, the API community had similar cultural and language barriers but received less translation and bilingual services. As a result, OAPIA collaborated with key organizations to provide critical testimonies in a council hearing. The goal of this hearing was to encourage the amendment of the existing D.C. Spanish translation law to include the three major Asian languages used among the API community: Vietnamese, Chinese, and Korean. Passage of this amendment would require D.C. agencies to hire personnel who could speak any of these languages and to translate their literature into all three languages.

Inside the office, I learned a lot about myself in a professional setting; outside the office, I learned more about myself as an individual. I experienced a different level of responsibility because I was living on my own in a different city. Most of my social scene in D.C. was with the API community; this was my first encounter with Asians in a political setting, and the experience was comforting. It showed me that it is possible to have a career in public service as an Asian American even though the journey will not be easy. The only issue that I did not feel was fully addressed was API women in politics, because not only do we face discrimination as Asians, we face bias as women. At the time, out of the seven API congressional members, only one was female, Patsy Mink of Hawaii. After Mink's death in 2002, Rep. Doris Okada Matsui of California has been the only API female to hold a seat in the 110th U.S. Congress. This is why I cannot feel fully represented in my nation's government. This is an issue that I am still trying to understand and explore.

Institute for Women's Leadership and Everything Else Politics

The D.C. internship was a life-changing experience; I was exposed to public service firsthand and underwent personal growth within a short period. Part of the internship included a weekly seminar conducted by the program director, which featured accomplished women in various political positions including lobbying, nonprofit organizations, grassroots advocacy, and public office. I felt that the classes gave a taste of women's leadership in politics because they focused on women who had already "made it," but there was not enough focus on how they made it or what steps they took to get there.

I did not fully appreciate my internship experience until I was accepted as a scholar of the Institute for Women's Leadership (IWL) at Rutgers. This opportunity came unexpectedly when I applied after being encouraged by college deans, classmates, and professors and after seeing plenty of ads for the program. I have to admit, I was intimidated when reading the curriculum of the program: over the course of two years, scholars would have to take three high-level undergraduate seminars; undergo a part-time, fourteen-week internship; execute a social action project; and take two advanced courses in women's studies. I found the program overwhelming but not impossible because the directors, staff, and my fellow scholars were supportive and constantly offered guidance along the way.

The interesting and unique quality about the IWL program was interacting with my fellow scholars. At the beginning of the program, we were a group of strong leaders with various interests, but eventually we became confidantes, supporters, and friends. Even though we all had different interests on women in leadership, I felt that we were mentoring each other. We were a group of intelligent and driven young women who gave unconditional support and encouragement whenever it was needed. That was the missing link; having female allies was a critical aspect of succeeding in politics, or in any professional field where women's leadership was limited. This became very apparent during my junior year of college when I interned for the White House Project (WHP), founded in 1998 by Marie Wilson, president of the Ms. Foundation for Women. WHP works to place more women in high-level leadership positions in all professional fields, most specifically in politics because the highest leadership position in the nation is the U.S. presidency.

This internship experience was very interesting, and I really pushed myself to reach my goal. One challenge was commuting out of state; the White House Project is located on Wall Street in New York City. Every Friday morning, I commuted from central Jersey for a ninety-minute bus ride, and every Friday afternoon I would make the same commute, sometimes longer depending on rush hour traffic. This helped me appreciate two things: my work for the office and my parents for making commutes like this six times a week for more than twenty-five years. For fourteen weeks, I commuted so that I could work on WHP's young women's leadership in politics project, which eventually became my passion.

It was the first time I had worked for a nonprofit organization or in an office of women where a hierarchy was obvious. The initial project plan was to create an information packet on young women's activism to be sent out to university women's studies departments throughout the nation. Instead, the executive director decided to create an inspirational poster that would outline the steps young women could take to facilitate their paths into politics. These would be mailed to universities in hopes that young women would use them. The project morphed again: to save money and to reach out to as many people as we could, the executive director decided to make the poster into an online guide to be featured on their Web site. At the end of my internship, I handed in a draft for the Web site that I titled "Steps to The White House." Through many weeks of commuting and off-site work that added to my regular college coursework, I was able to develop something tangible. In addition to that, I created the backbone of a future project.

While interning at WHP, I also worked part-time on campus for the Eagleton Institute of Politics as a paid intern for their Young Elected Leaders Conference. This gave me the opportunity to contribute to groundbreaking research on the nation's young elected officials as well as the chance to see the importance of civic participation at an early age and the impact it has on the community. Working with IWL and Douglass alumna Jessica Roberts was the most rewarding experience; her enthusiasm, dedication, and passion were a result of two institutions that I was a member of. Seeing her fine leadership skills as a program director was inspirational; I looked up to her as a role model and am very grateful that I was able to learn from her.

The project included extensive research and a conference with fifty young (twenty-one to thirty-five-year-old) elected officials throughout the country. The four days of the conference gave me a glimpse of the lives of young politicians. Interestingly (though not surprising), only a handful of the participants were women. In their report, Eagleton Institute noted that only 14 percent of the nation's elected officials under age thirty-five were women.[2] And although both male and female politicians are married and raising families, holding office and balancing family life often proves to be more challenging for women. Some female conference participants who were mothers noted that women often wait until their children are grown to a certain age before running for office.

The need for young women politicians did not strike a chord with me until I was asked by a Douglass classmate to help start a student chapter of the New Jersey Women's Political Caucus (NJWPC). With five other classmates and friends and through many hours of meetings, networking with national and state board caucus members, and a lot of support, we opened the first student chapter of the NJWPC, the state chapter of the National Women's Political Caucus, which is dedicated to increasing women's political leadership throughout the nation to achieve gender equality.

At the same time, I was beginning to develop a social action project. From all of these eclectic contacts and experiences, I realized there was a need to provide a tangible resource for young women interested in community activism and politics. I decided to hold a conference focusing on young women's leadership in politics. My goal was to provide leadership skills to high school girls and to connect community involvement and politics in their minds. I wanted to target high school girls because, from my experience with the Young Elected Leaders Project, I learned that even though one has to be eighteen years old to be a voting citizen, there is no age requirement to be civically engaged and active. To increase the numbers of politically aware youths and youth voting, young people must be educated in the political process before they reach voting age. I believed there was a need to create a forum for young women to express themselves and learn from each other as women and leaders. My conference, "Walk the Walk: Steps to the White House," was held in November 2002. To mark the end of the conference, a luncheon was held featuring the keynote speaker Maya Enista, a Douglass student and East Coast coordinator for Rock the Vote, the multimedia voting campaign launched by MTV to reach out to young adults ages eighteen to twenty-five, the demographic (until the 2008 presidential primaries) with the lowest voting records. At the end of the conference, I could tell that the participants and those involved with conducting the conference left with a new attitude about their roles as young community leaders.

Plunging into Politics

Looking back on all of these leadership experiences, I realize that coordinating "Walk the Walk: Steps to the White House" required me to be my own conference's example. I used networking and public speaking skills that I learned as a Douglass student and IWL Scholar, which helped me to be a better citizen and activist. Throughout this growing process, I received support from friends, family, and colleagues, both male and female. Knowing that others believed in me kept me going.

Since graduating, I have continued to advocate for equal representation of women in national and local legislatures. I sustained my involvement in New Jersey politics by pursuing a career in state government where I learned from experienced, strong, and accomplished women. Within the New Jersey Department of State, I served as a program associate for the Office of Faith-Based Initiatives, where I helped faith-based and community-based nonprofit organizations develop working relationships with each other and with corporations, foundations, and state agencies. I am currently pursuing a master's degree in events management in business, which has broadened my views and my interest in women's leadership beyond the political arena—not as "jumping ship" from the public to the private sector, but in reverence that both sectors are interdependent and in need of women leaders.

As I reflect on my experiences, I am surprised because I never thought I could accomplish such things. In an interview I conducted with Debbie Walsh, director of the Center for American Women and Politics at Rutgers, she described the "plunging" factor as one reason that could explain the low numbers of women in politics. Women tend to assume leadership positions only when they feel confident enough to do the job. If they have any sense of doubt, they will not take on the responsibility. This is not unique to politics but applies to all professional fields. Men, conversely, plunge into leadership roles. When offered positions of leadership, men have the confidence to take them, whether or not they are knowledgeable or have the necessary skills to meet the job requirements.

Throughout my years at Douglass, the Institute for Women's Leadership, and beyond, I believe I plunged into many things and took on more than I should have. However, I never thought about this while I was doing it; each challenge was an opportunity to solve a problem, and each challenge led to progression. Although I had a few moments of insecurities and self-doubt, I did not let that diminish what I had already accomplished and learned from family, teachers, and peers. Diverse women's leadership in all sectors of society is necessary for equal representation in public leadership. Our presence is both a responsibility and an opportunity to be heard. Veteran women leaders are increasingly supporting today's emerging young women leaders. I am still reminded of my parents' beliefs in delayed gratification and their hopes for my future. Through my experiences as an Asian female, my growth as a young woman, my education as a feminist, and my efforts as a leader, I hope that I am on my way to accomplishing what my parents worked so hard for.

NOTES

1. On both sides of my family, generations prior to my parents have immigrated to the United States. For example, my great-grandfather successfully immigrated to the United States while his wife and children (including my grandmother) were still in China. My grandmother immigrated to the United States with her family when my father was a teenager. I am part of the first generation born in the United States.

2. Ruth B. Mandel and Katherine E. Kleeman, *Political Generation Next: America's Young Elected Leaders* (New Brunswick, N.J.: Eagleton Institute of Politics, Rutgers University, 2004), 8. http://www.eagleton.rutgers.edu/YELP/YELPFullReport.pdf.

20

Stories from the Sidelines

Career versus Family

MEGAN PINAND

When I left college, I thought I had it all figured out. I thought I would be able to do anything I set my mind to and had a clear picture of where my career was headed. My aspirations were very clear, and I saw my life as a timeline. Two months after graduation from college, I got married and started a new job. My husband and I bought a house about a year later. After the purchase of the house, I wanted to focus on advancing my career and my education and eventually starting a family in the upcoming years. It was perfect, and I was on my way to having two and a half kids, a house with a white picket fence, and a corner office by the time I was thirty. That is what I had planned, but from the day I set foot in my new job the summer after I graduated, I have learned many lessons about women in the workforce and how their personal lives, especially their families, are perceived. Particularly, I have learned that women have to work very hard to maintain their professional stature at the office while balancing the responsibilities at home. I have also understood that support in a woman's personal life is essential to achieve work and family balance. Most important, I have learned that there are no easy answers to work–life balance, and women must decide if they are willing and able to achieve this in their lives.

In my undergraduate studies, I had decided to major in finance because I considered myself a "numbers person," and I was intrigued by the life of a business professional. In my sophomore year of college, I decided to take an introductory women's studies course as an elective requirement because I thought it would be an easy "A" and it would be insightful. That course was a pivotal point in my college career because it taught me a great deal about women's rights and gender differences that I never heard in history classes or on the news. To my surprise, this course was absolutely not an easy "A," and I left the semester with many questions concerning the status of women in this country, how they are treated in the workplace, and how they are treated in their home lives. After this course, I decided to apply for the Institute for Women's Leadership Scholars Program, a program that teaches women about leadership and social change. After I received my acceptance letter, I was excited not only to be a part of this prestigious program but also to begin finding answers to the questions I had concerning women and their status in society. In reality, these questions are never answered. In fact, in most cases a woman in the workforce or a woman with a family must find her own answers to these questions while she works to change workplace cultures and social policies that still make it difficult for women to "balance" work and family.

My first job after graduation was at a large telecommunications company. Over the course of the year and a half I worked at that company, I had two different bosses who held two divergent opinions of women in the workforce. I remember a conversation with my first boss, who was a single father for most of his career. We were discussing his strategy for maintaining a successful career and taking care of two young children. He told me that he made a choice. He could have either enjoyed his family life with his kids or continue on the management track he was on before his divorce. He continued to tell me that I would have to make a choice and that it is completely impossible to have both a successful career and a satisfying family life. He explained that either my career or my children would be forced to suffer and that I would have to decide which part of my life was more important. I was in disbelief. Everything I was taught led me to believe that I would be able to manage a family and a career at the same time. As a young woman growing up in the twenty-first century, I simply did not believe that I had to "make a choice" between having a career and a family. I was taught that women can have successful careers and at the same time care for their children.

I realize that my boss was correct in saying that it will be difficult; however, there are many policies, services, and benefits to help families find a balance between work and family life. To say that women have to make a choice to either work or have a family is to essentially give up the opportunity of having both, something men have rarely been asked to do. In addition, many mothers—including African American, immigrant, and working-class mothers—have always been expected to have both. In every job that I have had in my time outside of college, I have seen many women with families juggling careers. Of course it is difficult, but as more mothers of young children enter and rise up the ranks in corporations and the professions, public opinion will continue to change.

It is also possible that the difference in opinion between my boss and me is a generational issue. White, middle-class women raised in the years before the 1960s, for example, were taught that it is not possible to balance work and family. This is not the case for the new generation of female workers. We are taught that we can have a successful career and a family without making life-changing sacrifices. Another supervisor from my workplace provided an example of a woman successfully combining both.

My second boss was a female in middle management who had been working for the company since she was out of high school. Despite the fact that she did not have a college education, she worked among other managers who did. She had a son who is in his early teens, and she lived about sixty miles from work. Her husband was a blue-collar worker who often worked overtime and weekends. Her job was very demanding and often required her to take work home. Although we never had a specific conversation about the strategies she used to balance work and family, it was apparent to me that she was very successful at managing her life at home and her life at work. She told me many stories of her son, how he was doing in school, and what his hobbies were. She always seemed aware of what he did on a daily basis. Although he was now old enough to be at home alone, the years when he was young were the same years she was working hard to promote her career. I noticed that she always kept her cell phone close by so she could be in contact with her family whenever necessary, and she always had a positive attitude at work and never complained that she was not with her family enough. To me, she was a "super mom," and she set an example for all the women that work for her, including myself. Hers was a different model of how a family is structured. For middle-class families, the model was once a male breadwinner and a female homemaker. In the world today, it is increasingly common that two parents work to support a family. I think this is what many young woman professionals, including myself, strive for in their lives.

Based on the two perceptions of work and family from my supervisors, I sometimes think work–family balance is only achievable if a parent is in the correct state of mind. I also realize, however, that the parent's state of mind would be greatly aided by the creation of public policies such as governmental or work-subsidized child care. The structural constraints my boss who was a single father faced were different from those confronted by my second boss, who was in a dual-earner household. For myself, if I believe I can be a good mother and have a career at the same time, I am sure I can be successful. In the few years of experience I have in the "real world," I have surprised myself at what I can achieve. To me, success is not measured only by how I continue to reach the goals I have set for myself professionally; it is also measured by personal relationships, such as those of my family, my husband, and my friends. I consider myself a successful person not only when my career is growing but also when I am maintaining healthy relationships with my loved ones.

The way my grandmother lives her life is a good example of achieving work–family balance. When my mom and uncle were young, my grandfather fell ill with cancer. He was a factory worker at a mattress company, and at the time, my grandmother's main role was to care for her husband and children. My grandfather could not work when he fell ill, but the family needed money to survive. My grandmother decided that she had to get a job to sustain her family. While my grandfather battled cancer, she took care of him during the day and worked in a factory during the evening to make money for her family. She took sole responsibility for being the family breadwinner and taking care of two children and a very sick husband. It may not have been the most favorable situation for her, but she remained working this way for a few years. When my grandfather went back to work, her normal routine returned, and she became a homemaker again. It is obvious that this is an extreme situation and that not all women will have to face this in their lifetimes, but my grandmother's determination is a model I use in my life to prove to myself that I can achieve my goals of being a successful businessperson and a great mom. Despite what others may think, I constantly reassure myself that I can do whatever I put my mind to, including being a breadwinner, having a family, maintaining a house, and climbing up the corporate ladder.

After a year and a half of work at my first company, my husband and I decided to buy a house in southern New Jersey. Because my first job was in northern New Jersey, I needed to find a job closer to where our new home would be. I hired a "head hunter" to help me find a job that was closer so I would not have to commute a long distance when we moved in. I made the decision to change jobs based on personal reasons, and I hoped that my career would not suffer because of it. I was fortunate to find a job in the accounting department of an insurance company only about thirty miles from my new home.

The accounting department I work in is mainly made up of men. Upper management in accounting consists of all men, with the exception of one female vice president, who started work as a consultant in our department to help at busy times and was later promoted from the smallest cubicle on the floor to a large office with a great view. I had worked with her briefly, and my initial impression was that she was very nice, extremely smart, and had a commanding presence. When she was promoted, most people I talked to were upset that she was offered the position. They used the "B-word" that is associated with most female executives who are just as assertive as men are. They were disgruntled because she leaves at 5:30 p.m. at times (which is about a half hour before everyone else) for her son's baseball games. She is demanding, and she does take command of meetings, but she also gives direction, exhibits professionalism, and makes time to share her knowledge with her staff and other employees. Although I have not worked at the company long, I cannot understand the corporate culture that exists to allow this woman to be treated by her coworkers in this way. All I can do right now is ensure that I do not partake in the cruel tactics of others and try to make a good impression when working with her in the hopes that some day she is my manager.

Another female vice president who works outside of the accounting department recently gave birth to her second child. When I started with the company, she was about six months pregnant, and until the day she left on maternity leave (about a week before she gave birth), she worked long hours and took work home. She insisted that we give her the work our department needed complete before she left on maternity leave. After the baby was born, she returned to work after about three weeks of rest. I could not believe when I saw her car in her parking spot, nor could I believe when she left a work-related message on my boss's voicemail. What happened to the twelve weeks of maternity leave that I thought was customary?[1] Is this what women have to do in order to "have it all"? Is it really "having it all"?

Unfortunately, the company I work for has created a culture that makes women feel the need to appear so attached to their jobs that they cut their maternity leaves short. For employees to advance in the company, "face time" and "exposure" are critically important. Being in front of people and presenting your work and ideas are necessary. Although telecommuting is an approved work arrangement at my corporation, it is frowned upon behind closed doors. As employees advance, they are given added responsibilities yet no additional resources, and managers base performance evaluations on their observations rather than on results. To succeed, hard work, long hours in the office, and networking with the right people are expected.[2] These kinds of requirements can be very difficult for new mothers to fulfill. To keep their careers on track (and in some cases to retain their positions), some new mothers take abbreviated maternity leaves. My company is not alone in implicitly discouraging employees from taking advantage of family-friendly workplace policies. Marcie Pitt-Catsouphes and Bradley K. Googins write: "There is ample evidence that workplace culture and inflexible policies have limited the effectiveness of work-family initiatives, in some cases even when the workplace has attempted to create a family-responsive work environment."[3]

I have noticed in my short time with this company that most people are scared, myself included. I think about approaching management and voicing my concerns about the two women I discussed as well as other problems, but I remember how important this job is to my livelihood. Having a house is an enormous responsibility, especially in today's uncertain financial climate, and my income is necessary to pay the mortgage monthly. I have seen this company and my former employer fire people on the spot, and this is something I do not wish to risk. I enjoy the work I perform, and my department works very well together. For me to complain about this treatment would not only put my job at risk but would damage my reputation and my career. I think others feel this way as well, from lower management through upper management. This is why the "tone at the top" is very important for most corporations.

When I decide I am ready to have children, I hope there is a choice to stay home while the child is young, or to work part time after the baby is born. I can say that right now I am not sure which choice I would make. Still today there is much debate about mothers who stay home versus mothers in the workplace, even among mothers themselves.[4] Families do not always consist of a male breadwinner and a female homemaker. Often, they consist of two parents who work full time and children who stay in day care full time while they are young. Although women are not always seen as equals in corporate America, in my experience women are seen more as equal contributors in a family. My husband and I always ask each other, "Am I pulling my own weight today?" What he really wants to know is if I feel too burdened by the housework that needs to be done, or the bills that need to be paid, or the cooking that we need to do. Both my husband and I understand that we each work very hard for forty-plus hours a week and have little time to take care of all the duties outside of work. We made a commitment to each other when we married. We are committed to helping each other in any way possible. It is my job to make his life easier, and his job to make mine easier. We have learned to understand that the foundation of our relationship is support for one another.

In my short time in the corporate world, I have witnessed many examples of the tactics working mothers use to be in control of their professional and personal lives. I have seen how corporate America views women who decide to make their families a priority, and in some cases, they are indirectly penalized when they do so. When I finished college, I wanted to know if there was an answer to the question, "Can women efficiently manage their work lives and their family lives simultaneously?" What I have learned so far is that there is no perfect answer to this question. I would like to believe the answer is up to each individual person, but I know it is more complicated than that. The answer is not only about individuals; it also involves workplace policies, state and federal policies, family structure, stereotypes about gender roles, and the attitudes of coworkers and management. In this century, the tools are available for a woman to be able to achieve balance. Lines of communication are more open with the use of cell phones, text messaging, and e-mail. Working from home is becoming more popular as technology connects workplaces to households. Day care facilities also have programs for children of any age that accommodate any work schedule. Thanks to the 1993 Family and Medical Leave Act, companies are offering unpaid paternity leave for stay-at-home fathers, and some companies offer savings plans for their child's education. When you take these factors into account, it seems as if achieving balance should be getting easier for working parents.

Conversely, research has shown that flextime, telecommuting, parental leave, and on-site child care cannot do enough to address the heavy workloads and long hours of many workers in corporate positions today. Some scholars and work–life experts suggest that the serious recession of the early twenty-first century may lead to different work and family priorities and concerns.[5] I feel that combining work and family is one of the most challenging things I face as a working woman, and this will likely become even more difficult if I become a mother. It is hard for me now to make sure things at work are running smoothly and things at home are running smoothly as well. I feel guilty when I work overtime and should be spending time with my husband, and I feel guilty when I take a day off and my coworkers are putting in extra hours. I believe this guilt is a result of the emotional attachment that I feel toward both my family and my job, and once I become a mother I expect this guilt to worsen. During the years I have been out of school, I have come to realize that faulty messages of how to treat coworkers with families are being taught in corporate society. The well-being of employees is not addressed enough in business today, which forces harried parents to choose their work over their families. We need to find new ways to improve the options and quality of life for working families. As a young woman who plans to have children and work in the business world, I believe I can not only achieve my own goals but also advocate for broader structural changes that will make it easier for all of us to "balance" work and family.

NOTES

1. It is possible that my coworker returned to work so quickly because her family could not afford the loss of her income. Her maternity leave was before New Jersey passed the Family Leave Act, which allows workers to take up to six weeks off to care for a newborn or newly adopted child or a sick parent, spouse, or child while collecting up to two-thirds of their pay. This legislation passed the New Jersey Senate in April 2008 and was signed into law by Gov. Jon Corzine in May 2008, making New Jersey the third state in the nation (joining California and Washington) to give workers partial pay for time off to care for a new baby or a sick family member. "Paid Family Leave Act Clears State Senate," *The Star-Ledger*, April 7, 2008; "Gov. Corzine Signs Paid Family Leave," *The Star-Ledger*, May 2, 2008.

2. On the shortcomings of flextime and telecommuting see Sylvia Ann Hewlett, "Addressing the Time Crunch of High Earners," in *Unfinished Work: Building Equality and Democracy in an Era of Working Families*, Jody Heymann and Christoper Beem, eds. (New York and London: The New Press, 2005), 156–179.

3. Marcie Pitt-Catsouphes and Bradley K. Googins, "The Paradox of Corporate Solutions: Accomplishments, Limitations, and New Opportunities," in *Unfinished Work: Building Equality and Democracy in an Era of Working Families*, Jody Heymann and Christoper Beem, eds. (New York and London: The New Press, 2005), 224–250; at 242.

4. See, for example, Leslie Morgan Steiner, *The Mommy Wars: Stay-at-home and Career Moms Face Off on Their Choices, Their Lives, Their Families* (New York: Random House, 2006).

5. Hewlett, Addressing the Time Crunch," 163–164; Pitt-Catsouphes and Googins, "The Paradox," 229.

21

Creating Knowledge

Feminist Music Scholarship as Activism

MARY SIMONSON

My senior year of college was spent sprinting toward the future. I rushed to complete a thesis on nineteenth-century female amateur musicians, slaved over a heartfelt personal statement to include in my applications for Ph.D. programs in musicology, and jumped on plane after plane to visit the various graduate schools at which I had been accepted. At the same time, I hurried through my last few classes, including a seminar taught by a reputable feminist activist who was visiting my university for the year. One afternoon, as I rode the elevator with her and another professor in the women's studies department, she questioned my decision to pursue a career in musicology. "But why music?" she asked, noting that I was one of the "smart students" in the seminar. "You have the opportunity and brains to do something that matters." Shocked, I mumbled something about the need to do feminist work in all fields and got off at the next floor. Outwardly, I was stunned and defensive, my adrenaline surging. What an awful, insensitive, discouraging thing to say to a student! My fury, though, quickly faded to a familiar feeling of uncertainty and shame. Her question was one that had haunted me as I had surveyed grad programs and outlined my personal statement. What if she was right? What if an academic career—an academic career in music, no less—would not matter?

I am an activist, an agitator for social change, a leader. I am also a young woman embarking on a career in academia, a musicologist, a teacher. My research, my writing, my work in the classroom, and my presence in this field and in the academic world are my forms of activism. You are surprised? Sometimes I am too. For years, I struggled daily to imagine the intersection of feminism, musicology, and activism. I knew I was passionate about music, about thinking and theorizing, about learning and sharing what I had learned about women's rights, about feminist theory and critiques, about imagining and working toward a world in which power, privilege, and opportunity were more evenly dispersed. Yet somehow those passions just did not seem to fit together. Feminist activism, I had gathered (and had at times been explicitly told), involved being a community organizer, a lawyer, a doctor. It was about working for nonprofit organizations and nongovernmental organizations (NGOs), volunteering. It was about helping other people in a direct and transparent way. How could I claim to be "doing" feminism as I holed up in the library, reading and writing about music? Over the years, through discussions with other feminist scholars, by reading the words of feminist activists of all ages (especially those who ride the "third wave"), and by questioning myself and my work, I have come to realize that I *can* claim to be doing feminism. Feminist leadership, activism, and social change are not about carrying out a prescribed set of acts. Rather, they are about finding your own route and your own voice, exercising feminism in your own way, constantly striving to acknowledge and embrace new (or forgotten) sites for feminist activity.

Embarking on my college career, I never thought twice about my decision to study music. I was fascinated by the depth to which music touched me. I loved attending concerts, ripping into a new recording, stumbling across a previously unheard piece on the radio. I enjoyed the process of learning new piano pieces, ironing out difficult passages until they flowed smoothly from my fingers. Most of all, though, I loved learning the history behind these works: who had created them, why they had been written, and what they had meant to audiences. Most of my classmates complained that the required music history courses were boring and a waste of time, but I ate these classes up. I loved the steady stream of new compositions, the challenge of keeping track of dates and sequence, the anecdotes and myths and realities that come together in any history textbook. In the back of my head—or perhaps even unconsciously—I knew that the narratives we were being taught were incomplete, slanted toward particular composers, types of pieces, and musical traditions. After all, we focused on symphonies and string quartets, only glancing at vocal genres such as opera and lieder (art songs). We learned a lot about German music and a lot less about French, English, and even Italian music (we ignored non-European musics all together). And though I had sung the music of plenty of female composers in the women's choir I had joined, almost all of the composers we studied were male. I did not let these omissions trouble me though. After all, I knew there was more to the story, even if it went unspoken.

In the summer of 1999, I found myself sitting in an introductory women's studies class, and suddenly my perspective shifted. I had always been aware of feminism, of women's rights and struggles, and I felt that I was a strong female, descended from a line of educated, accomplished women. My mother was liberated. Her decision to stay at home with us as children was a choice that she made. She had given up her career because she "wanted" to, not because she felt it was her role. I had been encouraged to do whatever I wanted, to be strong and independent, to take control of situations and responsibility for myself. Yet my feminist ideologies remained largely unspoken. Of course women were equal; of course we deserved fair pay. Of course gender was socially constructed, of course. Everybody knew that! As my women's studies course progressed, though, I began to realize that it was not as easy as "of course." These were issues that needed to be revealed, acknowledged, fought for, shouted about. To silently assume and accept was just not enough: there was work to be done! Yet my fury and passion were tinged with dread. As crime after crime was committed against women, as inequality and discrimination persisted, did music history really matter? My friends, upon learning that I was a music major, had always wistfully replied, "That must be fun." How could I sit and study pieces of music everyday—sit and have fun—when there was so much work to be done? Feminist activism and music scholarship seemed miles apart.

My difficulty in linking feminist activism with music scholarship and teaching did not stem solely from the narrow definitions of feminism and feminist activism that dominate popular culture. The fact that the field of musicology has historically focused on close readings of the works of an exclusive group of composers has also contributed. Attempting to establish their work as legitimate (and important), musicologists have long tended to conflate their work with "science," adopting positivistic methods and claiming a canon of "great male composers."[1] Female figures were generally only introduced into the mix when they were related to famous men through familial ties, marriage, or patronage; there was little consideration of women's music-making, female composers, music education histories, and so forth.[2] Moreover, questions and issues that were beginning to be debated in women's studies and literature programs were (and at times continue to be) ignored in favor of studying "the works themselves."[3] Departments openly refused to consider or shied away from critical theory, topics that required subjective interpretation, and the notion and implications of music as a cultural phenomenon that affects and defines audiences as well as creators.

Beginning in the 1970s, a group of primarily female scholars began the project of uncovering female composers and their works, calling attention to various reasons why they had been excluded from the canon. By the 1980s, histories of women in music were being published, weaving webs of similarities that allowed for careful thinking about the ways in which female and male forms of musicking have traditionally been understood and valued.[4] Yet the landmark date for feminist music criticism was 1988: in this year, at the meeting of the American Musicological Society, a panel of papers in feminist criticism were presented, which instantaneously created a community that included women both involved in finding "lost" female musicians and composers and involved in a new kind of music criticism that attempted to rethink and reexamine the assumptions underlying the canon and music scholarship as a whole.[5]

Since 1988, a wealth of feminist work has taken place within the field. Specific pieces, musical forms, and, more generally, genres have been examined in terms of gender; female opera roles have been carefully critiqued and often reinterpreted; issues of power, vocality, and performativity have come to the fore; the cultural and social implications of a variety of types of music making are regularly addressed; and the ways in which music reflects (and helps to maintain or destroy) societal values has become a common inquiry. The fact that both music and music scholarship carry political weight (and are politically charged) is generally recognized, as is the problematic nature of the (male) canon and the concept of "Great Works." Yet despite these advances, a sector of the musicological field remains resistant, arguing that music criticism as a whole is invalid and unnecessary; that audience reactions to or interpretations of music are private, personal, and outside the realm of musicology; that valid music scholarship is positivistic, complete with right and wrong answers; that feminist interpretations of music do not examine musical nuances comprehensively; and that feminist music criticism threatens to descend into discussions of "feminine" styles of composition and listening rather than attempting to ignore—or better yet, transcend—these differences. As a result of such resistance, we are slower to understand the immense importance and cultural relevance of music, slower to alter society's general perception of music as apolitical, and slower to recover female musical actors and activities throughout history. At the same time, such resistance results in the continued presentation of the canon of musical "masterpieces" as an indisputable fact that requires no thought or discussion in Music History 101 and music appreciation classes, the continued separation of music from culture in many college classrooms. And indeed, as such messages are transmitted, feminist music scholars are forced to continue fighting, reminding themselves daily of the ways in which studying music is a feminist act of resistance, remembering not only the ways their research topics themselves will transform musicology but also how they relate to the wider world of feminist activism. As Ruth Solie writes, "For most of us, even the most abstract or theoretical musicological project retains its clear and material connection to our on-campus campaigns for maternity leaves and child care, our continuing surveillance of salary equity, and tenuring procedures on behalf of our junior colleagues, our determination to protect our students from sexual harassment, our activism outside the academy, and our allegiances with other women in our communities."[6]

My introduction to women's studies course left me hungry to learn more about women's rights and feminism. But what about music and music history, which continued to capture my imagination? I began thinking and exploring, hoping that there was some way to link the two. One day a women's studies faculty member who knew that I was a music student mentioned she had just come across an interesting book that explored music and music scholarship from a feminist perspective: *Feminine Endings* by Susan McClary. Published almost ten years earlier, the book was (and still is) considered highly controversial. McClary's injection of cultural criticism and gender-based analysis into musicology was largely unprecedented and, for some, hard to swallow. I immediately headed to the library, found a copy, and began wading through. Reading, I was alternately confused (semiotics? vocality?) and inspired. Here was the proof I had hoped to find: musicological inquiry could intersect with feminist theory!

My struggle was hardly over, however. In my backpack, I carried bound, published proof that music and feminism were not mutually exclusive, that music scholars could be feminists, that music history—like women's studies— was not static but constantly developing. The weight of the book, though, was not enough to reassure me. As I watched my fellow students fight for the establishment of a women's center at our university, develop tutoring programs for underprivileged youth, work for feminist nonprofit organizations— in short, doing whatever they could to change the lives of other people—I felt like a sell-out. That feeling deepened a bit more when I signed up for a women's studies course with a service learning component in which qualifying activities included volunteering at domestic violence shelters and hotlines, lobbying for pro-choice politics, working at a variety of nonprofit organizations called "The Women's [fill in the blank]," and working as a "Big Sister" to female preteens. And it deepened even further as I listened in class after class to debates over whether women's studies should be about feminist scholarship or activism, in which activism almost always came out on top, pinning feminist theory and academic inquiry beneath its weight, priority, and importance. I might have found feminist musicology, I told myself, but I was still miles from "doing" feminism.

Looking back, these assumptions were—regrettably—natural. Social action and activism are widely assumed to hinge on direct engagement with the political sphere. As a result, many of the forms of activism in which women have historically engaged—like community service—are cast as private, "nice" things to do for others rather than movements that are both inherently political and have frequently inspired change.[7] As service-learning advocate Tobi Walker notes, we must both redefine and resituate community service and similar activities as highly political acts that simultaneously affect public policy, create knowledge, and constitute a valid act of citizenship.[8] Feminist scholarship, particularly in the humanities, is in need of similar revisioning. Like community service, scholarship (and for that matter, music as well, although its gender politics are perhaps more complex) has historically been considered relatively nonpolitical. Indeed, in attempting to negotiate its insider–outsider relationship with academia, the field of women's studies has constructed activism and scholarship as binary opposites. It is time to escape this dichotomy. Scholarship and teaching, like other forms of community service, are inherently political acts that hold tremendous potential to galvanize and create change. We must begin to acknowledge feminist scholarship as a potential—and valid—site of activism, a source of theory *and* action.

Furthermore, it is crucial to expand our conceptions of feminist action and social change. Just as notions of what counts as activism and social change effectively forced women to the margins, we have allowed sound bites and stereotypes to limit our definitions of feminism and imaginations of what feminist action might look like. As the media reports on the death of feminism, how "feminism has devolved into the silly," how "feminism now stands miles from any important political matter," we listen and nod instead of protesting and offering counterexamples.[9] At the same time, we remain trapped in feminist agendas and acts of the past, unable (and perhaps unwilling) to step outside the tactics and styles of our predecessors and develop our own. As scholar Diane Elam has noted, "Daughters are not allowed to invent new ways of thinking and doing feminism for themselves; feminists' politics should take the same shape that it has always assumed. New agendas are regarded at best with suspicion on the part of seniors, at worst with outright hostility."[10] As a new generation, we must cease to be controlled by the media, the generation gap, and society as a whole. We must define our own feminisms, our own ways of acting as feminists as more inclusive, individual, and personal. Activism is "the doctrine or policy of taking positive, direct action to achieve an end." All means of reaching an end qualify, and all must be recognized.

With each year of graduate school, my commitment to—and understanding of—feminist musicology grew. Just as "of course" and unspoken assumptions were not enough in the women's studies classroom, neither were they enough in musicology. There was more story to tell, and it needed to be told, spoken aloud. Who had been overlooked, and why? What values and privileges did our narratives enact? What power structures and priorities were written into our histories? With each year, my perspective on activism and scholarship shifted as well. I met feminist scholars who firmly believed that their work was activism, and who freely discussed their own struggles and victories. I learned more about the scope and depth of musicology and, perhaps more importantly, about the gaps and omissions that persist in our ideologies, our methodologies, our agendas, and even our vocabulary. Slowly, I began to see the potential of my own research, writing, theorizing, and teaching. These activities, I have come to realize, are techniques of social change. These activities are forms of activism. Like many of my mentors and colleagues, I am "doing" feminism and creating change.

As I explore topics for papers and ideas for projects, I am drawn to topics that carry feminist potential: examining portrayals of women in opera, dance, and film; exploring the ways in which we define and value performance (gendered feminine) and composition (often the domain of males); understanding the music and reception of female popular performers; exploring the career—and self-promotion—of nineteenth- and early twentieth-century divas. I am equally drawn to projects that promise scholarly alternatives: thinking about music as a political tool; experimenting with new, more self-reflexive and intimate writing styles; learning about how people learn and use music in their everyday lives. These divergent topics are all sites in which the scholarly, the creative, the political and the radical meet to create (and recreate) feminist knowledge.

Now, as I make my transition from student to faculty member at a small liberal arts college, from being taught to being a teacher, I am forced to think carefully each day about my philosophies and what messages I believe are most important to share with my students and those who read my work. I am faced with the enormous responsibility of being a creator (and disseminator) of knowledge. How do I convey my own feminist alliances to my students? How do I open doors for them to begin understanding traditional musicology and the musical canon not as sets of pieces written by men but as a culturally constructed web of power and authority designed to privilege a few? I ask them to think about the cult that surrounds Beethoven and declares him a hero; I remind them that popular music is as valid to study as Mozart or Haydn. We discuss musical experiences (dancing at parties, shopping for CDs, and playing air guitar count), think about different ways of listening to music, talk about *American Idol* and the merits of covering other people's songs as opposed to writing one's own. We move away from the scientific, the objective, from dead white men in wigs, and begin questioning our own perceptions, valuing our own experiences.

In *Feminist Academics: Creative Agents for Change*, Val Walsh asks, "What does it mean to be effective as feminist academics, while also challenging the roots of our complicity in our own and other people's oppression? This is the practice of revolt, against how we are positioned historically and socially in relation to each other as women, which bubbles at the heart of any feminism."[11] For me, the mere act of standing in front of a classroom, of writing and submitting articles for publication, are acts of resistance against patriarchal norms. I am a female demanding to construct and produce knowledge, and to share that knowledge with others. To focus my work and teaching on problematizing a Euro-centric male canon, and attempting to validate alternative, more women-centered, more comfortable approaches to music scholarship deepens my resistance. To encourage and contribute to a field of scholarship in a way that may validate the ways in which other women engage in music (as performers, listeners, as members of the music industry), and celebrate and strengthen female musical practices and institutions (such as women-run recording companies and record labels and women-only concert venues), further expands my revolution. In these ways, scholarship is a means of creating social change. Creating and revising knowledge as someone who, by virtue of being a woman, does not occupy a privileged position within academia forces a revisioning of the field for those inside of it; sharing that knowledge and those ways of thinking with students (who often are not majoring in music but merely looking to fill requirements), inspires people outside of the field to question their assumptions; applying that knowledge and work to real life musical experiences and practices further calls into question traditional cultural values.

Yet social change comes not only with creating and sharing knowledge, but with altering what it means to be a feminist academic as well. Perhaps the ultimate activism of scholars (male and female alike) is continued agitation within the academy. As Jane Martin notes, "The fact that we are being accepted into the academy [does not] mean that, feeling forever grateful to those who tried so hard to keep us out, we must now accede to even its most undemocratic and inegalitarian tendencies. There is no reason . . . why we cannot in good conscience direct our *collective* energies to changing the academy's core values and its basic mores."[12] Feminist scholars must protest the strict standards of language and communication strategies that academics are held to, finding words and ways of writing that fit our own ways of thinking and working, not the shallow values of "academic-speak." We must embrace and trust our own voices and experiences when they are part of the story, adopting narrative strategies that allow the personal to interlace with the theoretical. We must actively question and protest research/teaching and theory/practice hierarchies (attempting not only to level these binaries but also to move past superimposing male/female figures over top of each), envisioning new ways of creating and transmitting knowledge. Just as feminism must recognize the endless variety of types of social action and activism, academia too must begin to encourage a wider variety of ways of learning, knowing, teaching, researching, writing, and creating, striving to become a place in which female scholars will not have to guard against taking up research subjects related to women and feminist theory, or being "too excited" about teaching for fear of "refeminization."[13]

"But why music?" From the distance of several years, my professor's question still echoes most days. Some days, it is louder than others. Most days, though, I welcome it. This question is a reminder, a challenge, a pedagogical tool. My response to it changes and grows with each paper I write, each class that I teach, each essay and book I read. Now I realize that my activism is my choice. I do not need the approval of the rest of the world; I need merely to embrace my work as my own, meaningful contribution.

As I read more and more accounts by third-wave feminists, I am drawn to a common message: we need to stop questioning what is and is not true feminist activism, what counts and what doesn't count, which acts are the most important and which don't matter at all. We need to ignore charges that young women (and our generation as a whole) are inward-looking slackers, and follow our own passions, whether they fit into the socially constructed boxes of "feminist action" and "social change" or not. Val Walsh writes, "Only by transgressing the limits and constraints placed upon us as women can we survive and thrive."[14] These limits come from multiple directions: the media, culture, society, other women; our mothers, our fathers, our friends. Social change, though, comes by breaking though these constraints, exploring the answers to our own questions, understanding why we are passionate about our work, and sharing these passions, these beliefs, these ideas with everyone around us. Activism, according to third-wavers Jennifer Baumgardner and Amy Richards, is "everyday acts of defiance."[15] For me, this means musicological research, teaching, and claiming a place within the academy; for others, it will mean something else. As we each act in our own ways, staking claims, naming fields and works as places for feminist change, we redefine what it means to be feminists in our time.

NOTES

1. Musicology is a term used to signify the study of music that is separate from performance or composition; a committee of the American Musicological Society defined it in 1955 as "a field of knowledge having as its object the investigation of the art of music as a physical, psychological, aesthetic, and cultural phenomenon." More recently this definition has been extended by some to include the study not only of music but of the entire process of the creation and reception of that music (thus the study of composers, performers, and consumers/listeners). For a more complete discussion of musicology, see Stanley Sadie and John Tyrrell, *The New Grove Dictionary of Music and Musicians* (London, 2001); or Oxford Music Online, http://www.oxfordmusiconline.com/public/.

2. Suzanne G. Cusick, " 'Eve . . . Blowing in Our Ears'? Towards a History of Music Scholarship on Women in the Twentieth Century," *Women and Music* 5 (2001): 131. The major exception to this is the appearance of female performers such as singers Jenny Lind and Maria Malibran or pianist Theresa Carreno in musicological accounts.

3. Studying "the works themselves" implies examining the music as an isolated creation that is unaffected by surrounding conditions, historical moments, and any other type of cultural referent.

4. Musicking is a term that Christopher Small uses to describe any participation in a musical activity, whether it be publicly performing, practicing, sitting in an

audience, listening at home, and so on. See Christopher Small, *Musicking: The Meanings of Performance and Listening* (Hanover, NH: Wesleyan University Press, 1998).

5. For an account of this panel, which featured James Briscoe, Elizabeth Wood, and Susan McClary, and was chaired by Susan Cook, see Susan C. Cook, "Women, Women's Studies, Music and Musicology: Issues of Pedagogy and Scholarship," *College Music Symposium* 29 (1989): 93–100.

6. Ruth Solie, "Defining Feminism: Conundrums, Contexts, Communities," *Women and Music* 1 (1997): 10.

7. Tobi Walker, "A Feminist Challenge to Community Service: A Call to Politicize Service Learning" in *The Practice of Change*, eds. Barbara J. Balliet and Kerissa Heffernan (Washington, D.C.: American Association for Higher Education, 2000), 30.

8. Ibid., 25–27.

9. Ginia Bellafante has written on the increasing gap between "Old Guard feminists" and the self-centered feminism of the 1990s. See Bellafante, "Feminism: It's All About Me!" *Time* 151, no. 25 (June 29, 1998): 54–60.

10. Diane Elam, "Sisters Doing It to Themselves," in *Generations: Academic Feminists in Dialogue*, reprinted in Jennifer Baumgardener and Amy Richards, *Manifesta: Young Women, Feminism, and the Future* (New York: Farrar, Straus, and Giroux, 2000), 224.

11. Val Walsh, "Transgression and the Academy: Feminists and Institutionalization," in *Feminist Academics: Creative Agents for Change* (London: Taylor and Francis Ltd., 1995), 86.

12. Jane Roland Martin, *Coming of Age in Academe: Rekindling Women's Hopes and Reforming the Academy* (New York: Routledge, 2000), 41.

13. Ibid., 59.

14. Walsh, "Transgression and the Academy," 96.

15. Baumgardener and Richards, *Manifesta*, 283.

CONTRIBUTORS

ALLISON M. ATTENELLO is the program director for Girls Learn International, a nonprofit organization that works to give American students a voice in the movement for universal girls' education. She holds B.A. and M.S. degrees from Rutgers University. Attenello spent the last several years working for the United Nations–affiliated University for Peace in Costa Rica, where she developed curricula on topics including gender and peace building; peace education, religious identity, and Islam; and peace education and library science.

LIZA BRICE, a magna cum laude graduate of Rutgers University, looks to media in all its forms to dismantle oppression at every level. Working to transform herself and the world around her, she has been a part of organizations such as WBAI Pacifica Radio, Democracy Now!, and The New Press. She is currently the online marketing and outreach coordinator at Women Make Movies in New York City. She plans to pursue graduate work in media, and hopes to create content that will drive human progress.

ALANNA CHAN graduated from Douglass College, Rutgers University. She has worked as a project manager and corporate events coordinator for Christ Church in Rockaway, New Jersey. Currently she is a graduate student at George Washington University, working toward a master's degree in tourism administration with a concentration in event management.

INGRID HU DAHL is a founding member of the Willie Mae Rock Camp for Girls, a nonprofit organization that promotes the empowerment of girls. Speaking at camps and lecturing across the nation and around the globe on gender, media representation, and "acting rather than appearing," Dahl is dedicated to inspiring young people and their allies to create change. She received her B.A. and M.A. degrees from Rutgers University where she served as an adjunct instructor from 2004–6. She is currently a program officer of youth media at the Academy for Educational Development and editor-in-chief of the professional journal *Youth Media Reporter*. Dahl plays guitar in the all-girl band Boyskout and plans to open a buy-sell-trade and community-uniting store in Brooklyn, New York, where she lives.

ROSANNA EANG is a graduate of the Edward J. Bloustein School of Planning and Public Policy at Rutgers University. She has worked at the Institute for Women's Leadership on the Community Leadership, Action & Service Project (CLASP). She is currently studying at the Ohio University College of Osteopathic Medicine and plans to become a doctor of Osteopathic Medicine practicing in Camden City, New Jersey.

DAHLIA GOLDENBERG works for GROOTS International (Grassroots Organizations Operating Together in Sisterhood) and the Huairou Commission, two networks that advance the work of grassroots women in their communities and support them to have a voice at the global level. She holds a B.A. from Rutgers College, Rutgers University, and an M.A. in gender and development from the Institute of Development Studies, Sussex University.

JESSICA H. GREENSTONE is currently pursuing her Ph.D. at Tufts University. At Tufts, she works as a research analyst on program evaluation projects and studies the social, emotional, and intellectual development of girls. Last year, she co-authored a report titled *From Gaps to Opportunities: Meeting the Needs of Girls in the Worcester Area.* She earned an M.S. degree from Cornell University, where she conducted research on the ways adolescent girls learn about themselves and their social roles through messages from the media. After earning her B.A. from Douglass College, Rutgers University, she worked for four years as the education director for the New Jersey region of the Anti-Defamation League (ADL).

MARY S. HARTMAN is a professor and director of the Institute for Women's Leadership at Douglass Residential College, Rutgers University. Dr. Hartman served as the dean of Douglass College from 1982 to 1994. As dean, she initiated a number of nationally recognized programs for women including the Douglass Project for Rutgers Women in Math, Science and Engineering; the Center for Women's Global Leadership; the Laurie New Jersey Chair in Women's Studies; and the Institute for Women's Leadership. Dr. Hartman is a social historian specializing in women's history and gender studies. She is the author of numerous books and publications, including *Victorian Murderesses: A True History of Thirteen Respectable French and English Women Accused of Unspeakable Crimes* (New York: Schocken, 1977); and *Talking Leadership: Conversations with Powerful Women*, editor and introduction (Rutgers Press, 1999). Her latest book, *The Household and the Making of History: A Subversive View of the Western Past*, was published in 2004 by Cambridge University Press.

ARWA IBRAHIM, a graduate of Rutgers University, is currently a coordinator at Direct Aid Iraq, a humanitarian relief and peace-building project intended to build bridges of friendship and support with Iraqi refugees. As an undergraduate, she organized numerous actions and educational events on her campus about the U.S.-led occupation of Iraq and other crises. She continues to advocate for the rights of Arabs and Muslims in America and to speak publicly about her experiences as an Iraqi refugee and human rights advocate.

EDNA ISHAYIK was a political campaign operative for eight years. She has worked for candidates at various levels of government. After working on Eliot Spitzer's successful campaign for governor she became the executive director of the New York State Democratic Party. Currently she is the communications director for the Institute for Policy Integrity, an environmental nonprofit organization. She earned a B.S. degree from Douglass College, Rutgers University.

JAN OOSTING KAMINSKY is a registered nurse and a Ph.D. student at Johns Hopkins University. A graduate of Douglass College at Rutgers University, she has worked as a research assistant for Memorial Sloan-Kettering Cancer Center and holds a second bachelor's degree in nursing, also from Johns Hopkins. She works as a pediatric intensive care nurse at Saint Barnabas Medical Center in Livingston, New Jersey. Kaminsky is currently involved with the New York City Mayor's Office to Combat Domestic Violence, which is researching the effect that exposure to domestic violence has on children in the home. In her free time, she is raising two feminist sons with her partner, Samantha.

KRISTEN LYONS MARAVI graduated with highest honors from Rutgers College, Rutgers University. She is a high school French teacher in Rockaway, New Jersey, and has completed an M.A. degree in teaching. She is active both in the school community and in her local church. She lives in New Jersey with her husband, José.

CAROL MENDEZ is currently a medical student at Robert Wood Johnson Medical School–University of Medicine and Dentistry of New Jersey. She graduated from Douglass College at Rutgers. During her undergraduate studies, Carol started a series of classes at a local health center in New Brunswick, New Jersey, to teach local immigrant Hispanic women about healthy lifestyles and preventing illnesses. She has also worked with immigrant communities in Philadelphia and Morristown, New Jersey.

KRISTY CLEMENTINA PEREZ is a poet, writer, educator, and community activist. After graduating from Douglass College at Rutgers University, she chose to return to her community in Perth Amboy, New Jersey, to teach. She taught writing, poetry, and literature for six years at Samuel E. Shull Middle School and Perth Amboy High School, where she created and implemented a poetry curriculum and course. She and her students also created the school's first literary magazine in twenty-five years titled *The Maverick*. She is pursuing a master's degree in community organization and planning at Hunter College School of Social Work in New York City.

MEGAN PINAND graduated from the Rutgers School of Business at Douglass College, Rutgers University. After college, she was hired into AT&T's Financial Leadership Program as a financial analyst. After two years with AT&T, she accepted a position with AIG as a financial analyst. Recently, she has been promoted to manager of financial planning and analysis in the international life insurance division in Wilmington, Delaware. She received her MBA from the University of Phoenix in March 2007 and resides with her husband, Dave, and dog, Shea.

SHIRA LYNN PRUCE works at the Jerusalem Open House for Pride and Tolerance, where she coordinated the Jerusalem Pride March in 2007, oversees the LGBT Leadership School and runs Israel's only LGBT health clinic. She graduated from Douglass College, Rutgers University, where she founded Israel Inspires, an initiative to inspire Jewish pride and Zionism in Jewish students across North America. After graduation she moved to Israel where she worked at the Israeli Knesset (parliament) as a lobbyist. She is currently living in Jerusalem, Israel, with her dog, Jersey.

ANURADHA "ANU" SHYAM graduated from the Business School at Rutgers University, where she completed a thesis on accounting standards and how companies like Enron and Worldcom used them to commit fraud. She presently works as a CPA with PricewaterhouseCoopers (PwC). While associated with the Institute for Women's Leadership, she worked closely with Manavi, an organization for South Asian women committed to social change and to addressing violence against women.

MARY SIMONSON teaches at Colgate University in Hamilton, New York. She completed her Ph.D. in Critical and Comparative Studies in Music at the University of Virginia in 2007, and has a B.A. in music and women's studies from Rutgers University. Her research and teaching focus on nineteenth- and early twentieth-century opera, dance, and popular culture in the United States; issues of performance and embodiment; film music; and feminist theory. Her article "The Call of Salome: American Adaptations and Re-creations of the Female Body in the Early Twentieth-Century" has been published in the journal *Women and Music*, and an essay on the film careers of early twentieth-century opera divas is forthcoming in the edited volume *The Arts of the Prima Donna in the Long Nineteenth Century*.

SASHA TANER is the acting associate director of leadership programs and research at the Institute for Women's Leadership at Rutgers University. She holds M.A. and B.A. degrees from Rutgers University. She has worked for more than six years in the field of education and as a domestic violence advocate. She also contributed to the IWL High School Leadership Program where she focused on enhancing the mentoring component of the program.

MARY K. TRIGG is an associate professor in the department of women's and gender studies and director of leadership programs and research at the Institute for Women's Leadership, Rutgers University. She cofounded multiple leadership programs for women at Rutgers, including the Rutgers Senior Leadership Program for Professional Women and the WINGS college-to-career mentoring program. She is a Fellow at the Center for Women and Work, where she was a staff member for eight years. Trigg has published articles in *Liberal Education*, the *Journal of Women's History*, *Initiatives*, *Transformations*, *American National Biography*, and *Community, Work & Family*, and she is currently working on a collective biography of four American women who were feminists between 1910–1940. She earned a B.S. from the University of Michigan, an M.A. from Carnegie-Mellon University, and an M.A. and Ph.D. in American civilization from Brown University.

COURTNEY S. TURNER graduated from Douglass College, Rutgers University. In addition to being an IWL Scholar, she was also a member of the Rutgers gymnastics team where she remains the team's record holder in the floor exercise with a 10.0. Turner was the first gymnast in Rutgers' history to qualify for the NCAA Division I National Championships and received the 2002 Headly-Singer Award, given to the top graduating female student athlete. She attended Emory University's Rollins School of Public Health where she earned a master's degree in public health, focusing on health policy and management. Currently Turner is a health policy analyst at the Centers for Medicare and Medicaid Services in Baltimore, Maryland, and is pursuing her doctoral degree in health and social policy.

ANDREA E. VACCARO currently uses her social justice leadership in her role as an instructor of English as a second language (ESL) at Union County College as well as in her adjunct work in sociology and teacher education at Seton Hall University and Fordham University. She is currently working toward a Ph.D. in language, literacy, and learning at Fordham University; her research interests include how social justice and critical literacy curriculum interact with the second language acquisition of writing at the community college level. She received her B.A. from Douglass College, Rutgers University, and her M.A. from the University of San Francisco.

SIVAN YOSEF is a senior research assistant at the International Food Policy Research Institute in Washington, D.C. She has previously worked in nonprofit management, editing, and research for United Way of America, the American Society of International Law, and FINCA International, and she serves on the board of the Global Literacy Project. She holds a B.A. from Rutgers College and an M.A. from the George Washington University.

INDEX

academia, 172–173, 212, 214–215, 217–220

Ackerman, Chantal, 53

action, 219; in activism, 33, 69, 102, 149, 192, 216, 219; in communities, 2, 67, 143; as individuals, 46, 52, 72, 83–84; and leadership, 7, 141, 193; for social change, 125, 217; and theory, 88, 92, 97. *See also* activism

activism, 3, 44–47, 148, 167, 184, 191; campus, 187–190, 194–195; community, 135; definitions of, 10–11, 144–145, 193, 219–220; as dynamic and changing, 72, 74, 139; examples of, 67–70, 76–79, 96–106, 170; feminist, 67, 212–213; and leadership, 58; LGBT, 30–39, 192–193; racial, 108, 114; and theory, 215–217; young women and, 201–203. *See also* action; organizing

Adair, Vivyan, 135–137

Addams, Jane, 122–123

advocacy, 44–45, 109, 172, 186, 189, 191, 200, 203

Africa: Democratic Republic of Congo, 143, 144; Kenya, 7, 87–95; South Africa, 167–168

African Americans, xvi, 21–29, 53, 107–108, 111, 132–136, 206

Aguilera, Christina, 82

AIDS, 34, 89, 91, 109–115, 167

Alcott, Louisa May, 170

allies, xvii, 32–33, 51, 53, 120, 191, 201

ambition, 4, 11, 15

American Dream Act, 69

American Musicological Society, 214

American Nurses Association, 172

Angelou, Maya, 130–132, 151

Anti-Defamation League (ADL), 80–82

anti-Semitism, 77–78, 80, 187–189. *See also* Judaism/Jewish Americans

Anzaldua, Gloria, 97

apathy, 34, 37, 95, 186

Arab Americans, 39, 44–46

Arabs, 185

Arafat, Yasser, 185

arts, 53–57, 141, 143–144, 146, 179, 212–221

Asian Americans, 49–50, 195–196, 198–200, 204. *See also* Chinese Americans

ASPIRA, 25–26

athletics, 107–108

Atlanta, Ga., 114–115

autobiography, 3, 10, 14

baby boomers, 2, 173

Baltimore, Md., 109, 111, 114–115, 168

Baltimore City Health Department, 109, 111, 114

Barak, Ehud, 185

Baumgardner, Jennifer, 72, 220

beauty, female images of, 55, 82

Bellafante, Ginia, 14, 217

Bikini Kill, 139

Bisexual, Gay, and Lesbian Alliance of Rutgers University (BiGLARU), 33–35

Bodega Dreams (Quinonez), 27

body, female, 82–83, 139–140, 156, 189

Bogotá, Colombia, 67. *See also* Colombia

Bolen, Jean Shinoda, 151

Brooke, Edward, xv

Buchanan, Pat, 164

Bureau of Labor Statistics (BLS), 171–172

business, 167, 169, 171, 174–175, 178–181, 196–197, 203, 205–211

Cambodia, xiv, 58–59; war in, 58; women in, 59, 65

Camden, N.J., xiv, 61–62, 66

campaigns, 155–160, 163–165

candidates, 155–160, 163–165, 192

careers: choosing, 127, 150, 156, 167–173, 200, 212–220; and family, xvii, 178–182, 205–211, 218; and women, xi, 4, 15, 109, 157–158, 161, 175; and young women, 81, 143, 191. *See also* business; nursing; work

Carmichael, Stokely, 96–97

Catalyst, 181

Catching a Wave (Dicker and Piepmeier), 1–2, 9

Caucasians, 80, 97, 104–105, 119, 122, 124, 126–127, 132, 206

Center for American Women and Politics, 162, 203. *See also* Rutgers University

Centers for Disease Control and Prevention, 112

Central American Free Trade Agreement, 105

Chen Kaige, 53

child care, 67, 74, 157, 181, 215

children, xiv, 4, 157, 161, 171, 172, 174, 177, 179, 181–182, 185–186, 202, 206, 210, 213
Chinese Americans, 49–50, 53, 195–204. See also Asian Americans
Christians, 191–192. See also religious identity
citizenship, 104, 148, 151, 198, 203, 216
civil rights, 31, 33, 45, 80, 143, 192
civil unions, 30–31, 37
class: as category, 54, 64, 150, 156; changes in, 175–176; differences, 103–104, 118–119, 123–124, 129–138; in Ecuador, 121; and families, 206–207; in India, 175; personal experiences of, 139–142. See also poverty
Clinton, Bill, 31, 62, 185
Clinton, Hillary, xv-xvi, 65, 158–160, 163–165, 196
coalitions, 102, 135, 191
collaboration, 6, 109–110, 116, 151, 169. See also leadership
Collins, Patricia Hill, 55–56, 97
Colombia, 13, 67–68, 73
colonialism, 94, 118, 125–126
Columbia, Md., 107
community, 81, 107, 139, 141, 145, 165, 170, 177, 179, 184–185, 189; activism in, 202, 213; Asian, 199–200; gay, 31, 34–35, 192–193; Latina/o, 67–74, 96–106, 200; leaders in, 90, 127, 160, 178, 186–188, 190; local, 7, 63–64; and localized knowledge, 90–94; low-income, 29, 65, 118, 120, 122, 124, 130; organizations in, 117, 203; preservation of, 8; sense of, 133, 137, 148, 214–215; South Asian, 176; and voluntarism, 2, 143, 216–217
Congo. See Democratic Republic of Congo
Congress, U.S. See U.S. Congress
consciousness raising, 9, 39–41, 46, 119, 140, 144, 151
consumption, 118, 120–123, 125–127
Conway, Jill Kerr, 14
corporations, xvii, 160, 174–175, 178–181, 206–211
Costa Rica, 105–106
Council on American Islamic Relations (CAIR), 45
culture, 197, 200, 209, 214–216, 219–220

Dasgupta, Shamita Das, 176–179
Davis, Angela, 115
Defense of Marriage Act (DOMA), 31. See also legislation
DeLauro, Rosa, 162
Democracy Now!, 143
Democratic Republic of Congo, 143, 144. See also Africa
development, 93, 118, 122, 127
Development, Relief, and Education for Alien Minors Act (DREAM Act), 69. See also legislation

differences, 187, 215; in power, 92, 106; in privilege, 124–125, 128, 133–134, 137; race and identity, 51–54, 56, 118, 144; in religion, 190, 194
DiFranco, Ani, 3, 139–140
diversity, 10, 49, 80, 151
Dix, Dorothea, 170
Dodd, Christopher, 164
domestic violence: and children, 172; in families, 62, 67; organizations, 106, 119, 124, 150–151, 216; in South Asian community, 176–178; support groups, 64. See also Manavi; violence against women
Dominican Republic, 21
Douglass College, 34, 51, 81, 156, 186, 190, 199, 202–204. See also Rutgers University
drug users. See substance abuse
Du Bois, W.E.B., 108

Eagleton Institute of Politics, 202. See also Rutgers University
East Brunswick, N.J., 5, 195–196, 198–199
East Brunswick High School, 195, 198–199
eating disorders, 139–140. See also body, female
economics: in developing countries, 118–119, 122–124; in family finances, 209, 211; and financial independence, 177–178, 182; and inequality, 130, 190; and poor women, 134–136
Ecuador, 7, 117–128
education: 21–29, 62, 80–81, 90–93, 187, 191, 196; adult, 59, 62–63, 73; college women's studies, 12–13, 52, 71, 118, 141–142, 150, 156, 176, 215–216; graduate, 115, 150–151, 171–173, 203, 212, 217; health, 71; high school activism, 32–33, 68, 78; of high school girls, 82; high school women's studies, 12–13, 195, 198–199; in India, 182; in Iraq, 42–43; in Kenya, 87–95; and race, 21, 63; social justice, 76–77, 79–84; study abroad, 119–120, 124, 167; undergraduate, xii, 4, 115, 168, 212–213; in urban high schools, 21, 24–25, 28, 63; of women, 6, 23, 63, 146, 150, 155, 199–201, 204–205. See also educators; women's studies
Educational Opportunity Fund (EOF) Program, 63
educators, xiii, 80–81, 93–94, 151, 193–194, 198–199, 212, 214, 218. See also education
Edwards, John, 158, 164
Elam, Diane, 217
English as a Second Language (ESL), 68, 90, 103, 147, 149, 199
Enista, Maya, 203
equality, xvii–xviii, 6, 31, 39, 47, 64, 74, 162, 176, 214
equity, 28, 161; educational, 65, 83, 88, 190
Eric B. Chandler Health Center, 64, 70
ethnicity, 80, 100, 103–104, 150. See also race

families, 10, 168, 172, 190, 202; Dominican, 22–23; in Ecuador, 122; immigrant, 59–60, 74, 196–197; interracial, 49; South Asian, 174–177, 179, 181–182; in Turkey, 148; women's roles in, 159–160; and work, 205–211

Family and Medical Leave Act, 210. *See also* family leave; legislation

family leave, 205, 210, 215

fathers, 22, 50, 55, 107, 111, 116, 167, 175–176, 197, 206–207, 210, 220. *See also* men

Federation of Women of Sucumbíos, 118–119

The Feminine Mystique (Friedan), 140

feminism, 9, 143, 173, 190–191; and academia, 218–219; and activism, 97–106, 189, 193, 213–214; backlash against, 83; on campus, 100; death of, 2, 13–14, 217; definitions of, 13, 16, 62–65, 108, 114, 176, 198–199, 212–214, 215–217, 220; and diversity, 5, 142; first wave, 13, 199; history of U.S., 9–10, 12, 14–15, 52, 167, 169, 198; and leadership, 63, 113–114; reenvisioning, 1, 13–14; second wave, 9–11, 13, 15, 140, 169, 198–199; self-identifying as, 56, 63, 71, 116, 139–140; and single-sex institutions, 81; stereotypes of, 14; and theory, 51–52, 71, 187, 212, 216, 219; third wave, 2–3, 10–12, 83, 170, 213, 220; waves, 10; Western, 93, 118, 124–127; and women of color, 64; and young women, 10, 12, 14, 195, 204

feminist generations, 10–12, 14, 217, 220. *See also* feminism

film, 49–50, 53–57, 140, 142, 144–145, 218; filmmaking, 54–56, 143–144; and women, 53, 143

The Fire This Time (Labaton and Martin), 2

First Ladies, 160, 163, 196

First World, 118–119, 121–122, 125

Fortini, Amanda, 159, 163

Friedan, Betty, 140

Fulbright Program, 117, 120, 122–125

fundraising, 89, 102, 105, 111, 130, 157–158, 162, 177, 184, 187–189

gay (men), 157, 184

Gay and Lesbian Alliance Against Defamation (GLAAD), 34

Gay and Lesbian Political Action and Support Group (GayPASG), 33

Gay/Straight Alliance (G/SA), 32–33

gender roles, 59, 65, 83, 108, 160, 169, 175–176, 179, 198, 210

genocide, 78, 184

Ginsburg, Ruth Bader, xvii

girls, 59, 76, 82–83, 106, 148, 151, 182, 184, 216

glass ceiling, 50, 187

Global Literacy Project (GLP), 88, 94. *See also* literacy

Googins, Bradley K., 209

graduate equivalency degree (GED), 73

grandfathers, 196–197, 207–208

grandmothers, 23, 67–68, 74, 160, 167, 196, 207–208

grassroots, 72, 186, 200; activism, 188, 193–194; organizations, 7, 30, 45, 117–118, 122, 125–127

Grassroots: A Field Guide for Feminist Activism (Baumgardner and Richards), 72

The Greatest Silence: Rape in the Congo (film), 144

GROOTS International, 117

Gulf War, 39. *See also* Iraq

harm reduction programs, 108–116. *See also* substance abuse

Hartman, Mary S., xi–xviii, 6, 224

hate crimes, 60–61, 80

health care, 64–68, 167–173; disparities in, 67–74, 116; of Latina/os, 67–75; in Teso, Kenya, 91; women's, 112–113, 119, 161–163, 167, 171, 188. *See also* public health

Healthy New Jersey 2010, 73

heterosexism, 30, 37

Hezbollah, 192

Hillary's Class (television documentary), xv–xvi. *See also* Clinton, Hillary

Hillsborough, N.J., 50

HIV. *See* AIDS

Holocaust, 78–79, 185. *See also* Nazis

homelessness, 60, 130

homophobia, 31, 36, 192

Hong Kong, 196

hooks, bell, 97, 126–127, 139, 144, 152

housework, 59, 133–134, 174–176, 208; and career, 178–179, 210–211; in Ecuador, 120–122; and gender roles, 108; in India, 175, 178–179; men and, 55; in Turkey, 148

Huairou Commission, 117

human rights, 39–48, 68, 78, 93, 140, 143, 150

identity politics, 8, 47, 51, 54, 96–97, 101, 164

immigrants, 1–2, 5–6, 10, 23, 46–47, 58–66, 67–75, 97–98, 175–177; immigration policy, 64, 69–70, 74, 177, 196–200, 206; second-generation, 178, 197–198; undocumented, 67–69, 98, 100–101, 103, 150. *See also* American Dream Act; Development, Relief, and Education for Alien Minors Act

India, 175–176, 182

Indian Americans. *See* South Asian Americans

inequality, 22, 67

Institute for Women's Leadership: as consortium, xii, 6; education at, 71, 138, 140–142, 176–177, 188, 200–204; programs of, 34, 40, 52–54, 64, 130, 206; as women's space, 81, 146, 150–151, 201. *See also* Leadership Scholars Program

International World Pride March, 192

Internet, 140, 143, 201, 210

internships: experiences in government, 188, 199–200; experiences in health, 64, 111, 115; experiences in international, 123–124, 167–168; experiences in nonprofit, 25–26, 33–35, 130, 143, 177, 201–202; finding, 190–191; mentors in, 109; in undergraduate education, xii, 4, 70–71, 140–141

interpreters, 70, 73, 91, 103, 148, 200

interviewing, 41–44, 111–113, 120, 142, 148. *See also* research

Iran, 149

Iraq, 39–44, 149; Baghdad, 40–43; war in, 2, 40–46; youth in, 40–43

Israel, 185–186, 189–194. *See also* Zionism

Israel Inspires, 189–190

Johns Hopkins University, 109, 168

Johnson, Nancy, 161

Jonas Foundation, 172

Jordan, 40–42

Judaism/Jewish Americans, 76–80, 124, 184–194

Khalilzad, Zalmay, 144

Khandelwal, Madhulika, 176

Khmer Rouge regime, 58. *See also* Cambodia

The Knesset, 190–192. *See also* Israel

Lambda Legal Defense and Education Fund, 31, 35

Latina/os, 21–29, 67–75, 97–106, 200

law, 177, 179, 181, 197–198, 213

leadership: in activism, 100–106, 189; campus, 72, 96, 186, 189; collaborative, 6, 67, 109–110, 116; definitions of, 6, 94, 158, 160, 164–165; difference and women's, 6, 71–72, 151, 156, 188; feminist, 113–115, 144–145, 151–152, 188; grassroots women's, 90–94, 117, 126–127; and power, 186; practice of, 28–29, 43, 174, 195; preparation for, xii–xiv, 3, 107, 111, 137, 188, 193, 199, 206; reimagining, xii, 3, 6, 8, 141; requirements of, 65; rewards of, 37; and risk taking, 28, 56; self-definition as, 178, 184; sites of, xi, 54; skills, xii, xiv, 7–8, 63, 71, 103–105, 187, 202; for social change, 3, 6, 28–29, 100–106, 141, 176, 212; theories of, xii; traditional, 8, 32, 159–160, 181; and women of color, xvii, 9, 196, 200, 204; women's, 146, 159–165, 170, 173, 182, 190, 201, 203; women's under representation in, xiii–xiv, 3, 9, 65, 141, 143, 155, 192, 204; young women's, xi–xii, 3, 6, 9, 32, 70–71, 142, 151, 165, 193–194, 201–204, 212; and youth, 34

Leadership Scholars Program, 25, 40, 130, 150, 206; impact of, xiii–xiv, 52, 64–65, 71, 81, 140–142, 188; as model, 4, 6; structure of, xii, 200–201. *See also* Institute for Women's Leadership

Lebanon, 192

legislation, 160, 165, 188; federal, 31, 62, 69, 74, 161–162, 210; state, 200

legislators, xi, 155–156, 160–163, 165, 188, 200; in the Knesset, 190–191; young, 202–203

lesbianism, xvi–xvii, 30–38, 140, 143, 157

Les Rendez-vous d'Anna (film), 53

Lewinsky, Monica, 196

LGBT (lesbian-gay-bisexual-transgendered), xvii, 31–34, 187, 189, 192–193

literacy, 23, 43, 64–65, 88, 94

literature, 24–28, 96–97, 130, 135

local problem solving, 3, 7, 87, 94

Lorde, Audre, 142

Majdanek camp, 79. *See also* Poland

Management Interventions, Inc., 130–131, 137

Manavi, 177–178

March for Pride and Tolerance (Jerusalem), 192. *See also* Israel

March for Women's Lives, 189–190

March of the Living, 78

marriage, xvi, 175, 178–179, 182, 202, 205, 207, 210–211, 214; arranged, xv, 58, 65; interracial, 50; rights, 30–38; same sex, 30–38

Marriage Equality New Jersey (MENJ), 30, 35–37

Marriage Equality USA, 34

Martin, Jane, 219

The Martinsville Seven, 107

Matsui, Doris Okada, 200

Matthews, Chris, 164

McClary, Susan, 216

media, 192; accuracy in, 131, 158; independent, 140–145; mass, 41, 185; messages of, 2, 10–11, 52, 54–55, 80, 139, 217, 220; and Muslims, 45–46; and politics, 164, 196, 203; portrayal of young women in, 82–83; representation in, 12, 34, 126, 139

medicine, 63, 67, 73–74, 167–173, 179, 197, 213. *See also* health care; nursing; physicians

men, 141, 202; in Ecuador, 121–122; in elective office, 161–163, 193, 202; in the family, 210; in the history of music, 213–215, 218–219; rights of, 113; and social norms, 50, 54–55, 175–177, 179, 188, 198; in the workplace, 167, 169–170, 172–173, 181, 203, 206

mentors, 51, 69, 149, 151, 203; in college, 25, 64, 81, 150, 216; cross-generational, 12; feminist, 16; in high school, 70; in internships, 3, 109, 188; peer, 52, 201; as role models, 11; in the workplace, 180, 203. *See also* role models

Merian, Maria Sibylla, 146, 152

Mexican Americans, 97–106, 142. *See also* Latina/os

Middle East. *See* Israel; Palestine

Middlesex County, N.J., 70–71

millennial generation, xv, 1, 10

Mink, Patsy, 200

Montclair, N.J., 5, 31, 33
Morris County, N.J., 129
Morrison, Toni, 97
Morrissey, Patti, 157
Morristown, N.J., 5, 68, 72
motherhood, xvi, 3, 151, 181, 206–207,
   210–211. *See also* mothers
mothers, 9, 55, 90, 148, 167, 220; and
   daughters, 11, 22–24, 65–66, 157, 217; in
   developing countries, 122; immigrant,
   58–59, 61–62, 177–179, 197; as leaders,
   6–7, 160; low-income, 129, 132–134, 156;
   and the "opt-out revolution," 4; as role
   models, xiv–xv, 11, 50, 58–59, 61–62,
   107–108, 112, 116, 175–176, 213; teen,
   64; and work, 171, 174, 181, 202,
   206–207, 209–211. *See also*
   motherhood
Ms. Foundation for Women, 201
music, 139, 144, 179, 212–221; women in,
   214–216. *See also* arts
musicology, 212, 214–220. *See also* music
Muslim Americans, 39; discrimination
   against, 44–46
Muslims, 147, 149, 185, 192. *See also*
   religious identity

NAACP, 108. *See also* African Americans
Nairobi, Kenya, 89. *See also* Africa
Naples, Nancy, 193
Narayan, Uma, 125
National Institutes of Health, 170. *See also*
   health care
National Organization for Women (NOW),
   189. *See also* feminism
National Women's Political Caucus, 202
Nazis, 78–79, 184, 187
needle exchange. *See* harm reduction
   programs
networking, xv, 12, 105, 196, 202–203, 209
Newark, N.J., 5
New Brunswick, N.J., 5, 64, 70, 97–102, 130;
   Community Interpreter Project, 70;
   Healthy New Brunswick 2010, 73; Unidad
   de New Brunswick, 100–102
New Jersey Department of State, 203
New Jersey Division on Women, 188
New Jersey Women and AIDS Network
   (NJWAN), 109. *See also* AIDS
New Jersey Women's Political Caucus
   (NJWPC), 202
The New Press, 143
New York City, 33–35, 130, 142, 168, 172, 178,
   195–196, 201; New York City Gay and
   Lesbian Pride Parade, 33–35; New York
   City Mayor's Office to Combat Domestic
   Violence, 172
Nightingale, Florence, 170
9/11, 2, 44–45, 168, 185–186
nongovernmental organizations (NGOs), 31,
   117, 122–124, 149, 167, 182, 192, 213
nonprofit organizations, 33, 199–201, 203,
   213, 216
Norton, Eleanor Holmes, 161

nursing, 10, 23, 159, 167–173. *See also* health
   care

Obama, Barack, 2, 159, 164–165
Office of Faith-Based Initiatives, 203. *See also*
   New Jersey Department of State
Olsen, Tillie, 134–135
180-Turning Lives Around, 150
opting out, 4
organizing, 72, 141; on campus, 186–187, 189;
   in communities, 2, 98–106, 127, 213; in gay
   rights movement, 35; by grassroots
   women, 119–120; in immigrant rights
   movement, 68–69. *See also* activism

Palestine, 185–186, 189–190. *See also* Middle
   East
Palin, Sarah, 158, 160, 163–165
parental leave. *See* family leave
patriarchy, 67, 187–188, 218
peace, 186, 188, 192–193
pedagogy, 141, 219
personal and the political, 83, 140, 142, 151
Personal Responsibility and Work
   Opportunity Reconciliation Act, 62. *See
   also* legislation
Perth Amboy, N.J., 5, 21, 29
Philadelphia, Pa., 59–61, 73
physicians, 169–171. *See also* health care
Piper, Adrian, 53
Pitt-Catsouphes, Marcie, 209
poetry, 79, 130, 134–135. *See also* writing
Poland, 79, 184
policy issues, 140, 177, 216; in the arts, 53; in
   education, 29; and poverty, 64, 135–136; in
   public health, 107–109, 111–112, 114–116;
   urban, 105; women's, 161–165;
   work/family, 206–207, 209–210. *See also*
   legislation
politics, xiii, 141, 148, 155–166, 184, 186–188,
   190, 192–194; women in, 195–204, 216–218;
   women of color in, 196
Pol Pot, 58
popular culture, 140, 214, 218
poverty, 58–66, 95, 129–138, 140, 149; in
   Camden, N.J., 62; and education, 25, 29; in
   Ecuador, 117–121, 123–127; and health, 65,
   67–74, 162; in Kenya, 89, 91; study of, 64;
   in Trenton, N.J., 129, 132, 137; and women
   and children, 58, 134–136, 148
power, 141, 151, 155, 160, 173, 212, 215; and
   hierarchy, 34, 50, 92–94, 150, 217; and
   identity, 97, 103–106; inequalities in
   research, 41, 44, 96; and leadership, 186;
   personal, 58, 62, 140; study of, 51; and
   women, 165
prejudice, 76, 78–81, 113–114, 136
professionals, 176, 188, 197, 199–201; in
   academia, 212–221; business, 180–181,
   205–211; health, 109, 111, 113, 169–171, 173;
   women, 196; young women, 4
public assistance. *See* welfare
public health, 107–116, 172, 187. *See also*
   health care

Public Leadership Education Network (PLEN), 199. *See also* leadership
public office. *See* candidates; legislators
public protest. *See* action; activism; organizing
public service, xii, 197, 200

Quito, Ecuador, 117, 120–121, 123. *See also* Ecuador

Rabin, Yitzhak, 185–186
race, 142, 198; and activism, 108, 114; African Americans and, 107–108; as category, 52, 54, 64, 73, 80, 103, 150, 156, 162; and difference, 126; and identity politics, 51, 96, 103–104, 164; mixed, 49, 53, 55; racial profiling, 2, 44–45, 47. *See also* ethnicity
racism, 50, 52, 60–61, 96, 107–108, 120, 135–136, 140–142, 197. *See also* ethnicity; race
radio, 140, 143, 158, 213
rape, 98–100, 143–144, 150. *See also* violence against women
Reach Out and Read (ROAR), 64. *See also* literacy
refugees, 41, 46–47, 135, 149, 152, 185, 199. *See also* immigrants
religious identity, 77–80, 148, 175, 179, 184–194
reproductive rights, 161, 167, 189–191, 216
research, 4, 127, 161, 168, 172–173, 202, 210; and action, 3, 115; challenges of, 41–42, 44, 105–106, 124; feminist, 96, 120, 176, 182, 215, 217–220; in internships, xii, 71, 111–114; and leadership, 4
Richards, Amy, 72, 220
risk taking, xiii, 52, 56
Roberts, Jessica, 202
Robert Wood Johnson Medical School–UMDNJ, 70
Rock the Vote, 203
role models, xvi, 3, 10, 29, 67–68, 109, 202–203, 207–208. *See also* mentors
Roukema, Marge, 162
Rutgers University, 4, 70, 118, 149–150; BiGLARU at, 33; CAWP at, 162, 203; and diversity, xvii; Douglass College, 51, 81, 199; and the IWL, 6; Jewish campus life, 189; Mason Gross School of the Arts, 54; and New Brunswick, 98–100; women's studies at, xii, 56, 141

Sanger, Margaret, 170
scholarship, 214–220. *See also* academia
Schroeder, Pat, 163
science, women in, 146, 152, 168, 170
second wave. *See* feminism
service learning, 2, 7, 25, 65, 70, 88–95, 216
sexism, 50–52, 57, 82, 158–159, 163–164, 187, 211
sexual abuse, 60, 66. *See also* violence against women

sexual harassment, 161, 215
sexual health, 110
sexuality, 82–83, 156
Sharon, Ariel, 185
Singhania, Lisa, 181
Smith, Margaret Chase, 161–162
Smith, Patti, 139
social action projects, 193; examples of, 40–41, 54–56, 64–65, 177, 202–203; and Leadership Scholars Program, xii, 71, 141, 188, 200
social change, 184, 212; and action, 7, 16, 51, 79, 83–84, 125, 193, 217; creating, xii, 2, 8, 35, 74, 81, 108, 141, 187; feminist, 106, 126, 139, 144–145, 191, 213, 217; and leadership, 28, 52, 110, 127, 145, 150–151, 176, 206; measuring, 194, 220; organizations, 97; tools of, 47, 53, 56, 140, 143–145, 219; and women, 71, 128, 149, 150–152, 155–156, 160, 189, 211, 216; and youth, 54, 70, 78, 142, 152, 178, 211
social justice, 69, 72; and education, 76–84, 141, 143, 145, 152; and feminism, 13; and personal responsibility, 2, 6, 29, 39, 67, 74, 79
social movements, 144, 193, 216
Solie, Ruth, 215
South Africa, 167–168. *See also* Africa
South Asian Americans, 39, 44–46; women, 2, 55, 174–183
Spears, Britney, 82
Spitzer, Eliot, 157
standard of living, 121, 123
stereotypes, 51, 76–78, 81, 83, 131, 137, 180, 210, 217
study abroad, 119–120, 125, 167, 185. *See also* education
substance abuse, 60, 110–114
success, xvii, 111, 151, 163, 177, 180, 182, 198, 206–207

Tamir, Yuli, 191
teaching, 26–29, 148, 159–160, 167, 173, 217–220. *See also* education
technology, 55, 169–170, 210
teenagers, 54; and body image, 82–83, 139; gay, 32; high school girls, 195, 198, 202; immigrant, 197; Jewish, 78–79, 184; Latina/o and African American, 25–27; and music, 139; and racial identity, 50–51; teen mothers, 64; and voting, 202
Teichner, Martha, xvi
television, 22, 82, 140, 197, 203, 218
Temporary Assistance for Needy Families (TANF), 62. *See also* welfare
terrorism, 2, 148, 168, 185–187, 192
Teso, Kenya, 87–95. *See also* Africa
theory, 88, 212; and practice, 94, 115, 141, 216–217, 219
third wave. *See* feminism
Third Wave Foundation, 14
Third World, 118–122, 125
Title VII (Civil Rights Act of 1964), 161–162. *See also* legislation

Tolstoy, Leo, 123
Tots 'n Teens, 108
trafficking, 150, 182
travel, 95, 119–121, 125, 146–148, 157, 185
Trenton, N.J., 5, 25, 36, 129–133, 137, 188
Truth, Sojourner, 170
Tubman, Harriet, 170
Turkey, 148–151
twenty-first century, xiii, 1, 6, 15–16

undergraduates. *See* education
unions, 172. *See also* work; workplace
United Nations High Commissioner for
    Refugees (UNHCR), 149
United Nations Security Council, 144
Urban Storytellers writing workshop,
    131–138. *See also* writing
U.S. Congress, 155–156, 160–163, 165, 200
U.S. House of Representatives, 69
U.S. Senate, 69

Velazquez, Nydia, 161
violence against women, 66, 105, 139–141, 151;
    activism against, 97–100, 104; domestic
    violence, 2, 67, 106, 150, 176–179; in Iraq,
    42; rape, 98–100, 106, 143, 150; among
    South Asian immigrants in U.S., 176–178
volunteering, 174, 193, 213, 216; as college
    students, 64–65, 69–72, 88; in
    communities, 2; as graduate students,
    72–73; as high school students, 63, 68–69;
    in organizations, 109, 117; in study-abroad
    programs, 120; and welfare requirements,
    62
voters, 158–159, 198, 202–203

wages, 171–172, 174, 191, 197, 208–209; gender
    disparity in, 15, 29, 156, 161, 214–215
Walker, Rebecca, 1, 2
Walker, Tobi, 216
Walsh, Debbie, 203
Walsh, Val, 218, 220
war, 144, 152, 170, 186–187, 192
Washington, D.C., 199–200; D.C. Mayor's
    Office on Asian and Pacific Islander
    Affairs (OAPIA), 199
WBAI Radio, 143. *See also* radio
welfare, 62, 64, 130, 135–136, 156
Wellesley College, xv–xvii
White House Project (WHP), 201–202
Whitman, Christine Todd, 84
Wiesenthal, Simon, 79
Wilson, Marie, 201
Wind of the Spirit Immigrant Resource
    Center, 68, 72
Women Make Movies (WMM), 7, 142–144

women's movement. *See* feminism
women's organizations, 105–106, 117–118, 124,
    127, 150, 177, 182, 189, 192. *See also*
    feminism
women's rights, 63–64, 66, 189, 205, 212–213,
    215. *See also* feminism
women's studies, 172; academic department
    at Rutgers, xii, 56, 141; college courses in,
    xiii, 34, 51–52, 63–64, 140–141, 150, 156,
    187, 201, 205–206, 213–215; faculty, 212,
    216; field of, 216–217; in higher education,
    12–13, 216; high school courses in, 195,
    198–199; majoring in, 10, 34, 52, 63, 80–81,
    97, 168, 188; methodology, 6. *See also*
    education
work: child labor, 60–62, 66; and family, 4,
    15, 157–158, 167–173, 174–183, 202, 205–211;
    and immigrants, 63, 68–69, 101, 174–182,
    196–198, 200, 205–211; personal
    experiences of, 147–148, 218–220; and
    South Asian women, 174–182; and women,
    15–16, 156–157; and women of color, 196;
    and women in developing countries,
    121–122, 127; and women in female-
    dominated occupations, 67, 159, 167–173;
    and women in male-dominated
    occupations, xii, 143, 203; and young
    women, 4, 12, 190–191
*Working It Out: 23 Women Writers, Artists,
    Scientists, and Scholars Talk about Their
    Lives and Work* (Ruddick and Daniels),
    14–16
workplace, xi, 3, 4, 12; women in, 205–211;
    women of color in, 50, 116, 180–181, 196;
    young women in, 81–82, 111, 190–191, 201,
    207, 209. *See also* work
World AIDS Day, 34
WORLD OF DIFFERENCE Institute, 80
writers: Latina/o, 24–27; women, 24–27,
    129–138
writing, 24, 27, 43–44, 129–138, 143, 212–213,
    218–219

xenophobia, 2, 51, 53

Yellow Earth (film), 53
young women, 2, 52, 73, 147, 172, 184, 188, 195,
    202–204, 220; college-educated, 4; of
    color, 29; and feminism, 9–12, 151; and
    leadership, xi, 9, 142, 165, 178, 189; and
    older women, 11–12; in the workplace,
    81–82, 169–170, 173
youth, 54–56, 70, 78, 95, 126, 155, 186, 202,
    216–217; Iraqi, 40–41

Zionism, 184–187, 189, 193. *See also* Israel

CPSIA information can be obtained at www.ICGtesting.com
Printed in the USA
BVOW080719280613

324560BV00002B/12/P